The Junky Chronicles Present:
The Church of the Poisened Minds

The Junky Chronicles Present:
The Church of the Poisened Minds

Where Every Sinner Has a Future and Every Believer Has a Past!

BILLY

authorHOUSE®

AuthorHouse™
1663 Liberty Drive
Bloomington, IN 47403
www.authorhouse.com
Phone: 1 (800) 839-8640

Published by AuthorHouse 03/26/2015

ISBN: 978-1-5049-0321-9 (sc)
ISBN: 978-1-5049-0419-3 (e)

Print information available on the last page.

Any people depicted in stock imagery provided by Thinkstock are models, and such images are being used for illustrative purposes only. Certain stock imagery © *Thinkstock.*

This book is printed on acid-free paper.

CONTENTS

ACKNOWLEDGMENTS

To the usual suspects, Dad, Ma, Mel, Brittany, B.J., Frances, Heaven, Amaya, A'aliyah I love you all so very much. To my Grannies, Ma Dear and Ne Ne, thanks for being so beautiful and giving your grandson much love. A special something something to my Apostles, Cleveland and Frances Person for still believing in their #1 Son. To all of my brothers from other mothers, Rodney Currie, Montez Poe, Nate Mills, Danny Wright, Maurice Miles, Darnell Lee, Brian Liggett and Darryl Caffey & Denny Harris. Thanks for your support and brotherhood. You guys aren't just my brothers you are all my best men!

And to the greatest team ever assembled, the Cornerstone of Grace, Inc family! Marolyn Donald, Alice Hill-Richards, Tanya Posey, Pamela (Dove) Coley, Sharon Anne Brown, Jacqui Coney, Candice Malone and Kimberly Johnson-Miller thanks for being my go to gals. And my right hand man, Elder Dee McCauley. There are diamonds and pearls but nothing compares to any of you. Thanks for keeping me grounded and in line, ha!

And a good God bless you to Pastor Betty Fields and the Christ Revealed Family for being so warm and kind to me and Sister Geraldine Bedford. Love y'all! And a Holy Ghost shout out to my adopted pastor in Memphis TN, Pastor Ernest Howard & First Lady Cassandra Howard & the B.A.S.I.C. Family. Thank you for yielding the floor to me, someone you had never seen or heard about and that word of confirmation God gave you for me. See you and the church soon!

To the University Professors of Grit: my Forefathers in vision, Spike Lee, John Singleton, Tyler Perry and Mr. Bill Duke. And to my Godfathers who started my inspiration to write with true grit, Odie Hawkins, Iceberg Slim and Donald Goines. And a special shout out to the Dean of Dons, Mr. Melvin Van Peebles. Everything that I write, each one of you cats play an influential and integral part in it. Thank you all for paving the way for people like me. Thanks also for showing me that thinking outside the box keeps things fresh.

To my pinup girls, the hottest of the hot: Janet Jackson, Co Co, Deborah A. Bey, Mae West, Mariah Carey, Selma Hayek, Jessica Rabbitt, Patricia Carson, Madusa Miceli, Ericka Alexander, Kandi Burress, SWV, Reba, Nancy Grace, Elvira, Juanita Bynum, Dolly Parton, Jane Mansfield, Cheryl Burton, Katey Segal, Tamron Hall, Layla, Stephanie Mc Mahon, Taraji P. Henson, Ms. Jamie Lee Curtis, Ms. Anita Baker and Ms. Bernedette (Thelma) Standis.

And to the greatest superhero/crime fighter, Batman and his ultimate opposition Catwoman, from Julie Newmar to Halle Berry. No one does it better than the woman in the leather cat suit and heels! So, purrfect!! And a special shout out to the one and only Batgirl, Yvonne Craig. She made a chick on a bike, hot and sexy.

And by the way, there are seven other people that I would like to thank. Mrs. Joanne Huningan the greatest business counselor, ever! Ms. Kristin Travis business relations developer extraordinaire. Ms. Rhonda Chinn, my speech teacher. Mr. Omar Haddon, my writing teacher. Ms. Jackie Anderson, my english literature teacher. Mrs. Olivia Harvell, my business teacher. And to my counselor and fellow Chicago White Sox fan, Mrs. Stephanie Howard. Each one of you are so instrumental in getting me back to what I was called and ordained to do, write. I thank God for people of your caliber!

And to God who blessed with the vision and wisdom to succeed and for sending me Elizabeth (Liz) Mc Allister, Jermaine (Sweeney) Smith, Deborah (My Prayer Partner) Waters, Maureen (NeNe) Bolden & Mother Mildred Givens. Thank you Lord for my time with these wonderful people that are my angels. I miss and love all of you very much!

'If you're looking for greatness, look in the mirror.'

Billy

DEDICATION

I dedicate this book to all of the strong men who desire to be the very best that God has called us out to be! We are the ones that should be a shining example of what a good man is to be. It's tough for some of us, but we have to keep trying. Viva the revolution!

And to the women who have been my best friends, confidants, Dianne Jackson and Sharon Anne Brown & Tonoa Wilson. With you in my life, you have shown me what love and life is all about. You believed in me when all I had was a dream. When others walked away, you, my friends, stuck with me. Thanks for staying with me, even in my state of nothingness. May we grow old and gray together and forever, is my continual prayer. I love you and bless God for putting you in my life.

"Bill, I give because I have and I have because I give."

my girl, Yolanda Nolen

CHAPTER 1
Church Folk-Here They Come!

It was a beautiful Sunday morning. The skies were blue and cloudless. The leaves on the trees were a vibrant green. The leaves did a little dance as the wind gently blew. *Yes, a beautiful Sunday indeed,* he thought as the car slowed down to park. Soon the chatter of adults and children would fill the air. Many looking or hoping for something special to happen. This is where they came to exercise their right to believe.

The car sat idling as he prepared to get out for his short walk. He looked over at the driver and leaned towards her. He looked into her eyes with love and desire. Oh how this woman made him feel. She leaned forward as well and they embraced and kissed with passion and fury. She touched his face and he held her hand until the moment of passion passed. He said, "I'll see you in a little while." Then he got out of the car. She sat there for a few minutes watching her guy and her mind raced over the last couple of hours that she had spent with him. It was times like this that she never wanted to end.

He walked down the street about a block or so thinking about her as well. But the closer that he got to his destination he started to turn his focus towards his mission at hand. Hope wasn't just for a few, it was for everyone. This is what he wanted them to know, that you are not hopeless but you can be hopeful. This, he knew first hand, from experience.

When he thought that way, he knew that he could reach more than just a few. It was as if his life force was being amped up higher and higher. The power that flowed through him to be able to reach so many was incredible. They needed him and he surely needed them.

As he crossed the street to the parking lot a few people were there waiting for him to walk up. It wasn't unusual for him to walk. One of the young men stepped towards him with outstretched arms. They hugged and the fellow said, "Good morning, Pastor, nice day for a walk, eh?" "Yes, it is a very beautiful day for a walk." Pastor responded. They stood outside talking for a few minutes more before going into the church.

Pastor had come to really rely on these faithful few and he looked forward to seeing them. A couple of them he had personally helped to turn their lives around and the other one was his own flesh and blood. He often would tease them about them being like King David's mighty men, Jashoboam, Eleazar and Abishai. It was this brother that Pastor leaned on the most. The relationship that they held was much deeper than that of the others. He knew that if he needed someone to trust in, this was his man. Abishai had slain three hundred with just a spear. Pastor had witnessed this modern day warrior go out and witness to hundreds and thousands. On the streets he was just as anointed and many lives were snatched away from the hands of the enemy. He effectively called him, Brother #1.

Next was the brother he likened to Jashoboam. He was the fruit of the loins of Pastor. He had watched over him all of his life because he was his son. But, from a very young age, Pastor knew that this one was special. Pastor called him Brother Son. Jashoboam also slew three hundred with his spear. Pastor witnessed his abilities in worship and praise dance to rip lives away from a burning hell.

And then there was the brother he likened to Eleazar who Pastor called Brother #3. There were two reasons for this. First, Eleazar was with David at Pasdammim and they were very victorious against the Philistines. The second was that this brother was very smooth and laid back. Very few things could unnerve this brother, he was smooth and kept a cool head.

As they sat in Pastor's office they began to talk about upcoming events at the church and the surrounding neighborhoods. The church had always tried to be visible in the neighborhood and not just on Sundays. Pastor had always encouraged all to voice their opinions, be it good or bad. He just requested that it be done decently and in order. And it was fast approaching one of the more controversial annual events, The Shutdown.

This event was held for three days, Friday 12am–Monday 12am. The church would close its doors for these three days. Inside, there would be church volunteers and a host of the cast aside. For three days and nights they would be treated to meals and counseling for whatever they were dealing with. There wasn't going to be a heavy dose of "Get your life right with God or burn in hell forever" but more of a "We love you and care about you" atmosphere. Yes, the naysayers had already begun their busy bodying. Talking about how the church shouldn't be closed especially on a summer Sunday. And then there were the other churches that had something to say. Things like,"Shut-ins are for praying and fasting and such." Well, it didn't really matter what they had to say because it was highly successful.

Not only that, this year it would be covered by the media. A local newspaper was going to cover the event from beginning to end. Only places that were off limits were the washrooms and shower areas. Everywhere else was fair game. Pastor had not let the cat out of the bag about the media being there. But before the cameras were to roll he would have those that were participating to sign a release form that would be immediately notarized. He also kept it under wraps because each year it was always hard to get volunteers to stay one night, let alone a whole weekend. Had the masses known that there was going to be live coverage it would have been a feeding frenzy.

It was time for morning service to began, so the four of them ended the meeting in prayer. As they prepared to walk to the sanctuary one of the church mothers stopped the pastor, he knew what she was up to. He tried to avoid her but as usual he couldn't shake her. With this one, it was always important and it always couldn't wait. She always had to have her little say before the service started. "Reverend Pastor, I have been waiting all week to talk to you and you only. You know I can't trust nobody but you." said Church Mother. And as usual, she wanted or needed to tell him without revealing her sources about the latest goings on, in and around the church. As she finished she said, "I am only sharing this with you because all this reflects back on you."

He kissed her on the cheek and thanked her, they headed towards the sanctuary. Asst. Pastor was up leading the congregation in prayer. As prayer went forth, Pastor prepared himself mentally for this morning's sermon. As he and his men made their way toward the pulpit he looked out into the sea of faces. Young and old alike had come out looking for something, expecting something. As his eyes rolled over the sea of faces, his gaze landed on Church Mother. His mind jettisoned over the last couple of times that she had made her busy body reports. He smiled broadly as if to prevent busting out in laughter. He wondered how could she know so much and could tell so much about everything and everybody but she would conveniently leave out her very own activities. She was notorious for going to the casinos and not only attending the bingo games at the Veterans Center, but she was the life of the hall!

Sitting right next to her was her partner in crime, Church Mother Superior. The two of them were notorious for their opposition of everything that came after the Reverend James Cleveland era. No matter what it was, these two could find a fault in it. It was a known fact that these two were famous for their tongue lashings. They were called Thelma and Lois by the younger ones, but the older ones called them Arsenic and Old Lace. And don't get it twisted, they liked their mixed cocktails. *Old or young, you gotta love 'em,* he thought.

In front of them sat a beautifully adorned woman. Not much makeup, not to flashy, but this girl was sharp. Almost on instinct they caught each others eye. She smiled at him sheepishly, looking like an Egyptian goddess. She was his first lady. He smiled back with a little nod and a quick wink. That sent her ablaze. Her kisses and embraces from earlier shot through his mind, heart and soul. If he could, he'd rush out to her and grab her. Then he'd sweep her off of her feet and off they'd go.

First Lady got up from her seat and ascended the stairs of the pulpit. She took her seat right next to her husband and pastor. From the store front to the multifaceted, state of the art edifice that they sat in at this very moment, she had been with him every step of the way. She wasn't a puppet head or just a pretty face, *she* held it down. Not only that, she held it together. Together they were like concrete, hard, solid and able to withstand the worst that came their way.

Soon it was time for the word to come forth. Pastor steadied himself and stepped to the podium. The choir was nearing the end of their song and he joined in with them. This was always fun. Every once in a while he'd even take over the directing for a few minutes. With a strong anointing in the air he began to flow into his word for the day. The word of God was, Pardon My Dust. It was a hot word and it permeated the atmosphere. Another word of hope had been spoken.

After the service came to an end, Pastor and First Lady went out into the congregation and spoke with the people. This was a tradition that they had started from the beginning of their ministry. As they stood around talking to the congregants Top Notch stood with them. This, she had done ever since she had become the ministry's secretary. She was also his Executive Secretary for his own personal business.

After a while the three of them made their way out of the sanctuary to the office area. As usual, there was a small line of people waiting to talk to the Leaders. Some wanted counseling, others needed help or assistance. To keep lines down and feelings from getting hurt, the Leaders had put into place a policy to talk with seven individual cases apiece. If a congregant couldn't see them, they could schedule an appointment during the week.

This way was instituted because people do have emergencies and this would also free them up to go home at a decent time. The counseling, they would do together. Everyone knew that talking to First Lady was just as good as talking with Pastor. Even when he spoke to the congregation about ordaining her as Executive Pastor it was greeted with a great shout of approval and support. Even the Senior Circuit shockingly approved without as much as a single bah hum bug. She bought a flair to the ministry and the people loved on her for that.

From the beginning, the Leaders chose not to have a board to help make decisions. They wanted the people to have a conscience voice. All major decisions would be shared with the people because it involved the people. Plus, this way no one could say that the decision wasn't made public. Because of that, they even held town hall meetings to hear from the people. Of course, over the years there had been opposition, but it was met with little resistance, just a few people with their own agenda, mostly.

Now, with the meetings over, it was finally time to go home. On the way there, they stopped at one of their favorite fast food joints. They ordered and sat down in *their* booth. It didn't matter to them if it was a four/five star restaurant or a quick bite, they always preferred a booth. They loved the ambiance of the booth setting. They knew that when you go to four/five star restaurants the in thing is to sit at the tables in the middle, but not them. Of course, if they were guests or their party was too big, then tables it would be. But what really mattered to them most was that they were together. Yes, they preferred to have a bowl of herbs in love, than to have a stalled ox with strife.

They began to talk about her trip. Compared notes on the meetings and went over their schedules for the upcoming week. Tuesdays were usually designated for their courting day. There was not to be any business done unless it was an absolute crisis. Both of them were highly successful business owners. He owned and ran a Port a John company that he and a friend started when they were in college.

She started a teen advocacy group and within a few years she had successfully launched that into a major force in the region and state. Actually, she operated the third largest business in her arena and the number one business in the private sector. All of their business cards and marketing read '**Every good gift and every perfect gift is from above, and cometh down from the father of lights' James 1:17.** They had never forgotten who it was that had blessed them from up above.

After dinner, they headed home. They rode in silence with just the music playing holding hands. Often caressing the others knuckles or fingers. This wasn't unusual for them to do. They could go spells of time without talking and nothing would be wrong. It was when something was wrong that caused them to really interact. It wasn't the end of the world or uncommon for them to disagree but it was paramount that they resolved the issue as soon as possible. They tried not to pull any low blows or cheap shots, they tried to stick to the facts and deal with it in those confines. They tried to respect the others feelings.

CHAPTER 2
Shutting it Down!

Over the next couple of months they diligently worked towards the Shut Down event. This was a time for the ministry to really shine. It was never about them, they tried to keep the focus on the events and the outcomes of events like this one. God was to be glorified in all of this. They wanted to think outside of the believer's box and get away from doing all of the traditional church events. Even if the event had a traditional history they tried to keep it current with the times.

Actually, they had met at a traditional church service. Incidentally, that day neither wanted to attend that particular service but each had made a commitment to attend. At the end of the service they were introduced by a mutual friend. Coincidentally, the friend worked with her and attended the same church that he was attending. The two of them chatted for a short time and they exchanged beeper numbers. Within months they were inseparable. The king had truly found his queen.

The Shut Down event was finally here. Everyone was inside and the doors were closed. After everyone was informed that the event was going to be covered and everyone had signed the release the cameras began to roll. Actually, the coverage had been following various stages of the preparation leading up to now. This wasn't a novice event and it was successful to the point that many lives had really been changed. These were the ones that gave credit to this event. That in itself validated *its s*uccess.

One of these success stories compelled a down trodden prostitute to turn her life around and in a short time she joined the ministry. After joining she became involved with the praise and worship department. When the praise leader left she stepped in and never looked back. It was at an annual Summer Soulstice that Pastor introduced her as the acting praise leader. One night after she had given her powerful testimony and the praise and worship had gone forth, the leaders of the church all laid hands on her immediately. No one saw that one coming not even the pastor. He said, "It's just like God to bless even when you're not looking for a blessing." She said, "It all stemmed from the Shut Down. It was this life changing decision to attend, that made the difference in my life." She remained faithful to God and to the ministry. Later on she officially became Praise Leader.

This year's Shut Down was going to be something different with the cameras rolling. It was rather uneventful until a fight broke out. The cameras caught it all and continued to roll. Fights were not uncommon but they were a rarity. It usually involved someone defending their space or property, sometimes involved both. Even before the first event was held the committee discussed the pros and cons of holding such an event. Fighting and theft was at the top of the list.

Before anyone could intervene the fight was over before it really got out of hand. The protocol for fights, were to sit the combatants down and talk about what was happening. This was to be handled the same way, even if the cameras had caught it or not. Cook, the church's resident chef, was to be the mediator. His job as a mediator was to help both parties to reach an agreement, get an apology from the aggressor and an acceptance by the victim. This fight was over a bible of all things. There were many free bibles given away to those that didn't have one. This was quite strange to say the least. Most felt sensitive about their few possessions. Issues over various thefts had arisen over time but never a fist fight in regards to a bible.

Everything was resolved when the cameraman asked a couple of questions and wanted to interview the two. Both agreed to be interviewed. They weren't camera shy in the least bit. One was a down on his luck foreigner who had come to The States looking for a better opportunity for his family. But he had squandered everything that he had saved to try to succeed in America. Too ashamed to face his family, eventually he stopped all communications with them. He had left behind a beautiful and compassionate wife and six children.

The other one was a lifelong resident of the state who chose a life of crime to support his and his longtime boyfriend's drug and alcohol addiction. He had been recently released from prison after serving another sentence for various crimes. He relayed that his boyfriend would be getting out soon and they hoped to find work and a good church home. The victim admitted that he had over reacted when he saw the other fellow pick up his bible and just kind of flew into a rage. They both apologized and that was that.

Clean, the church's janitor stopped by to talk with Cook. Clean had volunteered the last few years to help with the event. During this time he didn't have cleaning duties he just kind of helped out where it was needed. This year he and his wife were assigned the overflow area. That's where the families were housed. It wasn't that he really chose to do it. It was more or less his wife's decision for them. He would have rather been home watching sports.

Truthfully, he preferred to be anywhere else other than here. Although he was a vet, he was no match for The Wrecker, his inside joke and pet name for his formidable and overbearing wife.

His wife, Missionary Clean, was the church's longest tenured missionary. She was a charter member of the ministry and she made it a point to let anyone and everyone knew this. Although she treated him bad openly, he still stayed with her. As a matter of fact he remarried her. Back in the day she was something special to him, now it was more or less it's just cheaper to keep her. They couldn't have kids of their own so they adopted two. They were grown now and off on their own. It's like after the kids left something went haywire between them. But all in all they remained together. They had been together for so long, ever since high school that no matter what happened, they stayed together. Being married to her wasn't all that bad as he tried to convince himself yet again. But others thought differently about that. They had seen firsthand how he'd cower to her. They witnessed her brazen tongue lashings that were directed towards him and each one surely hit its mark. Yet, he still tried to please her. Even when the attempt failed to satisfy her, he'd try something else. He knew that she was carrying past hurts from previous relationships, even after all of these years. But, he loved her anyway.

He too had been working for the ministry for many years. Over time, everyone relied on him to lead his team in having whatever event set up. They knew that it was in very capable hands. Over the years the church would hold so many events and had become a player in hosting big time events. He hung his hat on the fact that he was *the man* that the Leaders leaned on for these occasions. But if he wasn't at the church he could be found at the country club or out fishing.

That weekend several lives had accepted Christ as their Lord and Savior. As the event was winding down an unforeseen event was unfolding. Asst. Pastor was preparing to resign his post. After talking things out he reluctantly decided to stay on a little while longer. He had known for months that he wasn't happy and his heart really wasn't in it. Not only that, he had been jaded for so long that he even questioned the validity of God and salvation as a whole. He was no longer driven to excel in ministry and he had even slipped back into his cold dark world, a world that he had gotten away from. He was becoming and not to his horror an atheist all over again.

How much longer could he put on the mask and stand before the people and still proclaim love for something he himself questioned? But the lure of the perks would reel him back in when he wanted to walk away. The clout that such a title from such a prestigious ministry carried was just too much to give up. He had already achieved what many others had only wished to do. He had gone to many countries and been on more continents than he could remember preaching and spreading the Gospel abroad. He was called upon just like the leaders and he also held their trust in him. He had come a long way from nonbeliever to drummer to minister to asst. pastor. Could he just be going through a thing or something? Had he really lost the faith? What was his next move going to be? All of these questions plus so many more had been plaguing his mind for a while now. Then it finally hit him and it was as plain as the congregation itself.

What he needed was an ally, someone to help him in his devious quest for destruction. He would cripple the church one member at a time. He didn't want them for himself or for another church. He wanted them angry, so angry that they too would turn completely away from God. He had plans to fester the people into a frenzy and possibly anarchy would rule!

He figured that God could have avoided all of this but he didn't because his eyes were opened to see all of the injustices in the world. Was it too much for God to be so busy to see about the little things? Why did he have to suffer so many losses while malcontents run amok? Yes, he would switch his allegiance. At least the other team seemed to be paying off. Staying would be better than leaving, indeed, he thought.

CHAPTER 3
A New Flame

Now that the Shut Down was in the rear view mirror, it was time to plan for the event of the summer, The Summer Soulstice. What traditionally was called a revival they revamped it with a new name with a different spin. It was a time of refreshing and restoration. Each night a new and fresh face was given an opportunity to bring the message. Seven gifted and anointed would be on deck. Also each night a different choir would perform as well as a different worship team.

At first they tried the traditional revival thing using well known speakers but some of them ended up being prim a donna's. One so called big time preacher left a particularly bad taste in their mouths. He was more concerned with hawking his merchandise than really ministering to the people. And when he received a copy of the promotional flier, he called and complained that his full title and full church name, The RightReverendDrArchBishopApostle of The Churchthattakesitallbutdoesntgiveanyback, wasn't in black and white or highlighted. He was the final straw that lead them to try something different.

All of the guests would still get the rock star treatment. All of the accommodations were on the church. All participants were given hotel stays for two nights even though they were only appearing one night. They had carte blanche for dining during their stay and a love offering for their time helping towards the success of the event. What they tried to do was to learn from mistakes that they had made over the years. No one was to be the so called headliner, because that in itself was a monster. They found some ministers to be so petty and contrite that they wouldn't appear if they weren't getting top billing. God forbid you asking them to open the event.

Without all of that muckety-muck, these fresh and energetic rhema bearers would put it all out for the sake of the kingdom. One could see their hunger, like most that start out before they get too big for the pulpit. They were hand chosen by the committee, then a letter was sent to them and their pastor inviting them to appear. Most invitees were shocked and honored to even be considered to be participants for such an event.

All had gone well over the course of time. Not saying that everything went smoothly all of the time. But for the most part, something that they had put together and discussed with the people paid off. Many years ago Pastor said,

"We can't be like everybody else. We have to have our own identity and still be lead by the Holy Ghost."

All of the invitees for this year's Soustice had committed and confirmed. Every year the event was built up to a fever pitch. The anticipation was great. Especially after the line ups were made public. This is what it is all about. Believe it or not, people can get just as excited about local fellowships and lesser known speakers as they can about someone well known, was the way that the committee looked at it.

This year's event would be spearheaded by the Sr. Deacon and the deacon board, as he would jokingly address them. He used to be a local celebrity of sorts back in the day. He was in a cover band that performed Temptation songs. When the band folded he kept performing as David Ruffin. Not only that, he would only perform the songs that David sang lead on. Even though he didn't need glasses he went as far as to start wearing them to pay homage to his idol. Many thought that either he was crazy or just obsessed with being 'Ruff', as he liked to be called. If there was a costume party he was going to be one thing and one thing only, Mr. David Ruffin.

He and Church Mother stood firm with the Leaders. You could best be sure that the seniors would get their point across even if it would ruffle a few feathers. Their rally cry was 'I've been walking with the Lord longer than you and I've seen a lot of things.' So to keep the peace with the old guard the committee came up with the idea for the Senior Circuit. This gave them a united voice. Even that took awhile for them to except because it wasn't like that, traditionally.

When praise and worship replaced the testimonial part of service it was almost treated like a lynching. They even had threatened to walk out and go someplace else. But help came from the unlikeliest ally to help talk the seniors off of the ledge, Church Mother Supreme. She stood up and said to them, "It's time for the seniors to start supporting the juniors. We have had our time, let's pass the torch on to the young ones. They always support us, why can't we do the same for them? Besides that, how many more good Sundays do we have left anyway? I mean, I'm not raring to go but I'm ready to go."

After that Sunday the atmosphere around the church was totally different. The seniors had the ministry's back and all was well. The juniors promised the seniors their full support as well. And when that was said, the seniors took to that like a shark to blood in the water. Every chance that they got they'd get as involved as they possibly could. Always over looking everything just so that they could say something.

With the knowledge of having the run of the event led by Sr. Deacon, everybody knew that the seniors were going to run with it. Just how far, was anybody's guess? Every program for the event was top heavy with seniors. That was one of the perks. You could shape the program to your specifications. What the seniors were doing this year was to tell the history of the church, from their unique point of view. Each night, a group would talk on a decade starting at the beginning, so by the end of the event, a full seventy years of history would have been told. They were going to talk about the musical climate from the godfather of gospel, Thomas Dorsey/Mahalia Jackson era up to the Kirk Franklin/Mary Mary era. They had also gotten a few old school performers to split duty for the event. Yep, the seniors were going to show the juniors how it's really done.

The good thing about all of this was that nothing was going to be a surprise as far as appearances or what was to happen. They had to submit their program in advance to the committee. Everything was approved and the planning went forward. Being liberal in thinking was what the committee had always wanted. It believed in being diverse. It was truly going to be one for the books. It couldn't be one dimensional, that way it wouldn't be a carbon copy event. The theme chosen for this year's Summer Soulstice was, Looking Forward to the Past. It really seemed like the seniors were focused and on target this year. They had put on events before but this one seemed like they were going to try to take it to another level. They wanted to celebrate life and all that they had witnessed. They had plans to turn it up and out and put the pressure on whoever was going to handle next year's Soulstice.

They had held several secret meetings and gotten many of their friends and neighbors to promise that they'd come out and support them as many nights as possible. To accommodate so many seniors, the Senior Circuit asked for a special starting time of 6pm. When they gave their reason the committee agreed that it was a very good idea. They thought that it was such a good idea that they considered using that starting time from then on. What they didn't tell them was that all the seniors were instructed to arrive at a certain time and they would leave at a certain time. They had also chosen different colors for each night as well. This, was well thought out and planned.

When the event started the Senior Circuit began their program with a bang! At 5:50pm they all marched into the sanctuary and took their seats in the 'reserved seating' area. Canes, walkers, oxygen tanks and all, they marched in with all of their heads held high and each one was holding a candle. Then the lights were dimmed and one candle lit the next like a domino effect. When the last candle was lit they all sat down as one. Sr. Deacon and Church Mother Superior ascended the stairs to the pulpit acknowledging those in the pulpit with a slight bow and a blown kiss as they walked up to the podium. Settled behind the podium, they began to make their acknowledgments to the pulpit.

Then they addressed the seniors. The Senior Circuit stood up and they began to walk all through the sanctuary. Each senior took a youth/young adult by the hand. Once all the seniors were paired up with someone, the senior passed the candle to the youth/young adult. When the youth/young adult took the candle the senior took the youth by the hand and saluted the youth. This was so awesome that the congregation erupted in an enormous shout. The scene was set!

"Today, Pastor, we the Senior Circuit or as we have been called down through the years the Dorsey/Jacksons, salute you and the youth on today. As far as we are concerned that's anybody under fifty-five." Laughter rang throughout the sanctuary. "We now pass the torch to the younger, more energetic Juniors or the Franklin/Mary generation as we call y'all." This caused even more laughter. "Let the symbolism of these candles represent not only the passing of the torch but also the fleeting flame of life. We now ask each one that is holding a candle to bring your candle to the front and place it on the table because we don't want to be the blame if the church catches on fire." Even he had to laugh as the deafening laughter rang throughout the sanctuary.

The Leaders sat back in their chairs in amazement at the seniors. They knew firsthand how the Senior Circuit got down. Cross one of them was like crossing all of them. Hyenas had nothing on them. Cross one once, there wasn't any coming back across *that* bridge. It was a good as burnt. So if someone at the church called you 'burnt up' that meant that one of the seniors had gone in on you and everybody knew about it. They didn't play fair. And to see them so loose was a blessing in itself. They were actually laughing and joking. What happened to the serious seniors that they had come to know and love?

The service proceeded on and by the time it was for the speaker to come forth the atmosphere was on high. After the word was spoken and the benediction was done almost all of the seniors were gone. Only a few remained for the whole service. This was the way it was for the nights following except for the very last night.

On the last night of the Summer Soulstice there wasn't any reserved seating, there wasn't a sea of one coordinated color. The seniors sat where ever they could find a seat. This was by design as well. The seniors were to arrive late for a good reason. This was one of their last symbolic gestures of passing the torch, they were surrendering their familiar seats, where they normally could be found sitting.

Later on in the service when the church choir sang, most of the senior choir members joined in with them. They sang songs of old and of new with spirited full blown battles and tight duets. The anointing was so high that a shout and a dance broke out all through the sanctuary. Truly, this was one of God's masterpieces. The torch had been passed and now there was no longer a gap on this particular spiritual bridge. The church had been fasting and praying for years for something like this to happen and it finally did come to pass.

Now it was time for the word to come forth. Visiting Minister approached the podium without his bible and with the spirit in the air of expectation he turned to Pastor and said, "Pastor, I honor the spirit of Christ, you and the pulpit, but if it is alright with you, I would like to turn this back into the hands of this awesome choir. There is nothing that I could possibly minister, say or do that could top that." Pastor stood up and gestured that it was the minister's call and Visiting Minister took his seat and the choir went back at it.

As the service came to a close Pastor spoke for the first time all week. He said to Visiting Minister, "Hey man, I bless God for you and your humble spirit and I want to get you back here real soon because I know that you are going to bless the house. Family, let's get him back for the church's anniversary." Then a chant rang out "This Sunday, This Sunday, This Sunday" over and over again. "The people have spoken. We want you back this Sunday to come and wreck the place, amen," said the pastor. He gave the thumbs up and he and the pastor shook hands and embraced, then Visiting Minister gave the benediction and the service and the event had come to an end. As the Leaders attempted to hand him his love offering he stepped back and refused it. They pressed, he resisted. He took his things and left.

That Sunday, Visiting Minister came back and he brought the pain. God used him mightily for the first time in the spirit of prophesy and demonstration. His word for the house was, 'Get my God out of your Box'. He ministered about how people around you can't possibly see God's work in your life and for your life because their faith isn't your faith. Much confirmation was revealed by the time he was almost done. Before he took his seat, he said to the leaders, "Those rat droppings that were found in the pulpit, was symbolic that there is a rat in the house." And with that, he took his seat as a hush fell over the congregation.

CHAPTER 4
When a Woman Loves

For the next few months it would be business as usual for the ministry. This was a period of rest with so much having gone on over the past five months. The Leaders especially looked forward to this down time. For the next couple of weeks neither would be on the road or fulfilling obligations. It was a time to spend with each other. The first week they would stay home, the following week they would take a trip, some kind of mini vacation. Their first day at home, they called their 'Adam and Eve day'.

It was just like it sounded. They would be naked and unashamed. Their home was their Garden of Eden. With their privacy fence and their property yards away from any neighbors they could really act out. No electronics were to be used because there wasn't any in the garden. At first he opposed the no electronics rule because that meant there wouldn't be any television or music. No cell phones or computers he was cool with, but no tv was going to be torture. As he protested she said to him, "What do you need tv and music for when you have all of this?" Then she did a little shimmy and lay across his lap. After that, he it never came up again.

They tried to keep their sex life spiced up. They wanted to keep the home fires burning for each other, so each year they tried to introduce something new and exciting. This year they decided to start immediately after the Soulstice was over. Normally, they'd take a day to get their affairs together but they had been unusually busy of late that they couldn't wait any longer.

On the way home they set up their voice mails with new messages and instructions. Their assistants already knew the drill. If it wasn't an emergency emergency they were not to be bothered. After that was done they pulled over on the side of the rode and began to make out. This only heightened the anticipation for what was yet to come. He slid his hand under her blouse and she gently ran her first two fingers just a little below his waist and it was on! They always had a fiery relationship, they kept it hot.

When they got home he opened her car door, ran and opened the front door and ran back and swept her off of her feet and carried her inside. The door had barely closed and they were deep in it. Now, they were in their very own paradise. This would be the last night that he'd see her in heels for the next couple of days so he was going to enjoy this moment.

After their first round of love making, they stepped out into the warm evening air. They slipped into the pool and continued to enjoy each other. He watched as the water glistened off of her body and the soft rippling of the water splashed against her. He held her close just like fine china.

They talked for hours as they swam and played in the pool. As they got out of the pool he decided that it was time for him to talk to her about something he had needed to share with her. He hated keeping secrets from her. As they sat on the edge of the pool, a place where so many of their heart to heart talks had taken place, he said, "For the longest time I have wanted to talk to you about something." She motioned for him to continue. "I have an offer to sell the business. The offer is great and I would still hold shares and be on the board. Although we have more than we had ever dreamed of having, I don't know if I want to do it anymore." he shared.

"I have been waiting on you to finally open up to me. I have been with you so long that I know when there is something wrong or there's something going on with you. But honestly I thought you were finally going to tell me about your relationship with Top Notch. The business end of this will be addressed as well, but right now I feel that I am entitled to some kind of explanation." she said almost without emotion as she looked him directly in his eyes.

That gaze of hers reached beyond his eyes, it reached deep into his soul. Rarely at a loss for words, he struggled to address the body blow that she had just delivered. His life had been well crafted and prepared for times such as this. But, the difference here was that she would *not* have brought this up if she didn't have iron clad facts or proof. This shook him even harder. As he was still thinking she got up and went into the house.

When she reappeared she dropped an envelope on the table that separated them. "Open it." she commanded. He picked it up and pulled out a hotel registration and a receipt. What gave him away was the vehicle information. He sighed and asked her, "What do you wanna know?" "Everything." was her response. He went on to describe his treasonous act against her and their vows.

By the time that he had finished with his account about his misgivings she looked at him with pity. She knew that this could possibly ruin him in the gospel arena and on the circuit. She had also known just how hard he had worked to get where he was and became the man that he was today. She remembered how he had overcome so many personal battles and had won them all. But she also knew that she had played a very vital role in his and their success. He didn't do this alone, not by a long shot.

As they had done with so many other couples, they knew that they had to come to some kind of resolve. She said, "The other day I watched a couple standing across the street from the liquor store. I had seen them many times before but this time I realized that I had never seen one without the other. No matter what the weather was, they were always together. That's where I am with you. I wanted to exact revenge on you for your betrayal, but that couple ministered to me unlike anything I had witnessed before. I have been by your side when we didn't have anything and we were living on *your* dreams. I'm not gonna destroy what so many have tried to destroy, which is you or us."

She continued, "Remember it was me who handpicked her and she is my best friend's daughter. Even though I don't know how deep it is, I will not let this ruin the ministry, their family or us. I don't know if you are having a midlife crisis or what? But you have today and today only to end it." With that being said, she went back inside. As she sat on the recliner he came in and knelt down on the side of her. She placed her hand on top of his head and with her touch he began to cry like a baby. He not only begged for her forgiveness but he began to repent unto God.

She got off of the recliner and knelt with him and they began to pray together. It had seemed like an eternity since they had done this together. When they finished praying, he said to her, "You are my right shoe. Together we are better as a pair than single. Baby, I want to finish this race with you and you alone. Please forgive me for anything else that I have done or commissioned against you and your heart. I love you and I am very sorry."

He nestled his head in her bosom and she cradled him and caressed his body the way that she alone could do. This moment was what both had neglected, the intensity of the relationship in prayer. Somehow they were side tracked, but as of this day they knew that they were better together than apart. With that, they went to bed.

When they awoke, he picked up his phone and called Top Notch. He had the phone on speaker so his wife could hear the conversation. When she answered he let her know that his wife was present and that they needed to talk. He informed her that not only did his wife know about them but she had the proof. For the first time in ever, Top Notch addressed First Lady as First Lady. She always called her Auntie, because her mother and First Lady were like sisters instead of friends. "First Lady, I am sorry and there is nothing that I can say or do to make this go away. I thought that I was in love with him but now I know how wrong I was. I will clean out my areas at work and at the church." she tearfully whispered. "That won't be necessary, hon', we are keeping you on, only if you want to stay. And that you never mention any of this to anyone."

After thanking her she hung up. As Top Notch lay in the bed she began to cry uncontrollably. What had she been thinking all of this time? Why had she gone along with such a dastardly deed? And why would they still want her around? The more she thought the harder she cried. "What's the matter babe?" she was asked. She just shook her head. All she could think about was how much the Leaders had helped her throughout some of the worst times in her life. How she had such a good friend in First Lady. It was First Lady who held her up when she initially found out that she was a candidate for breast cancer. First Lady herself was a survivor of the dreaded disease. Pastor had championed a lot of the, Save the Boobies projects, bringing awareness to men as well as women. They were behind the awareness not only at the church but at their businesses. They had raised tons of money for the cause which they called, No Boobie Left Behind. They had also championed the awareness cause throughout the community.

She began to get ready for the day with her head still swimming in all that had happened in the last couple of hours. It almost seemed unreal, almost like a dream. But this wasn't a dream it was a real nightmare. She drove to the church in a daze and before she realized it she was sitting in the parking lot of the church. Although she knew what she had been doing was wrong all along, she really dreaded going into the church to go to work. Today was different. She wanted to wither up and blow away, letting the wind take her where ever it would.

They are going to see my scars, she thought. She had always been transparent in herself. Once she had gotten her composure she went inside. As usual she was the first one in the office. Soon the other ones would be filtering in. The only other people that were there were the Cleans and they were in the kitchen. Right now she really didn't want to see anybody.

CHAPTER 5
Reclaiming His Throne!

Down the hall in the kitchen, Clean was hanging up some of the big pots and pans. As he was hanging up the last pot the rack broke. The noise was deafening, it was so loud that it shocked Top Notch out of her funk and without thinking she ran down to the kitchen. When she got there Clean was standing there with a skillet in his hand looking at the mess in bewilderment. He thanked her for checking out what had happened and assured her that he was unharmed. As she prepared to help him pick up some of the things he kind of shooed her away with his hand that held the skillet. She backed off and returned to the office.

As he stood there looking at this mess he got angry. He walked past all of this and went into the dining area. He became even more enraged as he looked at the back of his wife's head as she continued to talk disparagingly about him on the phone. Before he knew it, he was standing right behind her with the skillet high above his head and said, "Get off the phone." She shrugged her shoulders as if to blow him off and continued to talk. He stepped in front of her and repeated himself. This time, she did something she hadn't done in years, she looked into his eyes. "I have to go," she said to the other person and put the phone down. Hearing her emasculate him wasn't anything new to him, this time it was just too much.

"Here it is that I am in the kitchen and something happens to me and you didn't even bother to come see about me. Even that gal from the office down the hall ran down here to see what had happened. You sat here and did absolutely nothing," he said to her almost in a whisper, but the words thundered inside of her. "From this day forward you will respect me, in this church, at home, everywhere, even if we are rowing on a river. You have disrespected me for the very last time. I have been good to you for the last twenty-one years. I made my mistakes, yes I have, but I tried to fix them. You claim to have forgiven me, but the way you treat me says something different. Not only have I apologized for my transgressions, I tried to help you deal with your issues that preceded me. I have tried to love you the best that I can but you don't want my love. No one's going to love you like I do, but that don't matter to you, Lil' Miss Perfect. Remember, you've done things as well but I stuck by you, even when I didn't want too. Well, I'm done now and I mean it."

As he talked to her, she realized that he was holding the skillet in his hand and the more he talked the tighter he gripped it. As to provoke him, she shouted, "Go ahead and hit me. I'm begging you to do it!" Almost Clint Eastwood-like, he said, "If I hit you I'll kill you and you ain't worth my freedom." As the venom from his words pierced her, she realized that she had finally pushed him too far.

He went back into the kitchen to attempt to put the rack back up, but he needed help. He walked down the hall to see if Cook's car was outside or if Fixx, the church's maintenance supervisor had made it in. He knew that they liked to have a good cigar before they started work for the day.

Since there wasn't anyone to help him, he stepped out into the parking lot and looked up into the sky. He began to laugh out loud, uncontrollably, as he looked up. He laughed at himself. He had held his head down for so long that he had forgotten what it was to really look up. "Did I just tell that woman that I'd kill her in the church?" He couldn't believe that he had done something like that in the bowels of the church. He tried to treat it and respect it like the sacred ground that it was. Even if he was to tell someone about what had happened, no one would believe him. That's just how long she had dominated his life.

As he stood there thinking about all of this, the rain began to fall but he still stood there. He didn't realize just how long he had been standing there in the rain, flash backing to his war days and thinking about all of the times he and his platoon had been caught in the cross fires and pinned down but by some miraculous way, he always made it home. A lot of good men lost their lives but God had *saved* him! "Hey there," a voice from the past rang out to him. "Get in here before you catch cold, you ain't as young as you used to be." Even with the wind and the rain he knew that voice. He turned around and looked at his wife of twenty plus years and for a brief moment he saw them young and in love, then he began to walk towards her. She held the door open for him just as he had done for years for her. As he went in she asked him, "Do you remember when we first met and I was about to open a door? And you said, 'If you touch that handle, I'll break your fingers.' He nodded yes and responded to her, "And I probably would have and I don't think you've touched another door since then, at least while you were with me." They shared a good laugh together. She took him by the hand and they walked hand in hand to the kitchen.

She had cleaned up the mess. He took her in his arms and dealt her a kiss that neither remembered existed. After the embrace she handed him his trusty old tool set that she had bought for him many a Christmas ago. Over the years he had become quit handy with them. At first he wouldn't even attempt to fix anything. She held the rack as he began to fix the support strut. She said, "I'm sorry for the way that I have treated you. Please forgive me." "I have, a long time ago," he answered. "Tonight, let's go downtown to one of our favorite spots and talk. Let's clear it all up so we can move forward, together." As he put the last screw in, she said, "You couldn't find someone to help you because I am suppose to be *your* help-meet." "This blooper happened for a reason. And you are my help meet, two times." he said with a smile.

Soon after they had finished, Cook and Fixx walked into the kitchen. Every morning the three of them got together to talk about what was going on for the day. They always tried to communicate with each other to see if there was anything new. After that, they would meet up with their teams. All three of them had put in many years not only at the church but in their own personal lives. On his way to his office, Fixx thought about how the Cooks were acting. "Maybe the black mamba, finally gave old dude some. You know she always saying that he aint getting none of that. Besides, who would want some of that venomous, war torn, old hot crotch. She so mean that if a snake was to bite her, it would die." "Naw, man. She so mean that if a snake bit her, it would attack another poisonous snake and they both would die." The two characters laughed, but made sure that they were out of her hearing range.

CHAPTER 6
Help-meeting! It Takes Two

Cook and his wife, Sister Cook had built a successful chain of catering businesses. She was the brains behind it all. She was always trying to create something new. Before she began her own business, she worked on the creative meal team for a major food chain. She was making very good money for something she loved to do. And then one day some coworkers and her boss, who she thought were her friends turned on her. They attempted to sabotage whatever she worked on with them. After a while, she got fed up with them and left. When people found out that she had quit her high paying job, they thought that she was nuts. What the naysayers and busybodies didn't know was, that she had been working on her own business for years. She had gone through the ups and downs as well as the failures, but she refused to let anything or anyone defeat her. The only other person she could confide in was her man.

While her old coworkers were trying to keep up with the Jones' and burying themselves in debt, she took a more practical way about it. Instead of throwing money away, she invested it into her own business. She had learned the hard way about who to trust with her first business venture. Once she was jaded it was a done deal. The walls went up and that was a fact. So with bulldog determination, she stepped out on faith. Her guy stood by her side all the way. He had gotten another job to support them because their income was going to take a big hit.

He told her on the day that she was quitting, "I got you." Without him having to say that, she knew this already. He had been committed to everything else but marriage. They had kids together and had been almost inseparable. They had a beautiful place to live, vacations a broad, wined and dined in the best restaurants, but had only talked about marriage sparingly. It wasn't until she had quit working that he proposed to her. She was blindsided when he knelt on one knee, proposed before offering her the ring.

They were at a baseball game with family and friends when the announcement came across the P.A. system. The announcer called their names and with a hidden mike, Cook asked her to be the future Mrs. Cook. She accepted his ring and his token of love with a resounding, "Yes!" There were high fives and the announcer saluted them. It was priceless. She was shocked and amazed at how he orchestrated this event. Later on when they got married they had her dream wedding and it didn't send them to the poor house. From the beginning they were open and honest with each other. They understood each other. To be in such a wonderful relationship was a blessing and they treated it that way. Out of all of the years that they had been married, there was only one night that they spent apart. They never let anything come between them. She once told her friends when she was asked how she defined their relationship, "I give it to him as many times as he needs it. So if he goes out and gets it anywhere else, he's just being greedy. I also respect his gangsta and he respects my queendom. That my friends, is how *we* get down."

Once, he was a speaker at a men retreat and was asked a similar question and he answered, "I put her first in everything that I do, on this side of heaven. Period. The only thing that goes before her is God. I'll describe my wife in a few words. She's accommodating to my needs. She's easy going, punctual, outspoken and very organized. Oh yeah, and she is very easy on the eyes." He made it a point to stress just how important it was for them to treat and respect each other. They went together like a hand in a glove.

When she began to work on her business he supported her all the way. She would bounce ideas off of him and use him as a guinea pig. She knew that he would tell her the truth, if he liked the idea or not. One time in particular, she made a dessert dish that she thought was going to be the next big thing. She had him to try it and he couldn't even get it down. She looked at him not sure if he was faking or not. When he spit it in his hand she knew that it was a miss. If he couldn't get it down, no one would be able to. He shared with her all that was wrong with her latest creation. He usually knew how to relay a miss to her but this time there wasn't any way to avoid it.

Finally, after a year of trial and error, she took her big leap of faith. But she didn't go it alone. The night before the opening of the first shop, she took him there. After she opened the door and turned off the alarm, she took him by the hand and led him to the office. As they turned to walk into the office she flipped the light on. There were two big desks side by side with an aisle between them. She said, "Would you be *our* company's president? You have been with me from day one and I trust you more than I trust myself." Before he could answer, she wrapped her arms around his neck and kissed him with everything that she had inside of her. He cupped her behind and lifted her up as she wrapped her legs around him. Throatily, he grunted his acceptance of her offer. That was twenty years ago and seven Britt's Bakery shops later and they were still growing strong.

All of these couples, the Cooks, the Fixx and the Cleans were a tight bunch. They often got together and triple dated. Their favorite thing as a group was to go fishing out on the Fixx family pontoon, The Elizabeth-Sweeney. They spent as much time out on the water as possible. They would also do boys night out, just like the girls had their nights. Although the Cooks were quit younger than the other two couples, they fit right in and they had the second longest marriage between them.

For the next few months, things were going alright all around the church, until it all just seemed to explode. Not only was it like an explosion, but it was like a domino effect. The ministry was about to go through one of the darkest transformation of its very own existence. No one was prepared for what was about to happen. No one could have foreseen the dark days that lie ahead for this body of believers.

CHAPTER 7
The Grand Finale

The first incident sent shock waves throughout the entire ministry as well as the community. Church Mother Superior was home alone and no one could reach her. Finally, someone called the sheriff's department to have a well being check done on her. Chief, personally took the call and went over to her house. She had fallen a few times lately and lay on the floor for a couple of days. After the last incident, her children tried to put her in a senior's village. The old gal wasn't going for that. She told them, "Your daddy died here and so will I." The children got together and asked the sheriff if he would take a set of keys and check on her occasionally, especially if there was another accident.

Chief was honored to do it for them. After all, she was his ex-mother-in-law and he was still a friend of the family. She still treated him just like one of her very own. He and Daughter had divorced years ago, they remained very good friends. Many thought that they should have remained together because they seemed tailor made for the other.

When he arrived at her house he knocked and rang the bell twice, just like he had done all of these years. After a few seconds and there wasn't any response, he put his key in the door. When he went inside, he noticed that the television was on. He knew that at this time of day she would be watching either the baseball game or the stock market channel. She always kept up with the economy and her portfolio that she claimed was her other child. He called out to her yet again as he made his way towards her bedroom. When he got to her door, he knocked and called her name. There wasn't any response so he slowly pushed the door open and he stopped in his tracks. The matriarch of this fine family, the senior mother and member of the church and one of his all time personal favorite friends sat dead in her vanity chair slumped over. She still had the brush in her hair. He noticed that the master bathroom door was opened and he went in. He thought that he was going to be sick. That's when he noticed that the tub was full of water. He touched the water and it was ice cold. He composed himself and went back into the bedroom.

He wanted to take the brush out of her hand and lay her on the bed, but he knew protocol was to call the coroner's office. He closed her eyes and called the coroner's office. He knew that now he had the unfortunate task of informing the family of his findings. It was sixteen years ago when he had to let the family know that he and daughter's baby was dead. Daughter was so distraught that the task was all his. He put his personal relationship aside and called his ex-wife. Before he could say anything she said, "Mother's gone, isn't she?" He choked out,"Yes." With those words they both began to cry. She was the closest to the region but she lived a couple of hours away. "I'll be there in a little while." "I love you, girl." he said and hung up. She took comfort that it was him that found her mother and not someone else.

The drive back home was the longest drive that she could remember. For the first time in her life, she would be in her hometown and her mother wasn't going to be there to greet her. The closer that she got, the stronger the anxiety became. She had always been high strung but this was too much. The anxiety was brutal. Why did she have to leave in such a huff and not have someone to ride with her? That was the way that she was and she knew that. What she needed was to learn how to allow others around her to help out and realize that she wasn't superwoman. She rationalized this latest action by it being the death of her mom, her last living parent. True, her siblings could have done most of the things that she did, but she felt like it was her duty to be involved in any and everything. She knew that her dominant attitude was her Achilles hill. It had cost her marriage and a lost child.

As she was thinking about this, she realized that she hadn't called anyone to tell them about what had happened. She drove a little further then pulled over. She began to call her siblings. Each reacted the way that she had expected. They all knew that Mother had far surpassed her life expectancy from breast cancer. Even after she had both breast removed, her recovery was nothing short of miraculous. The doctors marveled at her tenacity. She joked to the doctors before she went in for the removal surgery. "Boys, today is a sad day for men all across the world. The greatest set of jugs are soon to be no more." Then she cupped both breast and said, "Come on girls, last go for our last ride together. Now I'm gonna have to get a job." She and the doctors all laughed and they went in with all of her family looking on. Hours later as she came to, she asked the family about her boobs and their whereabouts. After they responded she said, "Man, I was gonna have them bronzed and sent to the Smithsonian. Wow, I ain't been this flat since I was six. Someone call the implant specialist. Daughter, you gonna have to teach me how to stuff a bra or something. I bet y'all daddy spinning in his grave right this very moment. Poor guy died right here where those girls used to be." She had always been proud of her natural and ample breast, especially for her tiny size, yes she was. That was almost twenty-five years ago. Now she was gone.

The more Daughter thought about her mom, the better she began to feel. Now she could continue on her way. She knew that her ex had everything under control. He had been very good to her and she didn't know how things had gotten so far out of hand. She constantly blamed him for the failure of their marriage. After a while he just had had enough. Often she would think about the 'what ifs'. She knew that submitting as a wife was the hardest thing ever for her to do. And it cost her, a good man. She tried to mask it, but even now she regretted being so obtuse.

With all of the different thoughts and the phone ringing nonstop she arrived before she knew it. When she pulled into the driveway and saw the coroner's vehicle she lost it. As she cried, her passenger's door opened and Sheriff got in. He pulled her to him and she cried even harder. He stroked her long graying hair. They had held each other before but this time was different. "They knew that you were in route and they just went in a few minutes ago," he said to her as he wiped away some of her tears from his face."If I would have put on makeup it would have ruined your clean white shirt." He laughed a little and brushed her hair back in place and dried her face with his handkerchief. He got out of the car and went to her side and opened her door. She extended her hand to him as she stepped out.

As she stood outside of her car, she realized that she is now the new matriarch of the family. If she had ever held it together before, she had to really tighten up her grip. Soon the wolves would be arriving."Brother probably has quit his job already." she said."Not yet, remember he gets a week's bereavement pay." he joked. He took her hand and they walked towards the house and all of the raw emotions began to overwhelm her again. He slid his arm around her waist and steadied her."Damn heels and tight jeans." she muttered, but he knew better. He knew his woman.

The closer they got to the master bedroom, the tighter she squeezed his hand. "Oh my, Mother Sister girl," she said to her mother. They stood over her body as she looked at her beautiful queen. She looked so peaceful, almost as if she was going to wake up. She touched her bejeweled right hand and began to caress it. Then she looked at her left hand and the ring that had commanded a hand of its own for over sixty years. She remembered a conversation with her mother as her mother explained the importance of a wedding ring. "It's not important where it came from or how much it costs. What matters is who's putting the ring on your hand. Would you rather have an expensive ring and the show or a simple ring from someone who really loves you and you love him back?"

Chief began to ease out of the room to allow Daughter to spend some alone time with her mother. She grabbed his hand and pulled him back. "I need you here with me, babe." He kissed her on the forehead and sat in one of the many chairs that adorned the bedroom. The old gal had pizzazz if she didn't have anything else. Every time that her portfolio did well she would purchase a piece of furniture and bless someone with the old piece. The good thing about receiving something from Mother Superior, you knew that you had been blessed. Everything that she owned had a *real* financial value. But the thing that she treasured the most was that ring. It wasn't worth much to anybody else but it meant the world to her.

As they attended to the fallen matriarch, a calm came over her. They wanted for her to look her best when the rest of the clan arrived. Mother had always looked impeccable in life and Daughter was determined to uphold that for her. She wouldn't dare be seen not looking her best. Mother was always the Grand Lady at all times.

Soon, the family began to trickle and Daughter welcomed everyone with hugs and pats on the back. She had decided it was best for the loved ones to see Mother in her glory in her grand home for the last time before the coroners took her out. That was one of the beauties of a place where everyone knows you. People would do their best to help you in your time of need.

Before long the house was full of people and chatter. It was very uplifting because she was the life of the family. No one was over dramatic or tried to pull the attention on themselves. Everyone sat around talking about Mother Superior, the mother like no other.

Once everyone had their time to spend with her, the coroner was called in. Coroner and his son came in and prepared her for removal. Once they had her on the gurney, the men of the family carried her out to the awaiting vehicle. As they passed through the house a silence prevailed. Great-great Grand Daughter opened the screen door and said, "Love you Mother Dear." And the tears and sobbing began. The closer that they got to the vehicle the louder the cries became.

Pastor and First Lady, who were among the first to arrive, comforted the family as best as they could. As the vehicle drove slowly down the long driveway, Daughter ushered the immediate family into the master study. "Let's get down to business, Lawyer is on his way. So that there is nothing left to chance, as we had all agreed upon, we will have the will unsealed when he gets here." This was not normal practice, but this clan was far from normal. After the passing of Father, all hell broke loose because there wasn't a will in place. Immediately, after his passing, Mother sat all of the children down and explained to them about Father's wishes not to have a will. He just didn't believe in them. What he *did* believe in was the fact that he knew that Mother was going to do right by her family. Like in life, even unto his death he trusted his wife.

As they made small talk Lawyer came in and gave his condolences and hugged everyone. As he took his seat and opened up his attache' case, he proceeded to pass an envelope to each sibling. He went through the necessary legal jargon before they opened their envelopes. He began to read the will as they read along. Occasionally, he would look at them with no one in particular in his sight. Before her death, Mother had the will updated and notarized.

As he ended the reading of the will he asked them, "Are there any questions?" When there wasn't any response he knew that all was well. He was there the first time and he knew how some of them acted after Father had passed away. He remembered how Mother was so distraught over the actions of her children. But in a way, the fruit didn't fall far from the tree. He stayed a little while longer thinking that there might be a backlash because of the amount of money she had left to the church and other organizations. For this brood of kids, they were uncharacteristically calm.

After he left, they returned to their guest and well wishers. Now the place was absolutely packed. People were on the porch, in the yard everywhere. The grand dame was really loved. The Cooks had brought over a ton of food as they had always done for their family and friends. The community always had a tendency to support one another when a crisis came about. That made the situation a little easier to deal with. One of the good things was the fact that Mother had everything planned out for this occasion all the way down to her dress and the order of service. The only thing that had to be done now was to call everyone and let them know when the funeral was. She had stipulated in the will that she was to be buried in four days of her death. She made Daughter promise her that she would fulfill her finally wishes.

With all of the activities surrounding them, Daughter pulled Chief back into the study. She was beginning to have another anxiety attack. He needed to find her pills. She said, "Whatever you do, do not give me those pills. What I need from you, my best friend is to reassure me that everything is going to be okay." He did as he was asked. He pulled her into his chest as the tears flowed from her eyes. He whispered sweet nothings and caressed her the way that only he could. She began to apologize over and over again. He knew her heart and what the apology was about. He also knew that going to the cemetery would mean that she wouldn't be able to run anymore.

He sat with her until she was ready to go back out among the people. Her childhood running buddy was the first person that she saw as she stepped out of the study. He grabbed her and they held one another. She and Assistant Pastor had been friends for as long as she could remember. They never lost touch. He would've been there sooner but he was detained until now. He took her by the hand and they went outside.

All that she had been through, he was with her through it all. Other than Chief, she had never loved another. For a while he and Chief were neck and neck courting her. She had shared her first kiss with him and lost her virginity to him. They had been through so much together and supported each other, that their relationship was something different. He knew what he did to her back in the day was wrong. He manned up and they called it quits. Had he married her instead of trying to turn her out things possibly could have been better for them as a unit. He toasted to the better man and bowed out gracefully.

They talked for a little while and he excused himself. She thought that that was odd because he always had time for her especially in her time of need. What was going on with him that he had to leave her in such a huff? What could be more important than this? He promised that he'd check on her later, kissed her on the cheek and left.

Pastor came over to where she was standing just as she was lighting a cigarette. "You remember when Mother Superior caught us smoking your daddy's cigarettes? She was so mad that she made us smoke half the pack, dip snuff and chew that nasty tobacco. Girl, you brave. I ain't had none of those since that day." They got a good laugh in together. Soon they were joined by others and someone turned the music up from inside. The sounds of Mother Superior permeated the atmosphere. It was her favorite collaboration of music. People began to jam and sing along with the music. Soon they broke out with the Soul Train line. This helped to keep their spirits up. As the others went down the line, Pastor and Daughter did their thing. That's what the congregants loved about the Leaders, they always seemed to be in a good mood and be there for them. They would be there for you, either one or both of them. They weren't stuffy and eternally sanctified.

Still, she just couldn't get over Assistant Pastor leaving the way he did. He knew that he was going to be the official presiding over her mother's funeral. As the day went into night, more people came over with more food and drinks.

CHAPTER 8
Brother Going to Work it Out

Brother was getting his fill in and he hadn't really spoken much to anyone. They kind of dismissed this as his way of coping with the loss of his beloved mother. Although he was as callous as they came, he had a soft spot for his family and friends. He was reliable but unpredictable. His gambling habits had cost him to the point that the Family had to cut him off, but they loved him deeply. Father's loss really took a toll on him. Daughter and Sista tried to keep him in the loop and keep him on track. After he was cut off, he finally went looking for work and landed a job at a slaughterhouse in a town a few states away.

He was proud of himself because he had gotten the job on his own. No one opened the door for him or pulled any strings to get him in. Not only that, he held this job a lot longer than anyone including himself ever thought he would. And to top it off, he had been promoted a couple of times and was actually in line for a front office job. He knew what they were thinking about him, but he didn't care. He had nothing to prove to them or anyone else. He promised himself that he would not be a cliche just to fit in. Love him or hate him he was going to stay true to himself.

The only one that knew about his change was his mother. He made her promise that she would keep his affairs private. That was one of the reasons that he moved so far away. He had to get his act together and survive or fail on his own. He recognized the damage that he had done in the community and he needed a fresh start. Gambling had controlled his life since he was a youth. At first it was back alley dice games then it was the ponies followed by the dogs. If there was a wager to be placed and he could put money on it he would. The worst thing that ever happened to him was the stock market. Determined to succeed like his father but in a different arena he dived into trading like a dung beetle to dodo.

When it all came crashing down on him and to save face, he began to secretly borrow money and invest it in get rich quick schemes. He never could get it right but he kept trying until the bottom fell out. When that happened he didn't run to the bottle or to drugs he admitted himself in to Gamblers Anonymous. He spent months in rehab and wouldn't except his release until he thought that he was better.

Upon his release, Chief picked him up on the request of Mother Superior. She had always worried about him. He was her 'gypsy baby' as she would tease at him. He knew that he was abandon at birth and was raised by this family. Father and Mother told him everything when he was very young. It was a very well kept secret because at the time that he was born Mother Superior was pregnant. A week before she was to give birth, she and Father got into a very physical altercation over his drinking. When she told him that she was going to tell the congregation, he went into a violent rage. He began to break everything that he could get his hands on and soon his attention turned to her. As he made his way towards her she attempted to pick up a heavy object and her water broke.

As the fluid ran down her legs, Father snapped out of his drunken rage and picked her up and rushed her to the hospital. When they arrived at the emergency room, he explained that her water had broken and they thought that she was about to give birth. Within minutes she was on a gurney and rushed her into surgery. As the baby was coming out she wasn't breathing. The doctor did everything that he could to revive the newborn but it was to no avail. He apologized and she began to cry. Father held her hand and began to curse the death of his child. The medical team left them alone to bear their grief as they held the baby doll sized infant and cried together.

Soon she was placed in a recovery room with another woman who had just given birth. All night the new mom cried and complained about how another baby was going to ruin her life and that no man would want a woman in her early twenties that had five kids. As the night progressed, Mother Superior began to minister to the woman about God's love for everyone and that no one was excluded from His love. "That sounds good, but you aren't in my shoes. You have your husband I'm still looking for someone to except me and my kids," she said in despair. "Besides that, you don't even know me." Mother Superior responded, "No, I don't know you, but I have two kids and I just lost my baby. Now I have to bury a baby that I never had a chance to hear cry, not once. I would love to have another one but that's it. I couldn't go through this pain and agony again. Ever. I'm done." With that she turned over and pulled her sheet around her neck and closed her eyes and began to weep.

When morning came Father and Doc came in to the room. As she woke up, she noticed that the woman was gone. When she inquired about the woman, Doc said, "She went out for a smoke late last night and disappeared. But if you can come with us we have something for you to look at." She got in a wheelchair and the three of them headed towards the nursery. Through the nursery window she observed two infants, a boy and a girl. She recognized the infant girl. She held Father's hand a said, "Thanks Doc. I'm okay now. Heaven has another angel." Doc asked her, "Look at that little boy and what do you think about him?"

Doc motioned for the nurse. Nurse picked up the baby and Father wheeled Mother into the nursery. Nurse placed the baby boy in Mother's arms. "His mother abandoned him. Do you think you could find it in your heart and home for a little boy who needs to be loved?" she was overwhelmed and overjoyed. "He's perfect, my little gypsy baby."

That was decades ago and the secret never got out. Now he was without his number one cheerleader. Life would never be the same for him. He loved and cherished his mother and father but it was the others that he had issues with. Maybe some issues were real and others weren't as real. All he had left was his siblings. His ex-wife had committed suicide on the old church grounds and he kind of went into protect mode and the walls went up on every side. Outside of his parents, he refused to let anyone in. He felt that every time he got close to someone they either left him or died. This seemed like a pattern from his birth.

He went over to where his siblings were and hugged them. "Tell me what you need me to do and I got your backs." They looked at him and smiled, because he had been so distant in the past. That's all that they had ever wanted, was for their brother to be a part of *their* family. He had missed out on so many special occasions over the past decade or so. He had moved to a town that was so remote that the only way around was by car and one had to go almost twenty-five miles to the bus depot and the airport was even farther away. Although he grew up in a rural area it had an urban appeal. Everything wasn't hard to get to. At the time, he knew that he had to get away, far away.

The next few days were eventful to say the least. Mother Superior had everything so together that they had very little to do. They had a feeling that she didn't trust them to follow her wishes. The only thing that she didn't do was write the eulogy. But they were sure that the official was briefed.

Chapter 9
Holding Back the Years

The day of the funeral was at hand. Since the church wasn't that far away, the family gathered at Superior Land. Although they had been there all week, it still was going to take time getting used to her not being there. There wasn't a family color scheme because she made it clear that she was more concerned with love & solidarity than appearances and being cliche for this occasion. When it was time to leave, everyone packed into the cars and went to the church as one big happy family.

The siblings went in first followed by the rest of the family. There was already a crowd gathering and the funeral still had well over two hours before it started. Once the family had entered and given the okay to the funeral director the people began to pour in. This was the first and only public viewing because she wanted it this way. She looked absolutely fabulous. Even in death she was stunning and graceful. Soon the church was packed out and the service was about to start when panic set in. Asst. Pastor hadn't made it yet and no one had heard from him either. Daughter turned to Chief to see what should be done. He took her by the hand and they approached the pulpit. Pastor had an idea about what they wanted to ask him. Before they could say anything he said, "I'm already ready." With those words he got up and began the service for the celebration of life of the one and only Church Mother Superior.

There was standing room only, just as it should have been. Not only were there many families and friends represented, but almost every organizations that she was affiliated with was in the number. She was so recognized that only three people were to have remarks, one would represent family, friends and the charities. There were only two resolutions to be read because that would have taken half a day in itself. Before Pastor presented the representative, he held up a giant stack of resolutions. As Church Mother and Sr. Deacon made their way to the podium they were almost overcome with grief and emotion. "We stand before you and the family with heavy hearts and emotions that are hard to express. We are to read a couple of resolutions from her two favorite organizations, this church and the breast cancer awareness foundations." They went on to read and before they took their seats they talked a little about her. "Family, the old belle will be greatly missed. She was here for all of us in one form or another. She was the first lady of ladies. She will be a hard act to follow. Daughter, you have great shoes to fill, but we are here for you and the family. We all love you all." They blew them kisses and bowed as they left the pulpit.

First Lady came up and spoke words of encouragement and held out her arm and pointed towards the beautiful casket. "This beautiful woman pulled me to the side the day that I became the first lady and took my arm and pulled this bejeweled bracelet off of her arm. She slid it over my wrist and said, 'If you're gonna replace me then you may as well have something of mine. I held that title and seat that is now yours for more years than I care to count. These people are not just people, they are your family. From the worst to the best, you have to love them all. Stand by your man and it will be a trial, but hang in there anyhow.' Everything that she said to me was not only true but it was valuable. She taught us ladies not to cast our pearls before swine. I'm not lying when I say this, but I will miss this jewel of a woman. I will miss the First Lady of ladies." As she wiped away her tears Pastor slid his arm around her waist. He too tried to hold back the tears but he knew that he had to step up to the plate not only for the family and the supporters but for Church Mother Superior.

"From the first day that I met her until her passing she has always shown her love to us. We had our differences but she was still good to us. When I succeeded her husband Father Pastor, I hadn't a clue how far I would be able to go, but those two supported me and my wife to the fullest. Rarely do you find people who are willing to groom their successors but they did. We have tried to continue in the integrity that they paved for us. After Father passed, she was just as faithful to God and her work as never before. If she was hurting she would still press her way to be here." He continued on until he was coming to his conclusion. "As of this day, the row of seats that are front and center will forever be called, Church Mother Superior's Row, out of respect for her and her vision." With that, two ushers came down the aisles and attached golden plaques on the outsides of the row. There was a sweet spirit in the air. As the plaques were being secured Pastor motioned for the directors to come for the final viewing. The family sat stoically as the beautiful hand crafted casket was opened for the final time. As the top of the casket opened, there was such a quiet and calm that it was almost eerie. The only time this sanctuary was ever quite was when there wasn't anyone there.

As the ushers began to direct the people for the parting view, the family looked at this sea of humanity and their collective tears began to run down their faces. They comforted one another and held hands in solidarity. Daughter knew that her mom would be proud of them and she began to smile broadly. As she began to smile, it seemed to effect others. "Now, that's what mama would be proud of." she said to Brother. He gripped his big sister's hand so tight that she felt his nails dig into her palm. Here she sat with two of her favorite guys in the world, but there was a void. A void that she hadn't been able to quite figure out. How could Asst. Pastor do this to their family? That's when the tears began to come back. Why was she digging so deep into this? Why was she still allowing things like this to take her focus off of the good things? Here was the true love of her life which had never turned his back on her and supported her through the worst of times standing right beside her. But this other one, she seemed unable to escape from. Even in a time such as this. She tried to convince herself that whenever he contacted her she wouldn't drop everything and go rushing to him. But she knew that was a lie. He held her hostage and she knew it.

Finally it was time for the family's turn for the final viewing. They all touched, kissed or caressed their mother's hair. The Grand Dame of the ball was really gone. When the family stepped back Undertaker proceeded with the closing of the casket and the processional instructions were given. They followed the casket as it was wheeled out of the sanctuary. The pallbearers went out and stood by the hearse, then they lifted the casket in and the door was closed.

Once everyone was lined up, her final ride was in progress. Although the burial site was only a few miles away it seemed like the procession was extraordinarily long. All the while, Chief held her hand and he would caress her arms occasionally. She would look his way but only at a glance, careful not to make eye contact with him. When they stopped at the grave site everyone began to get out. It was a very somber moment for everyone. The true finality of it all was upon them. Pastor lead the way towards the family vault. It was a replica of Superior Land. As the family was getting ready to follow she stopped. Chief said,"Babe, you have to be strong." He tried to reassure her by looking directly into her eyes."This is going to be a challenge for both of us."

With that having been said they began to follow the throng of people to the vault. Every step they took, she could feel her legs buckle underneath her as Chief tried to support her. When they got to the entrance of the vault it seemed as if all eyes were on her. Everyone knew that she hadn't been there for years. She just couldn't bring herself to come there because her child lay in there. After that loss, she couldn't bear children nor had a desire to do so. She had often felt that God himself had abandoned her. She couldn't understand why all of the females around her were so fruitful but she was barren.

As if to be reading her mind, Sista and Brother stood close to her and they walked into the vault. The pallbearers came inside with the casket and placed it the burial tomb. Pastor gave the last rights and the ceremonial bouquet of flowers was placed on top of the casket followed by the gloves of the pallbearers. The ceremony was over and the caretakers went to work sealing the casket and the tomb. When all that was done, everyone stepped out to gather with the others. The sun beat down on them and the wind blew ever so gently. It was almost perfect except for the fact that they were at a cemetery. As the doors were closing, Brother and Chief took out their keys and prepared to lock the doors. Before anyone knew it, Daughter stopped them and pushed passed them and reentered the vault closing the door behind her.

She turned to the crypt that had been her child's final resting place for what had seemed like an eternity. She looked at the recently cleaned nameplate and picture of her lost child and she began to shriek out in pain. Chief and Brother came in to try to comfort her. They knew what she had been battling since the death occurred. She had been so distraught that she couldn't even attend the service for her own child. The last time that she saw her child was on the morning of the death. She refused to accept the loss. It pushed her to the point of a mental breakdown and she had to be admitted. She spent months in recovery and when she was released, this man that held her so tight right now was there for her through it all.

They would spend as much time there as she needed. She needed this time and rushing her wasn't an option. The family had been praying for this to happen and it was finally happening! She needed a breakthrough. She had given up on prayer a long time ago. Why should she pray when the victories were few, far and in between? Her emotions were off the charts. Brother silently slid out to leave them alone. Finally, she got the breakthrough that she so desperately needed and fell to her knees. There she began to bless God and she surrendered herself to Him. As she began to repent she said to God,"Father, please forgive me. Daddy, I need you to help me. I am yours if you will take me back." Chief attempted to help her up but she stopped him as she pulled herself up."Babe, I have to do this on my own. Thank you."

Once she had regained her composure she took him by the face and kissed him. "I love you. Please forgive me for pushing you away." They walked out of the vault together and she was shocked to see that almost everyone was still there. This was so overwhelming to her. As the doors were closed she watched as Brother and Chief turned the keys to lock the doors. They walked towards the awaiting vehicles and as they passed the people, many smiled and spoke kind words her way. Once they were pulling down the path towards the exit she looked back one more time and realized that the hurting was bearable. The world was a much better place now.

When they arrived back at the church there were so many people there. It was as if a major event was happening. Once everyone was seated in the dining hall Daughter addressed the multitude and thanked them on behalf of the family. The smell of many foods permeated the air and the mood was festive. Soon the hall was filled with chatter and laughter. This went on for a few hours and it was time to leave and head back to Superior Land.

Brother and some of the other men set up a food tent and the extra food and drinks were placed inside. The sun was starting to make its decent, leaving just a couple of hours of sunlight. Daughter began to look for her cigarettes and realized that her phone wasn't in her purse. She asked around but no one recalled seeing it since earlier. Some others helped her search for it and it was found. She checked it and saw that a message had been left on it. The message contained three words 'git at me' and she slid out of the back door without hesitation. She took off down the trail behind the great house and cut down the dirt path that lead to the other side of the lake.

When she got to the boat launch she stepped on to the deck of the boat and it slowly pulled off. After the boat was on the other side of the opening, the motor turned off and the only sound was from the waves splashing against the boat. He walked over to where she stood and grabbed her. He began to go up her dress and have his way with her. She attempted to put up a fight but realized that it was futile. She gave in to her urges and surrendered herself to him. He violently took her and when he was finished with her he started the boat back up and steered it to the launch. As she got off of the boat she heard a splash in the water. She tied the boat to its dock cleats and began to walk slowly back towards the great house.

It was dusk now and as she was half way down the path when Sista stepped out in front of her."What are you doing? How could you still go to him after all that he has done to you and your family? I followed you to the back door and I knew where you were going. What is it going to take for you to get that devil out of your system? It's like the more that he takes from you the more you have to give to him. I covered for you for the last time. I know that we were in this together at first but I won't be a party to hurting Chief again. He loves you dearly and it seems that you only need him when it's convenient for you. He's been good to you. Not just you but all of us. We aren't kids or even teenagers anymore. I don't even know why I am even bothering with you about this." As Sista turned away from her, Daughter grabbed her arm and before she knew it, Sista slapped her across the face. In turn Daughter fired off a slap to Sista's face! They stood there looking the other in the eyes.

Not knowing what to expect next, they stood there locked in a sibling stare down both wondering about what had just happened. They had a relationship and secrets that only they knew. The depths of which could destroy the other or even worse, both! Soon, cooler heads prevailed and they started to walk back to the house. As they made their approach, they could hear all of the revelry that was going on. They acted as if nothing had happened but inside they were seething at the other. The emotional roller coaster continued because now they had to be involved and interact with their company but inside they were incensed. They refused to act out on their emotions, that had a time and place and they both knew how it was going to go down! Around their loved ones they put their game faces on faking it all the time. The festivities went on late into the night barely missing dawn.

CHAPTER 10
Welcome to My House of Pain

The dawning of a new day was at hand as they were finally able to close the doors for some much needed rest. That didn't last long. It seemed like they had only gotten a few minutes of sleep before they were up and about. The three of them had some decisions to make and discuss the recent events. "Let's go to church today," Sista suggested. "Me and you got some unfinished business to tend to and it can't wait until service is over. First, I'm gonna whoop that jackass of yours, then repent about it. That's what's up. I shoulda beat that last night, back on the path," spewed Daughter as she stood up.

Not to bullied, Sista jumped up and started walking towards the basement. Brother ran past them to block the door. "We just buried ma and you two are about to go into the Thunder-dome. I ain't even gonna ask 'Where they do that at?' evidently the at in question is right here. Go ahead, kill each other. For what? I don't know and don't even give a damn." He stepped aside and the sisters went in the basement closing the door behind them. As they went to the part of the basement that they had named Thunder-dome, no words were spoken and no one backed down. It was on!

Daughter walked past her sibling and walked up the stairs. She slid the security bar into its slot and walked back to her place. They nodded and rushed each other, sumo style. Although they had had many clashes before, this *one* was going to end it all. This time there wasn't a two minute all out brawl. This one had to have a clear cut victor. It wasn't going to be a fight to the death but one that was going to be as close to it as possible. They ripped into each other with savage disregard for the other. Their fury coming out in grunts and groans, as they attempted to gain control. It was an all out assault, so severe that one would not know that the two were blood sisters. Fist rained down as Sista mounted Daughter unleashing a brutal barrage never seen or felt before. Daughter tried to cover up to let her arms absorb the brutal attack. As she did this, Sista beat her in the chest and ribs with one fist and used her upper body for balance. When she threw a punch to the face and missed, she lost control and Daughter flipped her over and with catlike reflexes she began to kick her adversary unmercifully. She kicked and stomped her as if she were a dog in the street.

Sista began to beg for mercy. "B', you shoulda thought about that before you put your fn' hands on me. I ain't through with you by a long shot." She reared back her leg as far as she could and with a primal shriek she kicked her sister so hard that she broke her toe from the impact, the sound of the bone breaking cut through the basement bouncing off of the walls. As she went down in a heap grabbing her foot, her sister began to spit up blood. In all of their madness that didn't stop them. They still tried to get at the other. Finally, they had reached the point of no return. They knew that any further assault upon the other could be fatal and they had just lost the most influential person in their lives.

As the air cooled down, they heard the sound of banging on the door. Brother was pounding and yelling at them to stop. They could hear the anguish in his cracking and strained voice. That sound ripped deep into them both as they made their way off the floor and up the stairs. They were so exhausted that neither could speak. When they opened the door, Brother stood there with tears running down his face and his eyes were red from crying. He grabbed out to his battered sisters and tried to hold them both. With the voice of a wounded sibling he said to them, "Where do we go from here?" He helped them to the couch and began to tend to their wounds. He did something else, he picked up the phone and made a call.

As service was going into high gear, Doctor's cell began to buzz. Not one to ignore his phone he looked and saw that the call was coming from Superior Land. He stepped out of the pews and went into the hallway. The caller was frantic and he knew that it was serious. He went back in and handed his wife their tithes, whispered in her ear, kissed her and left heading out to the mansion. He feared the worse as he drove to his destination.

Pulling up to the house, he was met at the door by Brother. "They are in the main study." When he went in he was shocked at the scene that sat before him. He looked at Daughter's badly swollen foot and the bloody shirt of Sista. He began to work on them as Brother assisted him. When he had done all that he could, Brother said, "I called you instead of calling the paramedics because evidently my sisters hadn't seen today's paper." He held the newspaper up and to their surprise, Mother's funeral was on the front page!

"There is no way that I would've gotten the paramedics involved concerning this vicious act the day after our mom was laid to rest." Doctor understood. "They have got to get to the emergency room right away. Brother, you take Daughter and Sista will be transported by ambulance." He picked up the phone and called for help as they left.

They rode in silence as he sped to the hospital passing the ambulance along the way. It was usually him that kept the family on their collective toes and for once, it felt good that it wasn't him. He knew that his sister was in much pain but his mind stayed on Sista. He knew that she was in bad shape and he began to pray. Not realizing that he was praying aloud, he heard Daughter join in. Here was the person responsible for someone's injury that wanted to pray for the victim. He wanted to tell her to can it but he didn't. He just began to intercede and stand in the gap for them.

He rushed into the emergency room and got a nurse and a wheelchair. They went out and got her and admitted her in. When asked how the injury occurred he told them that she hurt herself helping her sister who would be arriving soon. He had been around his parents long enough to know that you keep it in the family and deal with it that way. As Daughter was being taken away he whispered, "Love you, girl."

No sooner had she been whisked away the ambulance pulled up. He watched as his other sister was being brought in. She did not look good at all. He knew that by the way that the paramedics were acting. Her eyes were closed and she had a chest compressor around her midsection. What the hell was happening to his family and all in such a short time? They had already called in to let the emergency room know that she was in serious need of attention. Doctor rushed in behind them heading toward the surgery room to get cleaned up. Fortunately for him his most trusted assistant was still there. They got prepped and went in to perform surgery on her. Brother gave the lady at the admitting desk as much information as he possibly could. He told her that she had had a bad fall in the basement and that was all that he knew and went into the waiting area all the while thinking about his sisters and the damage that was done.

Why were they acting out so bad? All sorts of thoughts raced through his head. Soon he was joined by Chief. He was the only one that they knew that wouldn't be poking around in their business. All he was told was to come to the hospital. As the two men sat, Nurse came over to them. She began to brief them on the patients and that Sista was still in surgery. It looked like it was going to be a long and rough day. After a few hours had passed they were allowed to see Daughter.

Inside her room, they sat by her bedside waiting on her to come to. Doctor had let them know that she had been given a heavy sedative. He didn't know that she hadn't much sleep over the last days. She was in bad physical shape and she needed much rest. He wanted to keep her for observations for a few days.

He didn't really go into detail but he knew that he was going to have to say something soon. With the little information that they had, the two men waited patiently, each in their own world.

She began to stir a little while later and they jumped up on each side of her. As her vision began to come into focus, she was barely able to speak. She motioned for some water. Taking a sip she asked about her sister. When told about Sista being in surgery a lot longer than expected she tried to get out of the bed. "I need to see my sister. I need to see my sister," she yelled. They tried to restrain her from getting out of the bed and not to hurt her. She didn't even notice the cast that her foot was in. She struggled in vain until finally giving in.

"We can't tell you much because we don't know what's going on other than the fact that she is in recovery. Doctor will talk with all of us. He wanted to wait until she was comfortable and recovering and that you were coherent. All we know is that she is alive after losing so much blood." The more that she heard the worse she felt about the whole thing. She began to relive the fight, blow by blow leading up to the near fatal kick. She recalled that her intention was to stomp unmercifully upon her fallen adversary but chose to deliver a brutally placed kick instead. The tears of compassion began to well in her eyes followed by a heart wrenching series of sobs.

While the men comforted her, she began to calm down. For a moment they thought that they would have to buzz for the nurse. She lay silently in her bed but continued to cry uncontrollably over her sister. Later Doctor came in to check on her but she had cried herself to sleep. The men themselves had also fallen into a light sleep. The events of the past week had taken a toll on them as well. Doctor woke Daughter and the men. He talked as he checked her out. "If you guys want to go and see Sista you can but she doesn't want to see you." pointing at Daughter.

This cut her deep. Then she began to rationalize with herself and said to no one in particular, "I wouldn't want to see me either." Her mind began to go back far in their lives. They had always had a sibling rivalry but they were also the others biggest supporter. Had they really come to a point of no return? As the men began to leave the room with Doctor, Chief leaned over her and kissed her on the forehead. Going out of the door he looked back at her once again before leaving. He wanted to stay but he knew that he had to go with Brother.

They walked down the narrow hall to the room that Sista was in. Nurse was in the room as they entered. She let Doctor know that she was stabilized and was still coming in and out of consciousness. He looked at her charts and had a quizzed look on his face. They wanted to know if everything was okay. He assured them that everything was fine but Brother wasn't reassured. Almost on que, Sista's eyes opened slowly. They stepped closer, anticipating that she was going to speak. "Hey Brother and Brother-in-law." Then she slipped back into unconsciousness. She would do this all night as Brother sat with her. Chief went back to stay with Daughter.

CHAPTER 11
Reach Beyond the Break

Over the next few months, there still seemed to be an unrest around the church. One day Pastor was in his office when First Lady came in with Top Notch. They all had felt it. Soon they were joined by others and they went into the great hall. The only thing that they could do was to pray. They began to intercede on behalf of the ministry. As they prayed they began to go into spiritual warfare.

The town hall meeting was today and that always was a challenge. Maybe some clarity or resolve would come forth. After prayer was over many went on to the work areas. Since the death of Church Mother Superior strange things were happening. One, was the fact that no one had talked to the family much and the other was the attitude of Asst. Pastor. He seemed so distant almost invisible. He had either not shown up or if he did come, he was late and the first to leave. His contact with the Leaders was strained at best. They couldn't put a finger on it.

Then there were the strange calls from other pastors. Many of them had called in regard to the question of congregation tampering. Some were very accusatory of them trying to pull people from their flock. With every call the frustration mounted. One thing that this ministry prided itself on was that they never tried to pull others from anywhere. God had truly blessed them with the fruit of their labor. He had shown favor on this body of believers unlike they had ever seen. A very large segment had joined the church looking for a Christian journey experience. They came from the streets, shelters, prisons and from the street ministry. Where the question of flock hustling came from was beyond their comprehension.

The town hall meeting was about to start. The Leaders were on their way to the overflow area where these meetings were held and noticed the amount of people there were already there and even more were coming in. At this rate they would have to move into the sanctuary. He had Brothers #1 and #3 to usher the people into the sanctuary. The time was at hand for the meeting to start and prayer went forth. Pastor thanked everyone for coming out as he began to share with them the addendum for the meeting. Many of the faces were not as familiar as were others. This was very strange because it almost, always, was the congregants and people from the neighborhood.

Once the books had been opened and all of the topics had been touched he came to the last part of the meeting, the reading of the names of the new members. After the latest additions were officially read he opened the floor to the people. A man and woman stood up. "Pastor, we thank you for allowing us to speak. We would like to address a very serious allegation of member tampering. We have several letters here that had been passed out to various churches encouraging our members to come over here to fellowship. Not only that, we have people that claim that someone from your ministry has personally called them trying to get them into your fold. At first we were going to go to the state board but we decided to come to you first." Then the murmuring began. "May I see those papers please?"

Brother #3 gathered the papers and brought them to the pulpit. First Lady began to look through them and she began to shake her head as she handed them to him. On official church letterhead, these letters were written with the church's seal and their names stamped on them. He took a moment before addressing the situation. "First I'd like to apologize for this. We have no knowledge about the genesis of this and we will get to the bottom of this, I promise. Those of you that have fellowship with us know that this is not our character. Never has been and never will. When a person joins, *we* sit with them and talk to them. We inquire if they are coming from another ministry or if they are coming on a Christian journey. If they are coming from another ministry we ask why they are leaving and if they hold any position in that ministry. So far we have never had any problems over all of these years. We have prided ourselves on that. Just like when one of ours leaves, we ask them if we or the ministry had a part in them leaving. We try to resolve any issue as best as we can. And yes we have lost members over the course of time. Some have even left us to join other ministries that we have fellowship with. We assist them in any way that we possibly can, even giving them a letter of release and accommodations. We want what's best for the kingdom and hijacking someone to stay some place that they are not happy at isn't worth it." As he spoke the murmurs had all but ceased. By now his wife was standing by his side holding his hand. She could feel his tension. He was not only her pastor and husband but he was her best friend and her covering. She pushed pass what they were dealing with personally and stood with him.

For a moment there was a clarity that she saw spiritually. Almost in that same moment of clarity reality had come back. "We promise to get back to you, expediently. If there isn't anything else we can close out." She prayed a short prayer and they went out among the people.

After they talked with the people they went into her office. As she closed the door behind them, she turned to him as he sat down on the couch by the window. "Let's go home." she said. He looked up at her as she stood by her desk. They had been separated since the incident. At first they slept in separate rooms then she decided to go to her girlfriend's house for a while. She had to get away. She turned off the lights and they left. In the parking lot they said their good-nights to those that were still lingering around. He opened her door and she got in. He watched as she pulled off. Brother #1 asked if all was well with him. He nodded as he got into his car and headed towards the house.

CHAPTER 12
There Goes My Baby

The drive home for him was one full of thoughts and anticipation. At first he thought to stop and get something for them to eat but he decided against that and proceeded home. When he pulled into drive way he noticed that her car was still running. He walked up to her car and she turned the music down. She had been listening to their favorite song. He opened her door as she turned the music back up. They embraced and began to slow dance, careful to hold each other as tight as possible. As the song went off she locked the car and turned back to him. "We have some work to do and it seems like it's going to be a lot. But first we have family business between you and I. When I step back through those doors I am stepping back in as your wife and your best friend. Before we can help anyone we have to help ourselves. We need, no, we *have* to get counseling. I have someone in mind that doesn't know us and who won't be easily persuaded. We have an appointment in the morning."

As she talked he listened. They walked towards the front door and she stopped. He opened the door and she went inside. She looked around and everything was in order. The place was really clean and neat. She knew how he was at times and she'd fuss at him about certain things. "I let the maid go for a while, at least until you came back. I didn't want any woman in here but you."

That made her feel good but that's all that it did. "I'm always preaching forgiveness, but I don't seem to possess what I preach. Why? I don't know. I know that I can be critical of others, but when it comes to me it's like a double standard. One for everyone else then there is one for me. We are the nucleus of the ministry, our businesses and our family. And people look to us for guidance. How can we lead if we don't have it together ourselves? When I knew that I was going to be your first lady, I fought that because I knew what the territory involved. All I ever wanted to be was just your wife. That was from the first time that I met you even until right now. Since I've been gone, I had time to talk to myself and my girl. You are the best thing that ever happened to me. When I got sick you were there with me all the time. When I had my issues with my drinking and pills, you stood with me. I left you when you needed me most. When you had your award ceremony and I wasn't there, Girlfriend got all over me for not going. She reminded me of the things that I had done, but you stayed the course with me. At the town hall meeting, I watched you. I knew that those were lies and I couldn't stand by idly and watch them attack you." He stopped her from continuing.

"There is something that I have to share with you. I thank God for you and all that you have done and all that you do. I wouldn't be who I am today had you not come into my life when you did. There isn't a woman or person walking this earth that could touch you. That's why what I have to tell you will be hard. I had time to think things over and I promised that I wouldn't hold anything from you." He joined her on the love seat and looked her in the eyes. "There never was anything between me and Top Notch. I was at the motel helping our son." He sat back and the tears began to well in his eyes. "He and she had been secretly seeing each other and I didn't even know about it. He called me there because he had done something wrong. When I got there I asked 'What is this?' She was badly hurt and he was only in his underwear. They had had a really bad fight and then he sexually assaulted her. I tried to calm them both. She was hysterical and he was high. I spent hours trying to sort this chaotic scene out. I told her that she needed to call the police and get medical attention. She refused to do either one. Their time for the room was getting close to an end so I went to the front desk and extended the stay. What I did was very stupid and shameful. I didn't want him to go to jail and have his life ruined because of this. So I came up with the idea about her and me, and she agreed to stick to it."

"Did you think about what would happen to her? Our son did this and he should be held accountable for this. You mean to tell me that almost ruining our marriage was more important than the actions of a grown man who committed a crime so vile against a living and breathing soul. I don't know which is worse, lying or cheating? Now, we have a real problem. We don't need counseling right now but what we do need is healing. What could be more damning?" For the next few hours they went over everything that had transpired then went to bed. Neither slept much. It was a lot to deal with.

Before they got out of bed, he pulled her close to him their bodies fitting perfectly together under the sheets. It was a special moment for them both. He needed her kisses and her as well. She was truly his one and only love. All the while that she was gone and their contact was very limited, he busied himself in prayer and fasting. He dreaded the fact that for the first time in his life being with her, he wasn't honest with her.

Some of the things that she stated the night before made so much sense. Why would he allow anything to come between them? But he knew that his decision would put him between a rock and a hard place. There never would be another lapse in judgment on his behalf. She was just too precious to let that happen. She had been his everything. He knew that their relationship was that important.

"What do you want for breakfast?" he asked her. "I want you!" she replied and pressed against him harder. They spent the next few hours enjoying themselves. Afterward, they went to the shower. As they were drying off she turned to him and smiled. "For some strange reason, I just couldn't believe that you would have done something so diabolical. But I kept letting it into my heart. When I told Girlfriend about it, she stood up for you. I didn't have the heart to tell her that it was her daughter that you were involved with. I just told her that I thought that you were tipping around. Now we have a bigger problem. What do we do, babe?" He took her hands and began to pray. After prayer he called Son and Top Notch.

CHAPTER 13
In the Bottle

As they waited for their guest, they busied themselves with medial tasks. It seemed like an eternity before the bell from the gate buzzed. They knew it was her because Son had the code so they opened the gate. After a few minutes he hadn't come through the door yet. Pastor went to look out and saw his son's car. He thought that to be strange. As he opened the door, Son and Top Notch got out of their cars. They spoke and walked towards the house.

First Lady welcomed them in. They all sat down in the living room. The air was a little stuffy even though the windows were open. "Son, I told your mother everything. I couldn't let this secret ruin our marriage. What I did was dumb. I shoulda told her from the beginning and we coulda dealt with it differently. Top Notch, it's not too late to pursue legal action against him. We will stand by you and your decision, but we will support our son as well." Son attempted to speak but his mother cut him off. He sat back in his chair because he knew that his mother was pissed at him. "We have bailed you out time after time and I made your father promise me that he would not use his influence in this case. We are prepared to weather the storm. We will not be held accountable for your actions, not this time."

"May I say something, please?" Top Notch asked. Without waiting for an answer she proceeded. "I don't want this to get out. This will have heavy ramifications. I have had time to think about all of this. He has called and apologized several times. I just want this to go away so I decided that I am leaving. It's too much for my heart to bear, but I thought that I was in love, I guess I know better now. I am stepping down from all of my posts. This is my notice and my decision is final. I will take care of the reason for my leaving. Let me handle that, please."

They sat in silence for a few minutes before she got up to leave. The Leaders went to where she stood and embraced her. She was like a daughter to them. And they hated to see her or anyone else hurt, especially at the hands of someone so close to them. They had gone through that, because of this horrible situation that their son had put them in. The ladies walked towards the door and hugged again. Then they went out to her car. The day was as beautiful as a picture. As she leaned to put her purse in the car First Lady took her by the hand. "My daughter, I love you and there isn't anything that will change that.

But do you really have to leave? You have been nothing short of a blessing to us." "Auntie, I have to do this for myself. I have been helping others for as long as I can remember. I learned a great deal from you. It was you and my mom that cultured me in every area of my life. I will be in contact, probably more than you would like." They laughed and hugged again. Before she pulled off, she handed her godmother her work cell phone. With a look of strength and determination she waved and drove off.

As she was walking towards the door, she heard a loud commotion. When she entered the house, she entered just in time. Her two men were going at it pretty bad. They had gotten within arms length of the other. How had this transpired into such a bloodbath of words and anger? She stepped in between the combatants fearing the worse. Their son had put them in compromising positions before, but this was the straw that finally broke the camel's back!

They had noticed that something was off about him. Whatever the situation was, it affected his praise dance. The anointing wasn't there as it had been before. His parents had noticed this and wondered how many others had as well. Secretly, they had talked about removing him, but they thought that praise dancing was his best hope for whatever was holding him hostage. They had also noticed that ever since he had hooked up with Asst. Pastor that his anointing in dance was lifeless. It had no effect, almost like someone who was just going through the motions, someone who wasn't doing it for God and the people, but more so to minister to the flesh.

Once he decided to forge a relationship with the likes of Asst. Pastor, his disposition began to change. He used to be so loving and thoughtful. Now, he was callous and abrasive. This was not just in his home life but in everything else. At work he had been suspended for insubordination, twice. He refused to do the work assigned to him because he didn't like the response that his boss give him in regard to his advances towards her. He created such an hostile environment that he had to be removed. Now he had gone and done this!

"I know that this is our fault, we have been protecting you from yourself for so long that we regret it. You have to answer for this, Boy. There is no way around it. We used to think that it was because of us that you rebelled so much. But we agreed that it was your choices and you always seemed to make the wrong one. You knew that we would bail you out of the jam that you got yourself in. I wish that we had never done that. After the first time, we should have let them lock you up. We have walked on eggshells when it involved you, but that is over. This time your actions have gone to far. She said that she forgives you and so do we, but as of today, you are being removed from your posts."

"That's cool, because I was getting tired of doing it anyway. Besides that, I was really doing it for you two. At first I thought that it was nice and I received a lot of love. But as time went by, I lost the love for it. Being removed is a relief, now I don't have to be phony." When he said that, he looked directly in his father's eyes. Before anyone knew it, Pastor had his son's neck in his hands. He began to squeeze as tight as he could. He wanted to choke the life out of him. In a moment of hate, all the ill feelings that had been boiling up inside of him began to surface. As he choked and squeezed he began to swear at him. He wanted to kill him!

Son began to fight back and couldn't quite pull away from his father's death grip. His eyes began to bulge out and his breath was getting shorter by the second. She stood there in horror as her guys engaged in a one sided death match. She began to plead with her husband to get off of him. But her words seemed to fall on death ears. She was truly in fear for her son's life and the future of her husband, if he succeeded in his quest to maim or even kill him. Fearing the worse, she entered in, trying to pull her man off of the son.

When he felt her on his back, he knew that he had to let go or risk hurting her. He never wanted to harm her in any way, shape, form or fashion. She was his everything. As he began to loosen his grip, he could see his own finger impressions left on his son's neck.

He stood over him and stepped back. What had he done? His own flesh and blood was almost annihilated by him. In all of his madness, he forgot about everything that mattered. "If you leave the church and I find out that you are operating in any kind of office, I will send a personal letter to that pastor and tell them that you were removed from your various positions because of the things that you have done. And I mean that!" His son began to regain his composure and it was apparent that he had finally worn out his welcome. Without saying a word he left his parents home for what he figured would be for the last time. He dropped his keys to their home and the church on the ground as a last act of defiance.

Neither parent went to him, they let him walk away. They knew that this was the best way to resolve this situation. Pastor went out and picked up the keys and went back inside. His wife was still very shaken and crying. He walked over to her and placed his arms around her and brushed her hair back. "Baby, we are all that we have and I will never allow anything or anyone to stop that. I need you more now than ever. You stood by me through thick and thin. When you were not here with me I felt so alone. Thank you, my love and please forgive me."

"When you asked me to marry you and I turned you down it was because I allowed other relationships to hold me back, I felt so bad. I had wanted you as my soul mate from day one. The day you said to me, 'I will never do you wrong and I will never break your heart', I knew that you were the one for me. The more that I fought loving you, the more you chased after me. One day I finally figured out for myself that you were serious about me. I will never forget our first date, you pulled my chair out and helped me with my coat. You sat there for a minute before you said another word. I thought that you were going to stop pursuing me. But you reached out for my hand and held it before speaking."

"And I said to you, 'You are worth my wait.' And nothing has changed that. Not this that has just happened or anything else. I made a vow to you and I meant what I said. I will never stop chasing you because I know that the grass isn't greener on the other side. Our pasture is the only place that I want to graze in, no one has loved me like you do. No one has nurtured us like we have for each other. I stopped being single a long time ago, that's when I first met you. You have shown me love like never before and I never want to loose that. You know, we like them jackals. They mate for life. They stay together until the death."

He knew what to say and when to say it to her. His words made the difference at times. Sometimes it just wasn't the words that he said but it was the way that he would say them to her. She recognized him as her pastor and covering, but she heralded him as her husband and best friend. The events of the day had really taken a toll on them. But as usual, they met on common ground. Their son had almost caused them to lose sight of that with his blatant attempt to blindside them with his callous actions.

As they began to straighten up the mess from the fight, she found some pills on the floor and a small flask not to far from them. She picked them up and turned to her husband and said, "My baby." He took them from her and went to the sink and turned to her as she began to cry. "Stop that, it isn't our fault. He swore to us that he would never take us through this again and we believed him. I will not allow this to overtake us! Please stop crying. I'm hurt just as much, but he is a grown man and has been for a very long time."

CHAPTER 14
What's Good?

At last it was time for the church picnic. This was a grand time for all. This years theme was 'What's Good?' Each year the committees were to hold different events. What ever event they presided over, they could not participate in judging. This years events were Best Barbecue-Ushers Board, Best Sides, non vegetable-Deacon Board, Best Deserts-Nurses Board, Best Side, vegetable-Pastors Aide Committee, Best Bread-Teachers.

Other events were the annual softball, volleyball, basketball and tag football games, all played in a round robin format. The gold, silver and bronze team medals were at stake. All defending teams were seeded number one. The trash talking had started months ago. The Elders had pulled the first punch at a bible study by revealing their new world championship jerseys. It seemed like every year something new was added to the picnic. The event was so large that it was held for two days, Saturday and Sunday. All of the finals were held on Sunday. It was another way of creating change but still recognizing tradition.

Each team that participated in sporting events had to have at least two youths and two seniors and could not be gendered dominate. Trash talking had been going on and on, but the days of recognizing was at hand. Also, this year was going to be a dunk contest and a volleyball skills contest. The dunk contest was always a big draw especially for the youth. That was their time to shine. But every once in awhile some of the older guys would absolutely steal the show. The last show stopper was by Brother #3. He had dunk after dunk that kept the audience on their feet in awe. He won the championship belt with a dunk off the head of his finals opponent. This brought out one of the loudest standing ovations ever in the history of the picnic. As he held up the championship belt, he raised the hand of his young opponent. They took pictures together and that memory was talked about for the longest time.

But the crown jewel of the weekend was the spoken word. Each night the Leaders tag teamed in bringing the word of God. One night she would open and the following evening he would open, but both nights were high times in the spirit. When they brought the idea to the committee about having different speakers on the nights of the picnic, the committee strongly objected. "Pastor and First Lady, we know how liberal you are in sharing the pulpit and helping people to share the word of God, but at something like this, we feel that it should be you two that should bring it. There will be many people there that are not familiar with our church and it would be good for them to hear the word coming from you two. When we invite others out, we share with them not only about the ministry but about our leaders and how God uses the two of you." So it was settled, and that was the way that it would go until further notice.

The Leaders prepared to leave for the picnic and they were filled with much excitement. All week long, they had been studying, praying and fasting seeking God's face for this blessed weekend. Ever since the altercation with their son, they had been in countless counseling meetings and running here and there. But the quality time that they had found for themselves was oh so sweet. They held hands and shared some of their passages with each other. They always loved the fellowship of studying, prayer and fasting together. All week long he addressed her as 'my good thing' and she referred to him as 'my covering'. They had gotten so much closer by bonding together, it helped them to weather the storm. On the way there, they listened to their favorite C.D. In silence, each one in their own world. This year they did something different, they dressed alike, all the way down to their shoes.

Earlier that week, he had picked her up from work and on the way home they saw a sign that read, BELIEVE. They looked at each other and laughed. She said to her husband, "Let's get a pair of running shoes alike. We haven't dressed alike in a while. I think that would be nice, show the devil we are stronger than ever." He thought that that was a good idea and they drove to the sporting goods store.

Inside, they picked out a pair of running shoes and matching sweatsuits and shirts. As they were leaving, she was in front of him and when she got to the door she stood there waiting on him. He walked up with their bags and she waited for him to open the door for her. He looked at her and smiled,"Yeah, you wouldn't look right at the picnic with broken fingers." Even though it was an electronic sliding door, she always considered his wish to open her doors for her and she had long since conformed to that. She knew that he loved her even if he never opened another door for her again. They acted like teenagers in love.

Because of so much that had been going on in not only their personal lives but the amount of couple counseling that they had been doing of late prompted them to use as a theme for Saturday "It's not a breakup, it's a breakthrough!" and Sunday's theme was "It's a love thang!" Pastor would go first on Saturday and Sunday and First Lady would do her thing last.

He kicked it off in high gear talking about Brother Boaz and how he loved himself some Ruth. And cross referenced that with the love of Jesus the Christ. Just as he was hitting his stride, the spirit over came him and he began to cry. As the tears streamed down his face he said, "Brothers, I appeal to you on this day to love your woman. Not only tell her but show her. Never allow your woman to outshine you. What I mean is that it should be no contest, you should be the undisputed champion of love to her. Don't let her find it in a box of sweets or what ever she does to feel loved. You have to be her everything. Ladies, I am ministering right now to the men, my wife will minister to you all next. But my only advice to the women is, except him for who he is and help him to be the best man that he can be. Now back to the brothers, I want to share a little testimony about me and my wife. Prayerfully, I won't have to sleep on one of your couches, amen. One time we were not getting along. We slept in the same bed, ate in the same kitchen and went to the same church but we were so angry with each other that we allowed the enemy and fear to almost uproot us. Yes, she was mad at me and in retaliation I stopped speaking to her unless it was absolutely necessary. I even took it a step further, I stopped praying for *us.* That was a very foolish thing to do. I allowed whatever that had happened, to come between us and it evolved into a monster. Of course we put on our game faces for the public but we were making life miserable for the other. Then one day she was walking by me and I reached out to hold her hand and maybe it was on instinct but her little hand and fingers slid right into place. I call it the hand in glove syndrome. Your hands and love should be perfectly fitted to join the other. But before I made an attempt to get her attention, I got back on my knees and began to pray and repent. You see, I stopped praying, period. Hey you all, this is my first time speaking about this in public and my wife didn't even know that I had fallen back so far that I didn't want to even pray. Those of you that know me, know that I *love* me some prayer. I want you brothers to listen to me, God heard my prayers and He spoke to my spirit. He let me know that He wasn't pleased with my decisions. That I was a conditional servant. But His love for me was unconditional. I broke down even more. God had to minister to me personally in regard to the way that I was treating His chosen vessel for me. I knew that God put us together. I saw her face and her spirit. She did something to me from day one. She was and is everything that I hoped and prayed for. I stopped looking once I met her, because I knew in my heart that she was God's elect for me. What I am saying is, love your woman unlike you have loved anything before. Now brothers, take your girl by the hand and look up in the sky."

Against the evening clouds a Batman signal filled the sky over them. As he took his wife's hand he stepped back, kissed her and said, "Be her superhero!" Once the audience was settled, he introduced his 'very good thing' to them.

She was met with such a thunderous showering of love that she was almost overwhelmed. It was always an honor to her to be able to bring the word. Many had taken this privilege for granted, not her. She still got butterflies in her belly from the anticipation. As the audience quieted, she began to go forth in power and demonstration, using the topic of "You've got it!" She ministered using many references throughout the old and new testament in regards to many of those that overcame. "You cannot move God by fear. Being scared and talking about your faith in the same breath is like oil and water, the two don't mix. God moves on your faith. That's what turns him on to you. Your faith has everything invested in it that you need. Sarah, bless her soul, laughed when it was ministered to her that she would conceive in her old age. She laughed just like a lot of us would have. God doesn't look at your age, he looks at your ability. He looks at your faith. He sees things that he has to instill in you for the greater good. Sisters, there is a plan for you in this world, single as well as married. While you are single, enjoy it because when your Abraham comes, and he is going to come, prepare yourself for the vision that the Lord has for him that concerns you. If I were you I would be getting excited right now.

My husband shared some things about us that even I didn't know until now. All though I knew that he was the one for me, I still pushed him away. He didn't look like the ones I was used to, he didn't wear the cologne that I liked and he wasn't built the way that I wanted the man of my dreams and the future father to my children to be built. But he loved me and this man showed it from day one. I did every thing to discourage him, but he kept on after me. We did a lot of things together, but he was patient with me. I guess he finally got frustrated and he said to me, 'You are worth the wait.'

"What I am saying is that just like Sarah, I almost missed my blessings. Don't get it twisted that being married to a senior pastor isn't rough at times because it is. He brings his work, church and everything else home with him. I always try to listen to him because that is our job as a couple, to listen to each other. That's the beauty of being committed to the love of your life. I had to stop running from my fears and had to trust in my faith. Not just in my man, but in Jesus Christ."

"We were not meant to be alone. God created man and woman to be together for the furthering of His plan. It took a while but soon I too began to yield to

God's will for my life. Once we both yielded to God's authority, things began to get much better. Not every thing was fixed right away, but we tackled them as a team." She turned to him and held out her hand, he walked over to her and intertwined his fingers in hers.

She lifted up their hands and said, "If he doesn't hold my hand this way, I know that there is something wrong with him. I had to learn to look and watch before I took offense before knowing what the real deal was." The Leaders saluted the audience to a thunderous applause. They had to triumph, for love. They knew what many were dealing with and they blessed God that His love would prevail to all.

As they stepped out into the crowd they were greeted by so many couples. Some they knew, others were new faces. The bulk of the evening was filled with tons of talking and fellowship. Time was nearing for the beach to close so they made a hasty retreat over to the beach. Every year, they walked the shore line under the cover of night. Usually it would be just them as they walked looking out over the ocean and up into the stars. But this time something special happened. As they walked they were joined by a multitude of couples. Each couple either held hands, leaned on each other or just walked arms around waist. Many, often stopped to kiss and adore the other.

While watching this awesome exchange in love, they just smiled and glared into the others eyes."My love, you were worth the wait. Look at this all around us. That's whats good!"

CHAPTER 15
Cherish the Day

It was Sunday, the day of reckoning for all the finalists to bring home the gold and hold up the trophy with pride. There was still a hangover effect from the previous day's events and activities. All though it was relatively early, there were so many people all ready out and about. As the Leaders made their way to the picnic area, they listened to the music in the distance. They began to follow the rhythm of the music that filled the air. Soon they were in the midst of a group of musicians and a d j. They were doing a little warm up battle and the crowd was loving it.

The d j was pumping the deepest of house music, smacking it around with some hard hip-hop. The vibe and the energy was crazy. Soon they were bobbing their heads to the talent and skills of the beat maker. DJ knew that he was moving the small crowd when he started to scratch the vinyl. The harder that he jammed the more involved the people got. He took it to the next level by doubling Erik B. and Rakim's, Move the Crowd. When he did this, he stepped back from the tables, and hit the people with Eric B and Rakim's, Follow the Leader.

"Check one-two, one-two. People we have in our midst my pastor and my first lady. Give it up to the Leaders. They the truth, y'all, real talk. If you looking for a good church, step over to the church picnic area. We'd love to have you as a friend to the family. I've been there for a few years and it's been a blessing. Over at the picnic is a lot of food, fun and fellowship. God's got a blessing for you but you have to go get it." DJ went back to his task of keeping the music flowing.

On the way to the picnic area, Pastor said to his wife, "DJ has come a long way. It makes me proud to see the work of the Lord as it manifest itself. That boy wouldn't say a word unless he was forced to. Now he won't stop talking. That's my guy." She nodded her head in agreement. As they neared the picnic area, the smells of food found its way into their nostrils. "I can't wait to see who wins the cook-off, plus I'm starving." "I'm looking forward to tasting the spoils of the victors," she shared with him. "But sharing another day with you makes it even better." They stopped and began to kiss. A couple walked past them and smiled at the affectionate couple. The young man reached out and took the young lady's hand as the walked on.

When the Leaders finally made it to the area, they were approached by many of the members. They had a look of concern. "Whats going on over here?

Did something happen?" "Not really, we were just discussing some prayer topics and we thought about doing something special in memory of the fallen soldiers. We also want to remember those that we have lost spiritually. Do you have any suggestions?" They all went under the tent to talk about it. This wasn't going to take away but it would add to. They discussed this topic about an hour then it was off to the picnic and enjoyment.

Their first event would be the volleyball finals. He loved volleyball. He had played it all of his life. If it wasn't for his lower back problems he would've continued to pursue a professional career. He was in the top 30 in the country and volleyball helped to pay for his college education through scholarships. After his injury, he embraced it even more. He stood by his team and eventually became a student coach. Many were so proud of him but he was the most proud. By the time his back had totally healed, he knew that he didn't have the competitive fire in him to compete and he shared that with the team and his coach.

As they found a place to sit with a good view, they watched the finalist warm up. He set out their sling-chairs and as always he would drift in and out. He often thought about the what could have been. He kept it just short of being bitter. As he sat there Coach walked up to him. "It's gonna be a good one today. Both teams pummeled the competition. I haven't seen teams this fired up since my college coaching days. I remember this one kid though, he was a beast. He could drive the ball like David could sling a rock. I often wonder what happened to that kid?"

"It's good to see you too Dad." Pastor stood up and embraced his father. After that Coach leaned over and kissed his daughter-in-law on the forehead. "Where's Ma Dear?" "She'll be along in a bit. And you better believe that she will be making her presence felt. She's still got the determination to do things for herself, especially since her last doctors visit. Well, the title game is going to start soon so let me go so I can go over the rules with the teams." His father was one of his biggest supporters. What he lacked in affection he showed with his support. The thing that surprised them both was the fact that Coach didn't bring up their son. That's when they knew that his parents knew. Coach usually would ask about his grandson before anything else.

Soon the championship game was under way and it was a battle. This one had the feel of a sanctioned game. Like a prize fight of sorts. One of the blessings of playing the first title game was that it was held before the heat set in. Each year the games rotated. This encouraged others to participate. Another blessing was that whoever won, held the title and acclaim for that year. This also sparked a lot of trash talking. The winning team would usually go over to the next event and get good seats displaying their newly achieved success. Sometimes the debates would get hotter than the action, but it was done in competition and gamesmanship.

The weather this year was unusually mild. By now it would be scorching with people scrambling to find shelter or often going over to the beach for a quick, refreshing dip. Although the clouds would often bring relief, this year it didn't matter. The weather was perfect all day. As the leaders began to cruise the food row. Their first stop was to get a deep fried corn dog garnished with ketchup, grilled and raw onions. This was a treat for them. They acted like little kids all giddy and stuff. He handed her a steaming hot and freshly dipped corn dog done just the way she liked it. She took it and they tipped the corn dogs together like a toast and took a bite.

She loved her food and drink hot, just like the weather. He on the other hand preferred his food and drink a little cooler. But when it came to the corn dog toast he would bite the tip off and eat the rest a few minutes later. That was one of their favorite traditions for the weekend festivities. Next they made their way to the cider stand. They couldn't have the corn dog without washing it down with the finest cider independently manufactured. Actually, the cider stand was the only recognized business that participated in the annual event. The apple-orange cider tasted like the nectar of the angels. That was the company's slogan and it was right on target.

When Businessman was asked about the slogan he would say, "My wife wouldn't let me say it was the drink of the gods. She felt like it was to boastful and that she wanted it to be more approachable. So that's why its the nectar of the angels." They started the cider business within a few years of retiring. They knew that they had saved a very nice nest egg, but they didn't just want to retire without having something for them to do.

So they began to take classes in business and marketing. When they learned about how many successful businesses were launched well after the owners were past their so called prime, they were willing to at least give it a try. They had built a successful beverage business even though a couple of better known beverage companies had plants locally. They went into this venture without fear of the others because it was more or less something that they wanted to do. It wasn't something that they had to do.

Yet, they had a very marketable product and it was in the local stores and gas stations for about a fifty mile radius. They knew to keep cost down and prices affordable, they wanted to keep it local. The gamble paid off and soon they had four shops in four different regions. They stuck to the plan and had set up each one of their children with the opportunity to succeed in the family business. Sixteen total stores was the max for them. They had even turned down offers to sell the brand for a far more lucrative profit. They turned the offers down because they wanted their children to learn how to run a successful family business.

All though they had released much of the day to day operations to the children, they still ran the stand for the picnic and a few other yearly events around the city. They constantly tested the market for information at these events. The sales would dictate what the trend called for. For them, the people made the difference and the bottom line was secondary. "You can have the best brand in the world, but if you don't have the people to consume your product whats the point? Every bottle that we put out, we expect to sell it. But we want the person purchasing it to come back again and again. That's why we try to treat everyone who buys a bottle of our cider as if they had made the purchase of a lifetime. Some things are free and showing gratitude is one of them." He and his wife were so serious about this that they taught customer relations. That's something that they could do and still meet the people as well as the employees. After each employee went through the training and learning the different ciders, they were asked to choose three different ciders they personally preferred. They were given a four pack of those three drinks as a gift. They would be encouraged to bless others with some of the ciders. Not only that, the employee would have a recognition of the product first hand. All employees were given a chance to voice their opinions. They were treated like family.

With their drinks and corn dogs in their hands they went to sit under their favorite tree. Every year except for one, they did this. It was a time honored tradition and they loved it. Soon they were joined by a few people and they were engaged in spirited banter. The topics ranged from the food to last night. What was agreed on was the fact that last night was uncharacteristically filled with love and hope. "You guys brought a lot out last night and we appreciate that. I went home and held my family one by one and expressed my love for them. I hadn't done that in ages. Thanks. I really needed that." said one of the men.

This was what it was all about. Hope and deliverance. It just wasn't for the church folk but it was for the people at large."The one thing that we try to do as people is to show love and compassion for others. If God can love all of us unconditionally, we truly can at least try to do the same. Just continue to do what you're doing and bless God for that." They always attempted to at least keep the people encouraged. In the distance they could here the musicians jamming. The sound of the drums and the horns were intoxicating. He took her by the hand and they went back to where the music was.

They were belting out Cherish the Day by Sade. As they did this, a couple of ladies stepped out and began to sing. Some of the couples began to dance and make faces at each other. The Leaders did the same. Sade was one of their all time favorites. Actually, they had blown out a speaker or two pumping the sensual sounds of this great artist. Their first concert together was her's. They could talk about her in high regard.

Soon the singing divas asked for request. Someone requested Angel by Simply Red. Diva #1 replied, "That's my jam. We go deep with Mick Hucknall and Simply Red. As a matter of fact, if it's alright with you guys, we would like to do a mini-set." The crowd encouraged them and it was on. These two women sang with the passion as if it was their very own work. Even though it was late afternoon, the feeling of love was truly in the air.

They had gotten so caught up in the mix, that they had missed the basketball finals. What made them aware was the noise that was coming from the basketball courts. "Wanna go?" "Nope, I just want to enjoy the moment with you." They embraced even harder. They were no longer dancing, they were lost in emotion. The world was just them, alone. For the time being nothing else mattered. What they held in their arms was worth it all.

Finally, it was time to head back, but they knew that they would be back for another dose. They liked to be normal and not to be worried about what the do-gooders thought or said. They had been through all of that and they decided that it was up to them to be positive about how they portrayed *their* relationship. They refused to try to live up to other people's expectations of how their lives should be.

Since the crowd was still by the courts, they headed that way. It was just as raucous as it was about a half hour ago. The energy was high and the boy's were still going at it. Or so they thought. As they got closer, they realized that the girls were on the court, and they were ballin'! One of the girls was a highly recruited superstar forward. She had offers from all over the country, but she wanted to stay local so that she could help out with her siblings.

Even though her mom had backslid and fallen into despair well over three years ago, Superstar still came to church and made sure her sibs were in church as well. She was two years older than her next sibling and couldn't imagine leaving them behind. Not only that, she had to look out for her mom.

Coming down the court, she tripped over someones foot and collided with some others. She landed hard on the ground. There was a loud pop from the collision and the hush that came over the crowd was unbelievable. She rolled around in pain holding her leg. People ran over to the fallen athletes and tended to their injuries. Someone began to yell out for help. From the sound of the impact it had to be bad. It took a few minutes for the emergency treatment squad to get over to them. They began to work on the other girl that lay motionless on the ground. The sickening sound that was heard wasn't from a leg injury, it came from her head hitting the ground.

Superstar stood up hobbling, looking down at her baby sister. The tears began to run freely down her face as they began to pray for the girl. "Lord Father, please protect my baby sister with your love and cover her with the blood of your son Jesus Christ," she prayed aloud. Then she began to really weep for her sibling. This family had been through so much lately and all she could do was trust in the Lord. Now here she was again feeling that God was forsaking her and her family. With a loud voice she yelled, "Satan the blood of Jesus is against you and we rebuke you and your minions right now. We loose favor and healing on my sister and we bind every unruly spirit that is around her. My Father, please send and surround her with your warring angels." She stepped back and let the medical team work on Baby Sister.

Ma Dear appeared and held Superstar and began to comfort her as she looked at her grand baby while the paramedics placed her in a neck restraint and secured her to a gurney. "She's going to be alright. God has her. Love, just reach beyond the break. That's what I have always told your mom. Reach beyond the break and hold on." This made her cry even harder. Only God knew how deep her pain was. She felt so hopeless as her sister was being rushed away to the hospital. Pastor and Coach were following close behind. When they got to the ambulance, Coach turned to his son and said, "Stay here, I got this." Pastor kissed his niece and watched as the ambulance pulled off.

He and Brother #1 began to walk back to the basketball court and the people were still gathered there in prayer. They joined in on the prayer. When the prayer ended, #1 began to encourage his pastor. He knew that his pastor loved all of his nieces and nephews, but these two were his favorites. They had overcome such odds in their short time on earth. "Pastor, God knows." He really needed that word of encouragement from his best friend. They went out to the parking lot and sat in the church bus.

"We have to be strong at a time such as now. Go get my sister and take her to the hospital. If she has a bottle or needle in her hand slap it out of it. Don't take no for an answer and tell her what has happened." They sat in silence for a few moments before #1 left. Pastor stayed on the bus and looked up into the sky Many thoughts ran through his mind. He got up and turned the radio on and an oldie but goody played, it was Reverend Timothy Wright's, Master Can You Use Me? As he listened to the song, he thought about God's wonderful blessings and a calm and a peace engulfed him.

As he left the bus a cool breeze blew in his face. He went looking for his wife and mother. He found them in the picnic area sitting under a tree. What was so odd was that his mother was sitting out. She was usually inside of the tent. She didn't play when it came to bugs. He looked at these two women, and a smile came across his face. He sat with them and they had a pleasant conversation about what had happened. "Son, I was telling your wife that you have to do what's best for you two. I know you have done the best for my grandson but all you can do now is pray for him. Of course, you know that already, you are the pastor, right?" "Not now ma, I have too much to deal with besides him and his issues. We are having a good picnic this weekend and if I start thinking about that trifflin' joker I will let him ruin it and that ain't going to happen. Okay?" Ma Dear sat there and just looked at him. She saw the pain that was inside of him and she wasn't going to press him any further. Besides that, he and his wife would be ministering in a little while.

He stood up and reached for his wife's hand. She looked at her mother-in-law and winked at her. "Go ahead, I'm a big girl." They walked off towards the food area. Together, they knew that they could survive, anything. "I love you, my best friend." He smiled at her and took her hand and kissed it. "Man, you haven't done that one in a while. You trying to get something started, huh? Don't have me to tell Ma Dear that you are being mannish, ha."

They stopped and got some of the award winning food. All of the winners from each category put their items on a plate that would showcase all of the goodies. This was always a big hit and all of the proceeds went to the church and local charities. No one enjoyed food like these folk did. There hardly ever was any wasted food and drink.

Once they got their plates, they went to the area where the picnic tables were. As they sat down, he said, "I want you to bring the word. It looks like its going to be a very large crowd and I believe in my heart that you truly have a word for the people." "Thanks, my love, but we do this as a team. That's been our tradition." As she was saying that she looked in his eyes and said, "Our tradition, huh? I got it baby." They began to eat and talk. He always loved sharing meals with her. No other partner would do. As he watched her lick her lips he leaned across the table and kissed her sauce covered lips."Still being mannish? I'll take care of that later." "Preach girl!" he laughed. As he was laughing his eye's locked on to a couple of women coming their way. "Baby, don't look now but here comes the hellcats."

No sooner had he spoken, they approached them with that look only they could have."Pastor, First Lady. We were just in the neighborhood and we decided to stop by and check out the picnic. We aren't here to pick a fight or protest. We are here just to enjoy. We know that it's hard to believe, but we come in peace." With that being said they walked off. "There really is a God." he joked. "It ain't over yet. Them two right there, I wouldn't trust them if I was drowning and they rowed by to help me out of the water. Been there, done that with them two snakes. Even if God himself came down, He would have to tell me to trust them in three or four different languages and possible other ways. Time and time again they have been destructive towards us. Why do they feel we need to be their friends or associates, I will never get it. We should have been in the mob, you know what I mean?" she retorted. They ate in silence and soon were finished.

Eventually, they were walking towards the water. They watched as the kids frolicked and splashed each other in the water. Someone was playing Cherelle and Alexander O'Neal's, Saturday Love."Never on Sunday, Mondays to soon. Tuesday and Wednesday just won't do. Thursday and Friday we can begin but a Saturday love will never end......." "Now that's what's up!" he said to his wife. They laughed and danced to the music repeating the lines over and over again. *Their* love, was like a Saturday love, because neither wanted it to end! With that being said, she took her husband's hand and placed it on her heart. "My time is getting near and I need to go and get it together." He let her hold his hand there for a moment before stepping back. "Sure thing, my heart." He watched as his very good thing walked away. That walk of her's had always driven him nuts, now more than ever!

Within the hour he was back on the stage before the people. It had actually gotten hotter even though it was much later in the day. On the Sundays of the picnic, they tried to have the Word spoken early, because they wanted the people to be able to enjoy the last few hours of the event. He stood before the people and said, "We greet you with the words, Peace be multiplied. Today we have a special treat. My wife and the first lady of my life will bring the word alone today. For any of you that has not heard this awesome vessel, you and your spirit will surely be blessed. Now ladies and gentlemen, boys and girls and children of all ages, our ministry proudly brings to you, its undisputed champion of the word, our First Lady!"

The ovation was thunderous. "Why do I always feel like I'm at a wrestling event when he does that. Well, I bless the Lord for a mate that pumps me up like that. Girls, let me tell you, he is a work, that one is. He keeps me on my toes at all times. I want to speak to you on today about, A Love that Never Dies. If you will go with me to the new testament, the books of Romans 8:29 and 30 and Ephesians 1:3-12. The word of God in these passages of scripture teaches us that it is by His love and His love only, do we operate. He teaches us that His love is preordained and predestined only by Him. Get this, He swore this on Himself. He couldn't find anyone else, not in the heavens or the earth to swear by other than himself. Sometimes, baby you have to say to the Lord, It's just you and me, Daddy. You swore this about my life with your word that I was predestined to be with you. I know all hell is breaking loose in my life, but you swore that my life was covered by your word. Oh yeah, you are going to get there one day. But when you do repeat His words back to Him, you have to know what you are talking about. But if you don't know the word, how can you use the word? I had to go through some pretty tough times in my life before I could really use the word for a weapon against my situations. It's better to have it and not need it, than to need it and not have it. Before I go any further, I want to be obedient to the Spirit of Christ. Pastor, is that okay?" He nodded approval from in front of the stage.

"There are thirteen people who wants to be a financial blessing to this ministry. Only you thirteen know who you are. God says that He wants your soul and that your money won't do. You can't pay for what He has for you. I want those thirteen to come up here right now. God has a right now blessing for you." Only ten came up. "I will say this once again, then we are going to move on. There are thirteen that need to be up here and you know who you are." Soon the last three came up on the stage. "Now there is thirteen more that want to give but don't have it to give, God wants you to come forth as well." She waited and watched until the thirteen was there.

"Because of your obedience, those of you that has that special offering, place that offering in one of their hands that didn't have an offering but wanted to give. As you receive this gift of love from the Lord, embrace the angel that is blessing you. Remember, it was Jacob that wrestled with the angel until he was blessed." As the embraces were being applied, the yokes of bondage began to break apart. There was a rush that went through the audience and soon there was a great noise among the people. This outpouring of love and adulation for the move of God was so awe inspiring. Much tears ran as well as heart felt embraces. Some even fell to their knees while others held up outstretched arms. God was moving on the hearts of His people. First Lady began to hug each of the twenty-six, but when she got to a face that was all to familiar her heart began to grieve. It was her goddaughter, Top Notch. The two women embraced and kissed only like a mother and daughter could.

Feeling overwhelmed, First Lady finished hugging each one before they went back to the audience. But before Top Notch walked away, she grabbed her arm. "Let me show you all how good God is. Many of you know that this young lady right here has been by side since she was a very little girl. She was the daughter that I never was able to conceive. But God. We had a problem and I hadn't talked to my child ever since. I have been praying ever since then for us and the Lord has answered my prayer. Before you go, my daughter, I want you to know we miss you and love you very much." Top Notch walked away smiling. She knew returning was the best thing for her.

Pastor ascended the stairs and held his wife and began to pray for her. A couple of the nurses came to assist him. She was soaked with perspiration and her breathing wasn't normal. As they worked to restore her breathing, Pastor spoke to the people. "We don't normally do this, but I want to take up an offering for our First Lady. What ever you want to sow into her, it's all good, because she is very good soil to sow into."

Since there wasn't any offering baskets the people began to come up and place money at the foot of the podium. Soon the front of the stage was filled with money and coins. "Before we release from this service, woman of God please come and bless this offering and give us the benediction if you will." He handed her the mike and held her hand as she prayed. "Father we lift up this your people and we ask that you reward them for their obedience to the one and living God. Lord, you know all too well of what we are in need of. Bless us from the vaults of heaven. Give unto us until we can receive no more. In your son's Jesus' name, amen. Once the money was collected and given to her, they sat down as the people began to move on to do other things. "My daughter has come back to me, praise God for the victory. I will cherish the day."

Chapter 16
A Woman Got to Have it-Yeah Right

Chief sat on the hood of his car as he listened to the sounds of the night. Although their community was on the outskirt of town sometimes the city seemed so far away. Other times it seemed so much closer. For the last few weeks he couldn't get his ex out of his head. Even though it had been just about as long since they had last talked, he missed her. So many times he avoided going that way hoping not to run into her or one of her siblings. He knew that she was still here and hadn't yet planned on going back home. The last time he had heard from her, she was leaning heavily toward moving back into the big house.

Many nights and days he found himself missing her more and more. It wasn't like she held a Svengali curse over him but it was much worse than that. He loved her and his love for her was real. Like Heatwave sang, Always and Forever. That's the way he felt. He had tried time and again to convince her to give them a second chance. But each time his advances fell on deaf. He knew about his adversary and how she would run back to him over and over again. This frustrated him to no end.

Although, after their divorce, he did try to move on with his life, but he still loved her. In a way he even understood why she would consistently run to his rival. But when she needed him he was there for her. As he pulled into his driveway, his thoughts ran back to the beginning of their relationship.

He was a young campus guard for the university. There was this young lady that would drive erratically on the campus grounds. He had already issued her two verbal warnings about her driving. Each time, he had to ask her not to do it again and she would verbally comply. So one day he was talking to the guy that had trained him and inquired if she had given him any problems. He didn't even know who he was talking about. So he gave him her name and they looked her up in the log book. She was listed as an intern with a four year residency.

As fate would have it, he had switched shifts with one of his coworkers and that very day she committed another campus violation. He called to the gate so they wouldn't let her out. When he got to the gate, he walked up to her car. "Why must we keep doing this? I asked you kindly to ease up on the campus and you always agree. But here we are again. I need to see your campus id." She didn't say anything she just handed over her id. He took her id and went into the guard shack. "That's the one that I was talking about." he said to his coworker. "What you gonna do?" "Instead of issuing her a warning I'm going to ask her out." "Good luck with that, brother. She is a real doll, but she looks like she probably is high maintenance. You know you can't have caviar on a fish sandwich salary." As he walked out of the door, he said "Maybe she likes fish sandwiches."

He approached her car and handed her back the id plus an unfilled citation with his number on it. "We can do this one or two ways, ma'am. Either you can have lunch, breakfast or dinner with me within a week or I can put you on the campus bad driver's list. The choice is yours." She took the citation, "How about I let you do all three within a month. That will determine how I drive around here. How about that, sir?" "That's fine with me, you have my number, call me, soon." For the very first time he looked in her eyes. He definitely liked what he saw. She had the softest brown eyes and the perfect lips and eyebrows to compliment them. He watched as she cautiously drove away and returned to his car. He sat there for a moment wondering if she was going to call.

As it turned out, he wouldn't have to wait long. The next day when he returned to work, he had a message in his box. It was a small card inside of an envelop that read, 'Don't disappoint me' and her number. He picked up the phone and dialed the number. She answered the phone and they began to chat. "Do you like fish?" he asked her, looking at his coworker with a smile. He had gotten so caught up in the moment that he forgot to clock in. "I have to go but I will call you later, okay, I'll talk to you soon." He clocked in and floated on a cloud to his car.

After that they began to forge a nice relationship. After a few months they began to introduce each other to family and friends. They were on the fast track to love and happiness when something came their way that could disrupt everything. She was at work when she picked up a flier about civil service opportunities in their area. She took the flier with her and gave it to him that evening. The next day he went and signed up. Within in days he received the call and he was elated. He was one of five candidates to receive a paid trainee's spot for the local civil service organization that he had chosen. But the only catch was that he would have training at the main facility that was about three hours away.

When he shared this with her, she fully supported him and his decision. They mapped out how they would go about keeping their relationship in tact. He would come home twice a month for the weekend and they would talk daily. It seemed like everything was in order. As they went over this plan they noticed one major thing that they didn't do, and that was to pray about it. From their very first date, they had established a partnership in prayer. That Sunday he picked her up for church and at the family dinner they would make the announcement about his leaving. Her family had really taken a liking to him. Even her best guy friend supported them. At times the two of them would hang out and go boating.

When he made the announcement, her father stood up and said, "Take my daughter by the hand, my soon to be sir-in-law." Her father began to pray for their strength to endure the complications of a long distance relationship. As Chief reminisced about his daddy-in-law he thought about what a wonderful man he was and how he commanded respect without having to ask for it. He always addressed his son-in-law as Sir. That was the type of dude he was. Always treating people the way that he wanted to be treated.

By now Chief was sitting in his chair on the porch. It had been a while since he had pondered this hard about what more he possibly could have done to not only save his marriage but also to save his wife. Things between them wasn't always bad, they really had a good time for the most part. Their relationship was probably one of the most complicated in all of mankind's existence! Although he wanted her back, he wanted her unconditionally. He knew the power of love but he also knew that it takes two, not three, to make it successful.

Over the years he watched many of their closest friends fall apart but get it together. But, it just seemed like it wasn't going to happen for them. One minute up, another minute down. That was their cycle.

He had attempted many times to move forward with his life but it seemed meaningless. The women he found himself interested in wasn't interested in him or he would be approached by someone he wasn't interested in. This was baffling to him. One of his partners girlfriend took a abuse case for him so he wouldn't loose his job even though he openly referred to her as his common-law-wife and was non -committal to marrying her or anyone else.

For years he scratched his head over this. For years he wondered about what was wrong with him. Did he not deserve happiness like the next man? At times it frustrated him. All he desired was true love. It was getting late in the day for him even though he still held on to hope. It wasn't just the others and their relationship, it was also the ones that didn't want to be involved that seemed like they were constantly being chased after.

But no matter who he attempted to see or establish a relationship with, it either didn't manifest or they would tell him, "I need to get it together before I get involved." It just seemed like that was the way it was for him. Some of these women that rejected him, he saw on a regular basis. The funny thing is that it seemed like the ones that shunned him, who ever they got with seemed to offer them much less than what he had to offer.

He had been through a lot with Daughter. He felt that she was truly his soul mate. All night long he sat on the porch listening to Bobby Womack's greatest hits. This was one of their favorite artist. He thought about their first intimate time and how she insisted that 'The Poet' was playing. He listened and sang along to, A Woman Has to Have It. He stopped singing and yelled out,"Yeah right, but not from me?" His calmed demeanor quickly turned into rage and anger. He took the player and prepared to smash it to bits when a calming spirit came over him. The Lord spoke to his spirit,"Don't focus on man, focus on me." He lowered the player and sat back down and began to weep.

Soon he was laying prostrate on the porch and he began to worship the Lord his savior. He began to cry out to the Father and repent. Although he had walked away from the church, he still believed in God. "Father if you take me back, I'll run for you. Praise is what I do and order my steps, dear Lord." When the spirit allowed him, on bent knees he spoke to God, "I surrender, my life is in your hands." After a few more minutes he stood to his feet and went inside. Closing the door behind him, he looked around his humble abode and smiled. He could feel the presence of the Lord. He showered and went to bed.

When the morning came he awoke, but instead of doing his normal routine he just lay there and listened to the beautiful singing of the birds. He had always been a creature of habit, almost obsessively. He was going to stretch out on God, yet again. Today was all about Him. "Good morning Father. Let your will be done this day and grant me the grace to endure whatever comes my way, good and even better. Amen."

He started out in the bathroom then he made his way to the kitchen. He wasn't really hungry so he poured a himself a cup of juice. As he looked out in the backyard, he realized that he hadn't fired up the grill lately. Although it was very early, he set about prepping the grill for cooking. As he picked up the cleaning spray and brush, a familiar fragrance permeated the almost still air. And there she sat, with her over sized sunglasses on. Only Top Notch could look this great, this early in the morning. "We need to talk." she said as she walked past him. He followed her inside and closed the door.

Chapter 17
One Less Bell to Answer

She struggled to get herself together but she just couldn't seem to do it. Every time that she attempted to release herself, it seemed to prove more fruitless than the last attempt. For weeks now, she didn't have the drive or will that had defined her. She constantly lay in the bed and on the chaise lounge, barely eating or doing anything else. Since the passing of her mother, she turned almost reclusive. Her contact with her family was almost nil, even though all three still remained in the big house.

Over the years she had been so accessible to everybody but when it came to her needing people or excepting people's help she would allow her independence to step in. She realize that people were there to help her but she prevented them from helping. When someone needed a baby sitter, she was there front and center. If there was a major family event that had to be planned, she was there. When someone was going through something, she was there. When someone needed someone to talk to, she was there. But now she seemed all alone and the one person that she knew had her back she refused to allow him in.

Now the world seemed to be going by without her. At first she really didn't mind. She knew that she had herself. She had to grow up quick back in the day and allowing people in was just hard for her to do. She always guarded her heart except when it came to him. She lost a good man but held out hope for a man that only used her for his perverse pleasures. While one gave her hope and love the other one just took from her.

When Chief confronted her for the first time about them, she told him, "I don't think that I could leave him even if I wanted to." This was over twenty something years ago and his grip on her seemed stronger than ever. She never tried to resolve it and pushed good people away. She tried to keep their relationship a secret but he himself flaunted her and his doings for all to see. That was one of the breaking points between the sisters and most of the females in her family. Some even stopped talking to her because she refused to let him go. But the one person that stood by her side was her mom. She liked both of the men vying for her daughter's attention and refused to butt in. Family and friends were appalled at Mother for not interceding even though she knew more about what was going on than most.

Her daddy on the other hand was different. He came from a time when it was common practice for men to rival for a woman's affection. Some times it was for love other times the motive was less than honorable. He eventually shared with his soon to be sir-in-law that he himself won his wife's hand first, then later he won her heart. He was up against two others vying for her attention. She played it cool but it wasn't a secret that she was being courted by a gangster, a preacher's son and a very well to do young man from a good family.

This last fellow at one point had the inside track to her because he seemed to do and say all of the right things. The preacher's son was probably next and the gangster well he wanted her her for physical reasons at best. He didn't per-say swoon over her, but those two mammoth mountains had him drooling for her and he couldn't allow any other fellow to have her.

The gangster eventually won out and later she won his heart. He stayed true to himself, he didn't allow himself to be pushed out of what he felt was rightfully his. So one day he came home with an envelop and placed it on the table. He took his young wife by the hand and they went out into the backyard. They walked a few yards to where the small cemetery was that was literally in their backyard. He looked at her and softly said, "I have given up the gangster life for you and my babies. You could have chosen any one but you chose me. I may not say it enough, but you are the best thing that ever happened to me. That envelop on the table is from the mill. I been working there for a bit now and I want to be able to come home to the finest of creations, you. We're going to get out of this old shed and I'm going to get you in something you can be proud of."

All she could do was cry. It seemed to her that with those words coming from him they were standing in paradise and not in a cemetery. They went back inside and had dinner. After that night they were inseparable. But with every marriage trying times would come, but they always seemed to try and work it out. Over time he had given up gambling and horsing around and eventually they wound up in church together. Even though he was a known gangster he was known to be in church as well. He was going faithfully even when she stayed home. He had almost given up on asking her to go because he surely wasn't going to make her go. He knew that she was watching him, doing his gangster stuff during the week and then going to church as if that would wash away the dirtiness of his business.

He turned to his soon to be sir-in-law and shared with him, "If you believe in your heart that she is the one for you, let God and your heart lead you. And you can always come to me, that other joker, well he can't. I'm pulling for you, son." She remembered this precious moment as if it was yesterday. She had a fellow that truly loved her but she wasn't so sure that he was for her. If they went on ahead with everything maybe they could work out like their parents did. So she decided to postpone the wedding until she was absolutely sure that she wanted to spend the rest of her life with this man.

He was rock steady, but the other one, man did he have an edge on him. But there was only one problem, the one with the edge had never proposed. He had let her know from the start that he wasn't the marrying type. He worked when he needed to and felt that he should be compensated when he rolled out 'the long-fellow' as he referred to his man package. If it ain't broke why fix it? So she knew all along that marriage wasn't in his plans. Not only that, she knew about the others because at one point she and her sister vied for his attention. He played them both and they knew it. He let it all hang out. Besides them there were others. Rumor had it that he was messing around with one of his aunts. But none of that mattered to her because she wanted him!

But somehow on today, something came over her and it was a little different. She felt more compelled to do something. She wanted to get out and do more than just exist. She got up and went to her purse. She picked up her phone and hit one button. The person answered and she said, "I'm done." And with that she hung up. This she had done before, but this time she wasn't looking or waiting for a reply or anything.

As she began to get herself together her phone rang. She answered and listened to the person. "Don't come over or call me again. I'm done. I'm not going to block your number because you'll just call from somewhere else. Trust and believe that!" Usually, she would fold within minutes because she felt trapped and didn't know how to get out of it. But today was like a reawakening for her. After showering, she went into the closet and pulled out some of her favorite pieces. Once she had settled on the attire she quickly dressed and when she thought that she was looking fly she noticed something was missing. She opened her box that she kept her jewelry in and fingered a few items. When she saw the one that she was looking for she put it on. Before walking out of her room she looked in the mirror and said to her image, "Not bad for almost fifty."

She walked out and called for her brother. When there wasn't a response she called his phone. Still there wasn't an answer. She went out of the door and walked to her car. It was filthy and hadn't been washed in a very long time. She went to the garage and turned on the light. Inside was her parents prized vehicles. She decided on the classic '66 Chevy Malibu with it's sexy metallic green color and black interior. She removed the tarp that covered it and started it up. The motor sounded showroom ready.

She turned up the volume and listened to Garland Green's, Jealous Kind of Fellow, that was playing on the 8-track. Her dad was famous for making his family and friends custom 8-tracks and tapes. Many forgot that he was the one who started the tape ministry at the church. Although his formal education was limited, he kept up with the latest technologies of the time. Actually, it was investments in technology that helped to build his empire.

Although he did it for the love, he refused to take money for something that he enjoyed doing. But when someone gave him some money he would put it in the 'tip jar'. At the end of the year he would take it to the bank and put it in someones account. He knew almost everyone and he and his wife knew who was struggling. They would put a few names in a hat and pull out a name. That's how they did it, all the way until his death.

She cruised out of the garage and watched as the door closed while she drove down the driveway. She stopped at the entrance to the road for a second, she checked her 'drag' and proceeded to her destination. Her heart raced higher by the mile. She was almost like a kid going to the circus or something. Finally, she was trusting in what she had known all along.

CHAPTER 18
Proverbs 15:17

Pulling up to her destination, she noticed several cars that were there. Most notably was her brother's car. This wasn't unusual for him to be here, on the contrary, *her* appearance here wasn't the norm. She caught her breath and got out of the car. The closer she got, the colder her feet became. She literally had cold feet all of her life. It could be in the 80-90 degree range and her feet would be cold. But these cold feet were from nervousness. She listened as the music and the voices got louder. Each voice she was familiar with. The smell of fresh grilled meat had met her when she parked and now it was intoxicating to her.

She rang the bell and waited for a second. Sis Cook came to the door and looked at her. "Girl, you sho nuff looking good. Come on in. We all in the back." She followed as they walked to the backyard. As they went outside she saw him and he saw her. He stopped in the middle of his conversation and walked over to where she stood. "I didn't know you were having something today. I can come back another time if you want me to leave." "Why would I do that, seeing you look like you spent some time getting yourself together. You must have had a reason to look so fine. Even though you could have had on a suit of armor and I would have thought the same thing about you."

He took her by the hand and led her back inside. He took her straight to the basement. They began to kiss and embrace and their passion filled the air. As they got up against the dryer, she stopped him."He's gone." "But I've been here all along. The more you rebelled the more I stood by you. Of course you know this already. If you're here to make peace, I'm here to make it with you." They once again engaged in tongue to tongue combat. If they didn't have anything else in this world, they had the kiss that they had shared for umpteen years. When they finally broke it up, they straightened up their clothes. As she was going up the stairs he grabbed her butt. "Knock it off, sir." "I am, later."

Before they went outside he led her to their bedroom and closed the door behind them. She hadn't been in here in years and a lot of emotions came over her instantly. He went to the closet and pulled out a box and handed it to her. At first she was apprehensive and seeing this, he said to her, "I have never hurt you and why would I do something to you now. If you can't trust me then you need to push out." He turned from her and began to put the box back. "Can I have it, I'm sorry." He smiled and handed it to her. She opened it up and looked at him. She looked deeply into his eyes expecting to see hurt, but she saw something totally different. She saw compassion. "It's beautiful. Would you do me the honor of putting this around my neck?" "With pleasure." He placed the black velvet choker around her neck and she backed into him pressing against him. She could feel his excitement. "Later, remember?" She put her purse on the nightstand and they went out to join the others.

Cheryl Lynn's song Encore played and some people were dancing on the extended patio area. They were doing some of the popular dances that were out. They danced a little bit before sitting down at the table that Brother and his guest sat at. "This is my sister, you ladies may remember each other from the hospital." The ladies shook hands and sat down. Soon they were covering a wide range of topics. The ladies chatted as if they had been knowing one another for a long time. Daughter and Nurse seemed genuine as they talked.

Even though there was so much going on around them, Chief and Daughter couldn't take their eyes off of the other. Then the Neville Brothers' jam, Yellow Moon came on. Within an instant, he took her hand and they went to dance. Holding her close to him, he whispered to her, "Don't make a fool out of us. If this isn't what you want or you just want to go to the 'killin' floor for a few rounds I ain't to be played with. My faithfulness to you should speak for itself. Many a night I have waited for your return and we have the potential to do great things. I have forgiven you and I won't bring the past up ever again. But if you bounce, there is no coming back. I mean it this time." "I have been a fool before, but I know now that I am a fool for you." she spoke ever so softly into his ear. "You have always balanced me, babe. I am so sorry for all that I have done to you. Please forgive me. You have me, all of me."

He held her so tight that she winced. Realizing this, he loosed his embrace a little. By now everyone that was there was watching them intently. Sis. Fixer leaned over to her husband and winked at him. "What God has put together, let no man pull a sunder." "True that, my dear." Soon all the couples were dancing and laughing. At times switching off partners.

The timer went off and the men get really excited. They turned their attention to the newly built ground pit. They began to remove all of the palm branches and watched as the amazing smoke came up from the ground. The sweet smell of beef, pork and seafood filled the air. The men had been planning this event for months but their schedules had collided. So after a concentrated effort, all were finally able to participate. Each one was responsible for a particular food to be put into the pit. When Chief had approached each of them with an idea for the ground pit all were in favor. Soon they all got together and started digging the pit in his backyard. They hadn't gotten together on a big project in a while. The last thing that they built as a group was the three tree stands for hunting season. All of them shared a fondness for golf, baseball, archery and cooking.

As they began to remove the meats from the pit the women sat back in anticipation for the food that was coming their way. They credited their men on all of their cooking prowess. Sometimes, they would argue over which man prepared his meal this best. All of this was done in jest. No one really took anything too serious. Good clean fun was always on the menu. They realized that food was a good way to share with others.

Daughter and Nurse tried to assist the men but were soon rebuffed."Girl, you been out of the game that long that you forget that them over there, don't play when they get together on something new." "And as for you, newbie, there is a pecking order around here when it concerns the hens." The ladies high-fived each other and laughed at their innocence.

With the tables fully loaded, everyone gathered around the tables and joined hands for prayer. Since it was Chief's home, he was charged in leading prayer. Before he started, Sis. Cook spoke up, "Chief, I think that your better half should be by your side." All agreed as Daughter took her place next to her man. The radiance that these two generated was very apparent. "Father we bless you for the fellowship of love and spirit. Please cover us in our pursuit of righteousness. Remember the ones that are less fortunate and let us not forget about you. Your word says that it is better to enjoy a bowl of soup with someone you love than to have a stalled ox with someone you have strife with. I thank you for all of my brothers and sisters that surround me and my lady, not only today, but for the years of them standing in the gap for us. Amen."

Usually, everyone would just go for what they know, but this time no one moved. It took a few seconds as they reveled in the prayer that had just gone up. Over the past year, this close group had watched God do his things in all of their relationships. What many didn't know was that a certain seemingly strong couple was believing that it was the end of the road for them. But something happened in this prayer. As the glow began to fade, they started to make their plates. When Daughter began to make their plates, Chief looked at her and she smiled and said, "I got you, sit down."

When his plate was made, she took it to him and placed it before him. He watched in amazement at his woman. As the good vibration was coursing through his body his mind filtered some unwarranted thoughts. He silently began to pray asking God to remove all doubt and to give him the grace needed. As they ate she played footsie with him. This was their thing. He loved her feet. No prettier feet had God made. He often teased her when things were good, that an angel was missing a pair of feet because she had the feet of an angel.

"Hey, family, if it's alright my wife and I have an announcement. We have been going through some rough times in our marriage as of late. Tonight we were going to announce our separation. We wanted to let you all hear it straight from us. About six months ago we noticed that we were lacking in our communication with one another. We were talking at and not to each other. Once we addressed the scene we decided to get counseling and we were willing to do what was necessary to at least attempt to salvage what he had. But enough about that. As we watched the goings on here, on this day, instead of separating we are renewing our vows.

As a hush fell over them, Sis. Cook stood by her man holding his hand. "We still believe God. It's not that we want to be separate or go it alone but we have always had a good thing and neither wants to be the first to say goodbye. Sleeping in different rooms was hard on both of us. When our kids came to visit and decided to spend the night we slept in the same bed for the first time in months. We know that some of you look at us and know what we have been through. Just keep us in your prayers. We have seen relationships restored and new ones blossom. We are going to sit back and watch you all for a change. We have tried desperately to be glowing examples of a good christian couple to everyone except ourselves. When I watched Daughter fix Chief's plate I got a little jealous. Here it is that something that took so long, them being together, but God came through and we all were here to witness this. My heart grieved greatly but now through you all, we are compelled to finish this race together." The tears began to flow freely down her cheeks. Her man held her close.

Nurse spoke up, "Just enjoy the moment. All of us should just enjoy the moment. "Not bad for a newbie," Sis. Cook replied, laughing lightheartedly. They all began to eat and share in conversations. This went deep into the night. Before their guests prepared to leave, they held a little meeting to see what the next event was going to be. They agreed to do an aquarium or zoo outing. They set the date and soon the couples began to leave. The Cooks were the last to get going.

As the two couples walked towards the driveway they chattered about the results of the night. "Hey my friend, I got your back. You are my brother, but you are my best friend." The men hugged as did the women. "I love you." The women exchanged like they had done years and years ago."I love you more." The Cooks got in their car and drove away. They watched as the taillights disappeared into the darkness.

CHAPTER 19
Save a Horse, Ride a Cowboy

With everyone gone and everything put up and away it was time for the two of them to get down to business. They had been worked up since she had arrived. That choker was driving him to the brink of insanity. They were at a fever pitch and it was exciting. They turned to one another in the throngs of passion as if they were hooking up for the first time. The screams of passion, the excitement of it all overtook them. They tore into the other unlike ever before!

"I'm all yours. Do what you will to me. Take me. Take me now!" As she screamed and bit him, he turned her over on the couch. Her hands and nails dug deep into the interior of the couch. With her face buried in a pillow, her fingers clawed to grab something to hold on to. As she did this her fingertips felt something. Almost like an out of body experience, she grasped the item and opened her eyes. In her hand she held an all too familiar pair of sunglasses.

Within an instant she pulled away. Bewildered, he looked at her and his question was answered before he could even ask. "What the hell are these and why are they here? Not on the couch but in the couch. Everybody knows who rocks these glasses, Ms. Top Notch." As he prepared to answer, she stopped him. "Everyone knows she's the church ho, so I wouldn't be surprised if she hadn't made her way to you. It was only a matter of time, I guess. She has the gift, if she ain't got nothing else. Looking all young and fit, she know what she doing. I bet she slept with every man of prominence throughout the region." Preparing to speak again, she cut him off. "You are probably thinking, this woman has a lot of nerve, calling the skillet black. Well, in my defense, I knew what I was doing was wrong. But that didn't stop me. I'm still your wife..."

He held up his hand to stop her from rambling on. He took the sunglasses from her and set them on the table. "She was over here and wasn't feeling well. She laid on the couch and when she fell asleep I left. She wasn't looking good at all. That's it and that's all. Nothing more and nothing less." She looked up at him and reached out for him. He let her lead him back to where they were a few minutes ago.

At the big house Brother and Nurse sat on the porch listening to the creatures of the night and holding hands. They talked about the evening and how much fun they had, but they also spent time discussing the individual couples that were there. This took hours but she hung on to almost every word that they spoke. One thing that she noticed about him was the way that he spoke about each person individually and as a couple. Something in his voice sounded as if he was missing out on something.

As he talked, she laid her head in his lap. He caressed her hair and face. Although they hadn't been together long, they felt as if they had known each other for eternity. They often laughed about how they met and that maybe, just maybe, God had put them together.

In the still of the night air, he lifted her up and carried her to the backyard. He placed her on the patio couch and they began to kiss and carry on. Their kisses were to die for. They seem to do something unlike anything before and that something was felt between the two of them. Something about the other made them want to be better.

Nothing around them mattered, just this moment in time did. Looking down into his eyes, she spoke softly, "I'm your baby, tonight. You make me feel like a million dollar bill. My love is your love." This was the first time that the L-word had been spoken out loud between the two of them. Without a care in the world, they continued on their course to ecstasy.

As the momentous time came, he looked into her eyes and said, "I want you the right way baby, your love is just like music to my heart and soul. It's more precious than gold. I have to treat you like a lady and I will. So let's chill and take our time and do it right. I want you to be just fine when *we* get there. I don't want there to be any questions, where would I be. I don't want to be far away from you. I want to see the stars with you." "Man. I love it when you talk to Marvin and Kindred and to me." They snuggled and cuddled before falling asleep before the deed was done.

CHAPTER 20
You Can't Hide From Yourself

With the night turning into day she sat in the booth counting her tip money for the night. A man came up to her and requested a last minute dance. At first she thought to turn him down but agreed. She took his hand and walked him to the private area. She had danced for him before but this dance was going to be one for the ages. She gave him the lap dance unlike any other. When it was over he left and she was glad that the night had finally come to an end.

Returning home from a long night all she wanted to do was go to bed. Her life had been turned inside out ever since her daughter's injury. All along she wanted to be a mother to her children but life seem to run over her every time she seemed to advance. Even before the accident, she had secretly been trying to get her act together.

To get herself back in shape, she returned to the strip club where she once was the hottest act for years. She knew that being the sister of a prominent minister would hinder her chances locally, so she performed in other regions where her chances of being exposed would be slim to none. That lasted for a while but she realized that when God wants you He will send for you.

She had gotten it together before and had made her way back to the church to be with her family and friends. She needed a certain kind of love that she only could get from them. They were always there to receive her with open arms. Her mother worried about her the most. Ma Dear would say to her, "Your gift should bring you before great men. That's what the word says. Baby Girl, can't nobody do you like Jesus can."

She didn't have decent insurance and benefits for her kids, so when she needed money she went back to what she knew best. Seeing her own child hurting and suffering impacted her to the core. Unbeknownst to her family and friends, she was on the way to recovery. She allowed people to think the worst about her but she knew what was happening! She had returned to her knees in prayer and fellowship with God. She would take her time in revealing to her love ones about what was going on once she was absolutely sure that she was going to stay focused.

When she went into the house she began to pick up some of the stuff that lay around her apartment. As she made her way to the kitchen she sat a picture up that had been lying down so long that a dust outline formed where it once lay. In the kitchen she turned on a pot of water and got her favorite mug and tea. As she waited for the water to boil she went into her bedroom and began to hang up and sort through the pile of clothes that lay on the bed.

As she held up a shirt that used to be her favorite, she tossed it on her pillow and sat down on the floor. It was at this time that she knew she couldn't run any more. She had to face her fears and stand up on her own two feet. She remembered going to the hospital not knowing what to expect when she got there. Although #1 had told her what had happened she prepared herself for the worse. Up until that point that's all she expected, the absolute worse.

Deep in thought, the faint sound of the whistle from the teapot jarred her. She pulled herself off of the floor and went into the kitchen. As she stirred her tea and took a sip of the pipping hot blend she looked at her reflection in the mirror. She smiled at herself and spoke out loud, "That's right Lady Soul, I have got to find me an angel." She placed her index finger on the glass and blew herself a kiss. Sitting back down on her bedroom floor she held the hot cup and lay her head back on the bed. She began to smell the many different colognes that represented all of the men that she had brought home with her. She jumped up and threw the hot tea on the bed and began to scream and swear at her bed and what it represented the last years of her life.

Soon a banging at her door snapped her back into reality. Neighbor called out to her from the other side of the door. She opened it and let her in. "What's going on in here? Are you okay?" Baby Girl answered her, "I was just having a real housewives moment." The two began to laugh at each other. "Girl, I thought that one of them fools was over her snapping out or something. And if he was, I had that thing thing for him." Neighbor said holding up her chrome and pearl handled pistol. "Now put that away before I end up getting shot." They sat on the couch and began to chat. They talked about her being clean for this stretch of time and how she was making her way back. After a few minutes Neighbor left. She went in the bedroom and got her pillow and camped out on the couch. Looking up at the ceiling she saw an image of a finger pointing out of the window. She smiled and turned on her side and closed her eyes drifting off to sleep.

What only seemed like a few minutes actually were a few hours that she was asleep. She sat up and began to hum. She made her way to the bathroom and began her shower. As she pinned her hair up she thought that she heard a knock on the door. Looking out the peephole, she didn't see anyone so she went back in the bathroom and showered. She was excited because she was going to church. After all that she had endured it was the only thing left for her to do. Not a Sunday had passed that she didn't feel convicted about not being there. But God was giving her another chance and she wasn't going to blow it, again.

Half way dressed, she heard the door again. This time she was sure that someone was knocking. She looked out and to her horror it was her dealer. She knew that he would wait for her until she opened the door. "I'll call you later, I'm getting dressed" "Open this door right now or I'm kicking it in then I'm going to put the boots to you! Open up, dammit!" he screamed. Nervously, she opened the door. "Where the hell you think you going? We got bin'ess to take care off. You been dodging me for the longest. What's good?"

When she didn't answer him, he raised his foot as if to prepare to stomp her. She lowered her hands to block the foot that had done this to her time after time. She tried to scream but nothing came out. "I've been sitting outside your window all this time waiting for you. I knocked but you didn't answer. What you got to say for yourself?" "If you want to live, you will back up off her." Neighbor said as she cocked the hammer on her 'heater'. He stood motionless as if doing a self assessment. He came to his senses when he felt the gun on his neck. He knew that the women holding the gun was serious and would use it first then ask questions later. He backed down and straightened up."Push out or get carried out. The choice is yours." He turned to leave and mean mugged the two women as he left.

Slamming the door behind him, Neighbor looked at her shaken friend. She took her hand and said, "One step forward, one step back. Not here not now no more. Finish getting dressed 'cause your girl is going to church with you." Regaining her composure, Baby Girl returned to her bedroom and finished getting dressed. While she dressed Neighbor waited on the couch. She reached into her purse and put her pistol back in its holster. She was quietly thanking Jesus for not having to use it. Her brother had taught her to use it and use it well. She had always dreaded having to use it but she had been violated so many times that she took it everywhere she went.

Soon the two women were on their way back to their first love, God! As they rode to the church they talked about the events leading up to this point. The more they talked about the goodness of The Father the more their anticipation grew. "Girl, I been touched so many times by all of the wrong things that I hope that the very gates of hell don't swallow me up as I get out of the car." "You mean that both of us aren't swallowed up and consumed." They high-fived and rode in silence for the last couple of miles.

Pulling into the church's massive parking lot they looked at the throng of cars. Service had already started and they could hear the instruments thundering from inside. They got out of the car and held hands walking towards the main entrance doors. As they walked inside, both women sighed in relief that the ground didn't open up or a thunderbolt didn't come down from the heavens. People were standing and singing with the choir as they sat down.

Baby Girl thought about all of the wonderful times that she and her family shared in this very place. She reminisced about the day that her brother was installed as the senior pastor and how he insisted that she be right there helping to encourage the people through her ministry of praise dancing. Without thinking she jumped to her feet and began to get into the service. She felt good in spite of what had happened to her earlier. Neighbor sat there just looking at her best friend in amazement. Often times she reminded her friend that she needed to get back home before it was to late. She knew that Baby Girl had a calling on her life and she often feared that she might not make it back in time. But here she was, in her rightful place! Seeing this happen encouraged Neighbor and convicted her at the same time.

As the choir began to end their awe inspiring song, Pastor came to the podium. Opening his bible, he began to pray. The man of God began to bless God for his goodness and his faithfulness. He sang a little bit of one of his favorite songs before ministering the word. He didn't go forth with the word as long as he usually would have. The atmosphere was off, to say the least. Soon he and the intercessors were immersed in spiritual warfare. This had never happened before and the church began to bombard heaven with prayer from the depths of their souls. Observing this awesome event unfold, the two friends grabbed each others hands and began to pray out loud. This wasn't anything new to them, because they would often pray for their angels to protect them while they were doing their own thing. Soon there was a hold and then a shift in the spirit realm. Divers tongues began to come forth and visions were being seen by those who had never aspired to have these gifts to operate in their lives.

Once the order was restored, Pastor spoke to the congregation, "Today was a victory unlike we have ever seen or dreamed. We all have just witnessed a great manifestation of the Holy Spirit that moved on our behalf because somehow someway, we were all on one accord. Praise be unto God, because He is faithful and just even we are not." They finished with the rest of the service and the people began to fellowship with one another before leaving.

CHAPTER 21
Independent

The seasons had changed a few times and the situation between Brother and Nurse was at a virtual stand still. They still did things together but something was amiss. For the last few weeks he had beaten himself up for the lack of communication with his woman. He took the time to assess the pros and cons of staying in a seemingly one sided relationship. He knew that he loved her with his heart and soul, but sometimes, rather, often times she seem to push him away and he couldn't figure out why. He had called her and asked her out for a walk or a drive. She excepted and they arranged where the two were to meet.

It was funny to meet her like this because they would only arrive at a destination separately if they couldn't hook up and ride together. Usually, they would be happy riding together but something was wrong and he knew it. No longer could he tip toe around this fact and act like everything was okay because it wasn't. He needed to know where they stood and what the future held for them.

As she pulled into the parking lot of the mall, she checked herself out before getting out of the car. She saw him sitting on the bench wearing his coolest shades and looking only like the way that he could look. As she approached him, he stood up kissed her on the forehead. Before they went inside, they sat on the bench for a few. "I miss you when you aren't with me. Is there something that I should know or is there something that I have done to make you distance yourself from me?" "It's not you or anything that you have done. It's me and my mind. One minute I'm willing to ride or die then there are other times that my independence kicks in. I don't want to push you away but I also don't want to make you miserable with my indecisiveness."

"You have become such a constant in my life that sometimes I prepare myself for you to walk out on me. Even though you have not given me any hints that you are not happy, sometimes that's just the way that I handle it. When you held up our virtues that first night and the few other times that we got hot and heavy, I knew that you were my man and should have been thrilled but somehow I began to see you as being weak. For you not to be a church going man, sometimes you seem as if you still sitting on the pews and looking for a perfect way of life. Maybe some of the things that I had hoped for was coming my way through you. But as time would have it, I was more thrilled with the notion of someone loving me and I didn't really have to do much for it."

He sat there taking all of this in as she continued. She spoke so matter-of-fact, it almost seemed effortless and emotionless. She also began toying with the ring that he had placed on her finger and was expecting for her to place it in his hand, but she didn't. "When my family and friends ask about us I kind of tell them that we sort of drifted apart. I wouldn't go into details and they wouldn't pry But one night we were all hanging out down by the lake when they turned on me. My sisters and mother ganged up on me like never before. They tormented me for my callous nature when it came to you. How I would say and do things to tick you off but you wouldn't go in on me. When my oldest sister laid into me I thought that you and her had something going on because she stood up for you calling you 'the best damn thing that ever happened to me.' I went through all of the emotions that night, happy, angry, hate, resent, I mean the whole gambit, man. She got so close to me I thought that she was going to choke me. I had never seen my family in such a tizzy and it was all because of the way that I treated you."

"One day she and I were at the store when I ran into the Abuser. He began to tell me that he was seriously dating and close to getting married and that he was just promoted to be vice president of the company that he works for. We talked for a few minutes then he left. She even said to me, "You don't deserve someone like Brother. For you to keep in contact with a man who physically abused you and push away a man that hasn't as much as raised his voice to you is foul."

He looked at her and smiled. That's all that he could do for the moment. "So you have no problem pushing me away but you don't mind engaging conversation with someone who harmed you. That's kind of wild, ya know. If that was me, there was nothing that that person could say to me. Not even a hello. Let alone for me to engage that much conversation with him. Just how sanctified is that? Maybe now you will get your wings."

Saying this to her was the strongest thing that he had ever done before, but now he knew in his heart where he stood with her. No one had to tell him, he heard it from her himself. Yes, this did impact his feelings towards her, he wouldn't or couldn't deny that. He stood up and held his hand out. She began to pull the ring off of her finger, "That's not what I want. I bought that for you. I don't want it back." he said still holding out his hand. She looked at him in amazement as she stood up. "Let's spend today deciding on our future. No more in and out."

The two proceeded into the mall and walked with no certain destination in mind. In silence they seemed to be preoccupied with the recent dialogue between them. Often he would keep a lot inside that bothered him when she did something that rubbed him the wrong way. One thing he refused to do was to complain and fuss over everything. Been there done that. When he met her, he thought that his search was finally over. But recent events began to make him think a little harder. He knew that he had been very good to her and her children. They had become just like his own. He often took them with them.

He remembered the first time that they were talking about going out and she was preparing to send them to their father for the weekend to free up some time. He insisted that they come along and asked her if it was okay. She was shocked. She explained that she dated so infrequently that either the men hit and ran or they couldn't get pass the kids, even if *they* had kids of their own!

Walking slower than usual, he fell behind her. Maybe watching her walk would do the trick. That was one way that he dealt with his frustration when it came to her. He adored everything about her but that behind or 'punkin' was the deal breaker. He reached out and slid his hand across her hind part and she did a little wiggle. Before he knew it, she had stopped and he crashed into her. They tumbled to the floor and looked at each other. Sitting there on the mall floor they burst into laughter. People walked by and looked in amazement at the couple on the floor. He helped her up and they continued to walk.

They reached the point of having to turn around and he stopped her. "If we are going to make it, you have to give me more than what you have been giving me. It seems like you fuss about the smallest thing that happens when it comes to me. But you've told me time and again about being used and mistreated. Even had you not told me about your past experiences, I still would've treated you like a queen. I know that this sounds cliché but you are the best thing that has ever happened to me. You have given my life purpose and meaning. I love you for that and want to spend the rest of my life with you."

He took her by the hand and kissed it. Looking deep into her man's eyes she spoke with compassion and love. "You are a good man, I mean a very good man. All that your family and friends have said about you I have seen for myself. But right now, I am just not good enough for you or anyone else. It is true what I feel for you. It has never been this real for me in my life. But I have to let you go so that you can find someone who will truly give you what you need. I just don't feel that I am ready to let go of my independence right now. Maybe that's the reason for me running away so much. This isn't my first time letting someone go and it probably won't be my last. Just do me a favor. When the right girl comes along just be patient with her like you did with me." They stood there with nothing else to say.

Walking back to their cars seemed like an eternity. When they finally approached their vehicles she stood by her car door. "Well, I guess I better get back use to opening my own doors, huh." "Per your wish, Mrs. Independent." he said and got in his car and drove away. As he wiped the tears from his eyes he thought about going back but he knew that the best thing for him to do was to keep driving.

About a mile into his drive his phone rang, it was her. Answering could be bad, letting it go unanswered could be even worse. So he answered, "I seem to have forgotten how to open a door. Could you please come back to me and help me?" she asked. "Call the motor club, they specialize in this kind of stuff." he said and hung up.

That day seemed to drag on and on for him. He would have loved desperately to have had things to go in a different direction but it didn't. She walked out on him, he didn't push her away. For the rest of that day all he could do was think about what more could he have done to keep her. Finally after hours and hours of soul searching he stood up looking at a picture of them.

He grabbed the picture and was tempted to smash it into a gazillion pieces but at the last minute he decided that the picture wasn't at fault but it was the people inside of the frame! He grabbed his keys and the picture and jumped into his car. He drove like a mad man until he reached his destination.

As he got out of the car he tried to formulate what he was about to say. He rang the bell and she answered. He held up the picture and said, "I have wasted my entire life and I will not waste another moment, again. You have told me that I make you happy and all of that stuff and that made me feel good. So good that I gave up everything that would be harmful to our relationship. I wanted you to see that a good man was worth fighting for. But I was foolish to think that. You rather have your independence than have someone who love you because of your independence. But when you are in a working relationship, independence has to be checked at the front door. Me personally, I never want to rely on you or any other woman! I have my own money, car, life and everything else. The one thing that I don't have is you. I thought that you might see that, but when things don't go your way all you can do is run. Every time something went wrong you start talking about warning signs and such. Well, you haven't been the most upstanding girlfriend either. But I didn't run out on you. I wanted to work things out with you. I didn't hold every thing that you did against you. So this time, you don't have anything of mine in your place, car or work to give back to me like you always do. The thing about you is that you are scared and you don't have to be, not with me. I ain't like any one else. I'm me and that's all I can be."

She stood there visibly shaken. "I have been beaten on or down so many times that I figured it would only be a matter of time for you to do the same to me. I was walking away from love before it broke my heart." "Go and get your car keys." he said sternly to her. She went inside and came to the door way. He walked her to her car and took the keys from her hand and opened her door. "This can be the last door that I open for you or the first that I open for the rest of our lives, together. The choice is yours." "I chose you, I'm sorry." she said apologetically. "The only one you can trust is God. I had to find that out for myself. With Him we can make it, baby. I don't want to loose you or Him. Let's go to midweek service and get a little church in, what do you say?" She agreed by wrapping herself around him and kissing his face.

He kissed her back and they walked towards her front door. Opening the door for her, he looked inside and saw her twins lying on the couch. Although it hadn't been that long since he had seen them, he still missed them because just like her, they had become a part of his life as well. "I'll be here at 6:30 to get you guys, okay?" "I love you, man." she said kissing him on his nose before going inside. As he left he stopped to thank God for sweet love.

CHAPTER 22
Unbreakable

Family & Friends Month was going on at the church and the turnouts were unbelievable. The Leaders and the committee had been working at a break neck pace getting everything together. They all worked, almost to the point of exhaustion. This was the crown jewel of events that were held for the calender year. Out of all the events, this one seemed like the people really went out of their way to see that the church was shown in a good light.

Getting ready for church, Pastor and First Lady were having their morning coffee and tea when all of a sudden she dropped her head. Not realizing that anything was wrong he looked across the table at his wife. "You okay, honey?" he asked. She didn't respond so he got up and went to her. He lifted her head and to his horror, her ear was bleeding profusely. He went into panic mode add called 911. He frantically explained to the operator what had just happened and gave the best description of what was happening.

Within minutes the paramedics were inside working feverishly on her. All he could do was pray and get out of the way and allow the experts to do their thing. Not to set off a panic he decided to call only a few people to inform them of what was going on. She was still unconscious when Top Notch and Girlfriend rushed in. They came to his side and he tried to explain to them just as he had with the paramedics. He looked super worried and concerned for his wife. She had been tireless in her business and the church. He had asked her many times to slow down and kick her feet up. Things needed to be done and she felt that she needed to it.

She was so active and hands on with Family & Friends that her time and energy was well spent. At one point, he tried to put his foot down, but she wouldn't hear of it. He knew that many people relied heavily on her and there was a constant pull. Never one to want to disappoint anyone, she found herself being pulled in every direction that she could be pulled. Even if she had some rare down time she would find something to do. She always felt like there was something else to be done. Many nights he would pray and intercede for his best friend's strength and help.

The three began to pray as she was being taken out of the house and into the awaiting ambulance. "Sir, we have got to get her into emergency surgery right away. The swelling is getting worse by the minute. We are calling everything in, so that the emergency team will be ready to receive her upon arrival. If you are riding along you have to come right now." said the paramedic. Realizing that he was still half dressed, Girlfriend agreed to go with her. Top Notch would stay behind to help him get prepared. They knew that time was very precious, just like the woman who was being rushed to the hospital.

She watched as the ambulance blazed away with the sirens blaring. He rushed through the house into his bedroom to grab a shirt and get everything that he would possibly need. Half frazzled, he stopped dead in his tracks and looked up to God and said, "Father, we have come too far for you to leave us." What seemed like forever, in reality was just a few minutes since the ambulance had left. Soon they were on their way to the hospital, neither saying anything.

Pulling into the emergency entrance, he jumped out of the car almost before it came to a complete stop. Top Notch cringed as he bolted out of the car and rushed into the hospital. She pulled off to find a parking spot and within minutes she was right by his side. She had driven so fast that they were there almost as fast as the ambulance. But they had already rushed First Lady into emergency surgery. Girlfriend met the two in the waiting area, as she was about to speak, Doctor walked up to them."I have been briefed and its going to be a very delicate procedure. She still has not regained consciousness, but in this case that is good. Doc is on his way to assist me and the crew. Please, keep us in your prayers." Before he could say another word, he was called over the intercom and he hurried off down the hallway.

"Let me call Asst. Pastor and inform him that he will be officiating service today. Top Notch call the committee and #1 and #3 and let them know that we won't be in today and we will talk to them later. Do not tell them we are here." "Pastor, is there anything that I can do?" asked Girlfriend. "Just being here with me and your girl is more than enough. But eventually, one of you are going to have to go to the house and get her things for her." Top Notch stepped outside to make her calls so that the noise from the inside of the hospital would not betray them.

After every call was made the three began to pray. They didn't pray long and hard, because they knew that she was in God's hands. For some reason, maybe that reason alone there was a calm between them. Instead of worry and doubt, they began to think of all the things that she was going to need if she was going to have to stay for a spell. One thing that she wasn't afraid of was surgery or the hospital. She look forward to her doctor appointments and such, especially her mammograms. She had shown such courage and strength and proved to be a true survivor. They reminisced about the time when she went under the knife for the first time and he said to her, "Let this be the last time that something has to come out of you, because I need all of you with me."

After that procedure was done, they found out later, that she could have actually gotten better without having to have her organ removed. This angered them beyond their usual capacity. When they switched doctors, the new physician, Doctor, threw away almost all of the medications that she had been using. With this new find, they became diligent with their health care. After that, they went to all of their appointments together.

She became such an advocate about health care and concerns. She went as far as having an health care administrator installed at both of their businesses and at the church. She was a champion of life. She would often say, "If your gifts should bring you before great men, then your greatest gift should be your health." After people heard her say that, many began to rally behind her. Many knew about her many aliments and challenges, she wasn't bashful to tell about how God blesses her over and over again regardless to what the diagnosis said. And here she was, again, in the hospital.

They waited for hours before the doctors emerged from the surgery. The only information that they had been given up to this point was that she was in stable condition and all was well. Doc approached them, "We have done all that we can, she did well and is in ICU right now. I must let you know that her face is swollen because of the procedure. What happened was a rupture in her ear. What caused it we don't know and by me being her physician, she never spoke about ear aches or any thing related to it. Tomorrow we'll CAT scan and run a battery of test on her, but from where we stand, she should be back on her feet in no time. What I mean by that is, in a month or so. But first things first. She will be here for at least a couple of weeks, that much is for sure. Doctor, did an excellent job on her and all I did was assist."

"I know that you all are anxious to see her, but it won't be for a couple of hours at the earliest. She's very strong, and we believe that Jesus covered all of us as He has done so many times before." said Doctor. They talked for a little while longer before the doctors left them. The three rejoiced thanking the Lord for his favor. "Now we can let every one know what has happened, even our son." Pastor shared with them. "Man, God has done it again for us."

Within hours, there were so many people there for support. Family and friends alike. All was concerned and offered their assistance to help with what ever the needs were. When Asst. Pastor showed up he and Pastor went out side to talk. "Thanks for coming, I'm holding a meeting with the committee in the morning and you should be there, it's very important." As Pastor spoke to him, he noticed something strange about Asst. Pastor's demeanor. He was rather distant, even more than usual. There was something else going on, but he just couldn't put his finger on it. He shook his hand and they went back inside.

Most of their family was there, except their son. "Have any of you talked to our son lately? I've tried to call a couple of times but he hasn't answered." Pastor asked the family and friends. It seemed as if no one had had any contact with him as of late. Although they were not on speaking terms, they still tried to keep up with his coming and going. More often than not, people would just tell them what was happening with him. After this brief survey, many of them tried to contact him. But after a while, it was to no avail. He just seemed to have disappeared into thin air.

He shifted his attention back to his wife. He asked Girlfriend and Top Notch to go back to his house and get the things that she was going to need while in the hospital. The funny thing about his wife was that she had no fear or phobia about hospitals or surgeries. But this time she didn't have a chance to prepare for this. It happened so swift, without warning. All he could do was wait. The only thing that he wanted to do was not only see her, but to hold her in his arms. He hated times like this, when things were out of his control. This made the wait even more agonizing to him.

The time seemed to creep by when finally Doctor came out to where they were waiting. "She can see two of you right now, but that will be it for today and it has to be brief." Pastor and Ma Dear followed Doctor to the ICU area. Preparing himself for the worst, he held his mothers hand as they walked towards her.

As they stood looking at her, tears began to stream down his face. He knew that he couldn't touch her face so held her foot. He knew she couldn't stand her feet being touched but that just seemed logical to him. His mother held her hand and caressed it. She lay motionless but her breathing seemed normal and that was a relief to them. He kissed her hand and walked out of the room. Ma Dear soon followed him. Standing by the doorway, she looked in her son's eyes. "Trust God, He delivered one back and He's going to safely return this one as well. Her work and the mighty work that God has ordained you two to do is far from over. Do you hear me son?" He shook his head in agreement with what she had spoken to him.

Those words seem to wash him with the comfort of knowing that more than a few people had their backs. As they walked to the waiting area, everyone was still there. "She's doing fine and we know that all things work together for the good of them that believe." There was a collective sigh of relief throughout the area. With this news in hand people began to leave. He appreciated the supporters, but he knew that people had other obligations in their own lives to tend to.

Baby Girl and Neighbor inquired if there was anything that they could do to help out. It seemed like she was spending an enormous amount of time in this hospital lately. She had been in the hospital so much with her youngest child that the recruiters would meet her and Superstar there. Actually, Superstar signed her letter of commitment to play at Local University there. How proud she was of her daughter. She was highly touted and it showed. The day that she signed, she said to her mother, "I won't leave you, I'm staying local." She had said that from day one and she stayed true to her word. She learned a lot from her daughter and she appreciated all of the hard work that she had done and still kept her grades up.

Before Superstar signed the letter, Baby Girl took her daughter outside and explained to her that she would be able to handle the responsibility of being a parent again and that she deserved to get away and be on her own. Superstar acknowledged what she was hearing and they went back inside and she signed the letter. Most of her family was there for this monumental day. She felt like she was truly important, almost special.

But the reality came crashing back and she was sick of being in and around the hospital. It was getting tired and it was time for a rest from all of this tragedy and near misses. She got on her knees right where she stood and began to pray as Hannah had. Soon others were on their knees getting closer to God. The staff even got caught up in this awesome move. After a few minutes of prayer and interceding, many others left and within a few hours there was only a handful of them left. "You all can go on home, I'll be here." he said. Although they were tired and knew that they were needed elsewhere, they decided to stay on, at least until first Lady came to. He also hoped that she would come to before the meeting, but if she didn't he would still go forward with this all important meeting with the committee.

Someone went out and got some food for them. As they ate, to take their minds off of the situation, they began to talk about some of the events and happenings in the community. The annual couples walk was fast approaching and this year they were going to walk the zoo and its paths at sunrise. This was the first time that the zoo was involved and the directors of the zoo suggested that they do a sunrise walk. If they agreed, the zoo would open two hours later to the public. The counsel was so intrigued that they jumped on the opportunity. This walk was going to be something special. As the night progressed, they settled down and tried to get as comfortable as possible.

When morning came, Pastor inquired about his wife and her status. He was assured that she was in a stable state and he was allowed to see her again. He just looked at her and smiled. He knew that God had her and a true sense of comfort overcame him. He didn't have to touch her or do anything because he knew in his heart and soul that she was going to come out of this with flying colors. He walked back to the waiting area and woke Top Notch and Girlfriend, "We have to go. The meeting starts in a couple of hours and we both need to go home and do something with ourselves. Girlfriend, will you stay here until we get back?" "No problem, Pastor. We got this right here." With that being said, the two left.

On the way to the house he began to brief Top Notch about what was about to happen. She took a few mental notes and marveled at this man who had been going through one of the toughest period of time in his life. When many others would have folded, cracked or just thrown in the towel, he trudged onward. By the time he dropped her off, she was fully aware of the situation. This would be one for the books to say the least.

As he waited on his secretary to come out, he looked into the high clouds and let his mind drift away. He was early and had time to meditate on the happenings of late. The enemy seemed to be extra busy, all around him, his family and friends. He knew that God wouldn't let the enemy have the victory. He had brought them to far to leave them now. He began to pray for his son, especially. This thing had gone on far too long. No matter what, he was still their son.

He was so deep in thought that he didn't hear the door of the car open. Top Notch got in and that snapped him back into reality. "After the meeting, we'll go by my son's place. If that's alright with you." She nodded in agreement. They rode to the church in total silence, each in another zone. Pulling into his parking spot he looked around and noticed the cars that were there. They got out and went inside.

Turning the corner to the offices, they heard the collective chatter among the committee members. As he approached them he waved and went into his office. Closing the door behind him, he dropped to his knees and began to pray that his decisions be approved by God himself. Soon there was a knock on the door. He straightened himself and opened the door. Top Notch handed him a stack of papers and followed him as he walked towards the conference room.

Walking in the room he felt a pull on him. He shook it off and spoke to every one. Top Notch passed out the agenda for this meeting. She had added a few last minute notes. If she wasn't anything, she was thorough. She had proven herself time and again. Even in light of the last event she still shined. She was strong and she knew it, no man or woman could take that away from her.

Pastor started the meeting with prayer and began to go over the agenda. As usual the Cooks had prepared a very nice table of breakfast food, fruit and beverages. He had always like holding meetings that involved food. He stalled a little to give everyone a chance to serve themselves and get situated. They went over the basic stuff and then the newer things. He was pleased that everyone was there and accounted for, except his wife.

So far no one had brought that up and he was glad because he had a special announcement in regard to that alone. That's why he left that for last. But before he opened up to that subject he himself got something to eat. They took a mini break before going into the conclusion of the meeting. Before he was ready to start again, he felt that uneasy spirit again. Without drawing anyone's attention, he began to pray silently. Finishing his food he began, "As you all are aware of, our first lady had emergency surgery. She is doing well and will be laid up for a while. So with this development, I am going to be by her side every step of the way as I have done in the past. With that being said." He got out of his seat and continued. "In my absence Asst. Pastor will be in charge until we make our return. Asst. Pastor please stand." No one was more caught off guard than he was and it showed. Awkwardly, he approached his pastor. Pastor pulled his chair out and motioned for him to sit down at the head of the table. "We and the church are in your most capable hands until we return. The floor is yours."

Sitting in unbelief, he thought to himself, Finally. The king is wounded and he has given me the keys to the kingdom. Not just any kingdom, but to *his* kingdom. He thinks that all is well, but it isn't. He will truly regret not including me as one of his own. Looking at the people sitting around the table and feeling a sense of entitlement, he smiled and said, "United we stand, divided we will fall." With that being said the meeting was over. The committee began to embrace the temporary leader as he looked into the eyes of Top Notch and winked at her.

Turning away and following Pastor out of the door, she felt sick to her stomach. She wanted to question the logic behind his thinking. She understood that he wanted to be by his wife's side as she recovered, but she knew that this was a very bad idea. She knew all to well of what this man was very capable of doing. They walked in silence back to the office."I'll be ready to go in a few." he said to her going into his office. His mind focused on getting back to his wife and little else. In his office, he made a few necessary phone calls and canceled all of his appointments for the week. When he finished, he turned off the lights and locked his door. Before leaving he checked his wife's office and locked it as well.

Top Notch waited by the door as she watched him move around the office doing last minute mental checks to be sure that he had done everything that he needed to do. She knew that it was going to be a while before he came back. His wife was his life and everyone knew it. He often joked that he'd hurt a rock or kill a stone for his wife. With a final look around and a light sigh he walked out of the door with her following close by. When they reached the car he opened her door, "Let's grab a bite before heading back to the hospital. What do you have a taste for?" "A chili cheese dog with extra onions and some butter garlic fries, don't think I'll be kissing anyone tonight." she answered. They rode to the best greasy spoon known to man.

When they arrived and had placed their orders, he called Girlfriend to see who was there and what they wanted to eat. She text him their order and he placed it as well. Sitting down, before digging in, he reached out and touched her fingertips, in return she took his hand and patted it. "Pastor, every things going to be okay." They began to eat. "Man, there is nothing like these bg fries in this world." They ate in silence each in their own land of thought. Finished with their meal, he picked up their to go order and headed toward the hospital. As he parked he noticed a few people outside the door smoking cigarettes. He remembered when he was close to a pack a day, himself. Sometimes he'd find himself following someone smoking and catching a whiff or two of that sweet smell of tobacco.

Entering the hospital, they ran into Doc. He saluted acknowledgment and kept going. When they made it to the waiting area, Ma Dear said, "Good news son, your son is here and he's in there with his mother." He smiled and passed out the food and waited for his son to have some time with his mother. She took the fallout hard, but she knew it was for the best. If not now then when? Too many times they spent picking up the pieces or cleaning up his mess. It was well past all of that. He watched his small group of supporter eat and he was happy that he wasn't in this alone.

After a while, he wondered what was taking him so long to come out. Impatiently, he slid down the hallway to the ICU. When he walked in he noticed that only Girlfriend was with his wife. "Where's our son?" he asked her. "He left about ten/fifteen minutes ago." she answered. "I'll sit with her for a while. Your food is out there. Thanks, my friend." he said as she walked out. He looked down at his wife and the bandage that covered her head. He took her hand and caressed it. For a brief moment he thought that she flinched or maybe it was just wishful thinking on his part. Either way, he was happy to be by his wife's side, where he should be. Every thing else was secondary. I guess that's why they call it the blues, he thought to himself.

Soon he was joined by Doc and Doctor. They went over with him all that they were going to do with her. He shook their hands and watched as the nurses prepared to roll her down the hall. Yep, he thought, that's why they call it the blues. He decided to accompany his wife to the testing area. Whenever she came to, he wanted her to see his face first. After a battery of tests, she was finished and back in ICU. He was joined by various supporters as he waited for the results of her tests. Everyone seemed to be in good spirits which was good for the atmosphere. The doctors came back and went over the results with him. She was doing good and all the tests were positive. Her recovery time was reduced drastically compared to their initial diagnosis, barring any unforeseen complications. She was recovering so well that they were moving her into her own room sson. At least now her visitors could stay a little longer and not only that, everyone could breathe a little easier.

He had just enough time to go and let everyone know what was going on. As he gave them the update they began to thank God for the victory and hugged one another. He disappeared as fast as he appeared. He rushed back with excitement just as the nurses began wheeling her out of ICU. He checked to make sure that nothing was left behind and he followed them as they got on the elevator. Soon they were in her room and began to hook the IV's up. As they left, they assured him that she was going to bounce back before he knew it. He wanted to spend some quality and alone time with his baby now that she was out of danger.

He began to weep as he looked at his beautiful bride. It was short lived because one of the nurses came back to change her head bandages. For the first time, he was able to see what the doctors had talked to him about. To him, she was just as fine as the day that they married. Swollen or not. She was unbreakable and so was their love!

CHAPTER 23
The Walk

The walk at the zoo was at hand and all of the participants were assembled with their pledges awaiting the officials to open the gates for this historic event. There were even some that came that hadn't signed up and was hoping to get in on this walk. When Director came out to welcome everyone he sent security to close the parking gates so that no one else would be allowed into the zoo. He announced, "Welcome to The Zoo and our first walk-a-thon. Those of you who are coupled up and do not have registration forms will be permitted to participate as long as you have the required fee and a decent pledge. Those who are in this group please step over to the booth and we will get you registered. The rest of you proceed to the gates and enjoy the walk. We have some surprises in store for you. God bless and enjoy." Everybody applauded and began to go inside.

Brother and Nurse were with the Cooks and Fixx. All of them had been looking forward to this and they were as giddy as little kids. They didn't have any plan of attack as to what they wanted to see. They wanted to cover as much ground as possible before the zoo opened to the public. These three couples had weathered some really tough storms as of late, but that didn't stop them from still attempting to try. They all agreed that giving up was easy but hanging in there was the toughest to do. For one of these couples though, a lot was riding on this event!

As they entered the zoo they could hear the animals. "Sounds like the animals are out already. Lets start at the reptile house and work our way around." Fixx suggested. They looked at the maps that were given to each individual participant. The maps were specially made for this occasion. The really cool part was that each habitat had a tour guide or two depending on how large the habitat was.

Their first habitat was the reptile house. There were so many different species of snakes that it was going to take a little time to see them all. From the outside, the building didn't look as big as it seemed inside. They slowly walked along the exhibits critiquing the slithering devils until one snake caused them to stop. He was a giant boa constrictor, with two heads! "This guy right here is the star of the show. Most people are already fearful of snakes, but when you combine girth and hideousness, you get 'Stonie'. That's his name. It seems like everyday he gets bigger and bigger." addressed the tour guide. "Whats the difference between a snake and a two faced person? The snake knows that its a snake." quipped Brother looking at Nurse. They lightheartedly laughed and looked at him peculiarly because they were well aware of the goings on between he and Nurse. They shuffled up and down the exhibits until they reached the door to exit.

They ducked into a few smaller habitats and exhibits, making short work of them. As they walked down the path they could hear this loud pitched laughter. It was coming from the African Desert habitat. The closer that they got, the louder the laughter got. Fortunately for them most of the animals were outside. The noise maker was a spotted hyena named Maeverg. She was being attacked by a few of the other, younger female hyenas. "She must have been the dominant queen at one point. It appears that the old girl is being pushed out by the younger and stronger females. I have always loved hyenas, I once did a thesis on them. They are the most vicious predators alive. They can digest almost anything, hooves, horns, you name it, they can eat it. With them, nothing goes to waste." Nurse shared with them. As if on que, the aggressive hyena grabbed the old gal by the ear and ripped at it with viciousness and precision. With that attack, the old gal cowered with her tail between her legs and went into the 'surrender' stance. The other hyenas gathered around the new queen of the pack. Everyone that witnessed this was amazed. "My God. This is the stuff that you only see on TV and in the wild, but to actually witness an animal hostile takeover is one for the ages."

A little further down in the same habitat they observed a couple of buzzards high in the trees. They were lapped faced vultures. One was named Kemmiecoo, she was just sitting there looking around. "This buzzard here, Kemmiecoo, she has been through a lot. She was attacked by four male vultures, so we had to separate her from them. They are on the inside, but they still try to get at her. That's why she looks constantly around her surroundings." the guide for this exhibit shared with the crowd. They walked around the entire exhibit before going inside to see the animals that seemed to be uninterested in coming outside. As they were coming out of the habitat, Kimmiecoo, flew down from her perch and started wailing in the direction of the four aggressors who had been let out to get some air in the cage next to hers. "Looks like someone has a hot crotch today, eh?"

When they were finished with this exhibit they decided to keep going instead of getting something to eat. They had only visited a few good ones and wanted to get the most out of the time before the place was overrun by the public. They had come to an area where the zoo began to break into many different paths. They wanted to stay together but they also wanted to explore by themselves. So they decided to meet at the canteen for lunch, then they would finish the walk together. The weather was so beautiful, and it was nice to be out and about. The Cooks walked away holding hands. The Fixx walked away arm around waist and Brother and Nurse just walked. All on different paths and courses.

They walked in silence, something that seemed to define their relationship. The more one tried, it seemed as if the other pulled in another direction. Why were they so off? While it seemed that everyone else was working on their relationships and issues, they couldn't get pass seemingly minor issues. They approached the insect house. He knew that she was a big insect lover. She often would get on him for killing certain spiders and bugs. He opened the door for her and they went inside. He knew they would be in here for a while. Over time, he learned about himself when it concerned her. Instead of pooh pooh something that she wanted to do that he didn't necessarily want to do, he would do it just to make her happy. One thing he could do was to be there with her. He was an avid outdoors man but he could do without bugs and the like.

They navigated the displays one by one, not skipping anything. She was very partial to insects. She seemed to like them better than people at times. Although she was in the medical field, her heart really was with nature. Her uncle, before he passed, had set her up with an endowment that was for the field of medicine. When she told him about her passion for insects, he shared with her the importance of human life opposed to that of nature. He once said to her, "God takes care of nature, we are to take care of each other. That's what separates us from them." They approached the beetle displays. She got so excited that he thought that she was going to explode. This was a new exhibit. The zoo was breeding a new batch of dung beetles exclusively for the African animal exhibit.

"If you pay close attention to the dung beetle exhibit, in a few moments we will began to feed them. Fortunately for us, we are out here and they are in there. Over in the corner, we have JalvnCaxsin our resident thief. He doesn't play well with others, so we had to separate him. All he does is try to steal others hard work, so we give him a big mound of elephant dung to keep him happy." pointed out the tour guide. She continued to ramble on and on about this certain dung beetle and its kind. To break the monotony, he said, "Damn, even that poor bastard dung beetle has a hyphenated last name." She turned to him and grabbed his hand. They walked away from the small group that they were standing by.

"Listen, we've been through this time and again. I told you my reasons and I wish that you would respect that," she said as stern as possible. "It's too much to have to deal with to do all of that changing. Why can't you get that?" "That's exactly what I'm talking about. Answer me this then, when you were your father's daughter, you had one last name. When you were married to your husband, you had only one last name. So why in the hell would I allow you to bring in someone else last name. That ain't fair to me, hell I might consider that if he would have died or something, but he walked out on you. That's cool, keep his last name I'm done. You defend his raggedy ass last name but you're willing to lose someone who cares about you. Typical."

He pulled away from her for the final time and walked out of the building, not looking back. As he stood outside, he noticed how calm he was. Usually, arguments with her would have him all over the place. Not today! He sat on the bench waiting for her. Within a few minutes she was sitting by him. As she put her sunglasses on, she put her hand on his leg, something that she intentionally had not been doing lately. "Can we finish this walk? I want to get home with my man. I'm all in because I do love you. Why I act this way? Even I don't know sometimes. I'll be everything plus some, if you'll have me back." "We've been through a lot since we became serious about one another. Let's take a little time to get back to the basics and see where we land. I want you to respect me like you respect him." he answered. She nodded in agreement. With that they began to walk towards the next exhibit.

They cruised through the next hour checking out a lot of the attractions. Soon it was time to meet up with the gang for lunch. By now the gates had been opened to the public, but that didn't seem to matter to them. Today, a lot had been achieved and they could see the hand of God at work. Once the group was together they all compared the different animals that they had seen. Incredibly, no one had seen the primates. They ordered and ate so that they could get to see the great apes.

As they walked to the primate house they could hear Keith Sweat's jam, Twisted. They danced a little to the music on their way. They watched as two of the gorillas played with a tire. Another great ape sat on the banks of the fake rivers edge. When he turned around, with the precision of a skilled pitcher, he hurled a handful of dodo. As the crowd ducked for cover Sis. Cook said, "I guess he don't like Keith's whining either." After the coast was clear, they went inside. The smell hit them immediately. "Maybe we should have hit this boy first, cause it is foul in here." The heat was making the funk even funkier. They hurried through the habitat, but before they left they checked out an old silver-back. He looked shell shocked and defeated. Kind of made you feel sorry for the old boy. Not sorry enough to stay and listen to his story.

Now the safari vehicles were running so they decided to hop on one to get off of their feet. Ah, the feeling of love was truly in the air. The couples either held hands or simply embraced listening to the tour guide as he pointed out different things on the route. Of course, he didn't have a clue about all that they had already seen. It was refreshing to bask in the throes of love and being loved. The tour guide slowed the vehicle to a crawl. "We are coming near our turning point, but we have an exhibit that is my personal favorite. The rain forest exhibit is unlike anything you will probably witness, unless you go to see the real deal. But I personally promise you that you will enjoy it." As soon as he said that, a lovely woman came out of the doors of the habitat.

Almost everyone got off and lined up. "You are about to witness something special. This exhibit hasn't been open to the public yet, you will be the first group to have this experience. After you, it will be closed until Monday, it's official opening day. As you can see, we are a long way from everything else. You are in for quite a treat. Follow me." she said. With that, the few that remained on the vehicle jumped off including the driver.

As they entered, it seemed as if they had walked into another world. Nothing on TV or books came close to the sights and sounds of this place. The colors were vibrant and the constant mist gave the ambiance something unique. They watched and listened as this well informed woman walked them along the paths. When they reached the pond that was encased in glass so clear, that one wondered how the water was being held back. Soon they were looking up from near the bottom and that's where the real magic began. "If you look closely, you will see the worlds largest leech. We call him 'YB', that's short for Young Bloodsucker. He hasn't been here long, but he attaches himself to anything that gets close to him." They pushed on ahead basking in the beautiful surroundings. "This must be what the garden of Eden looked like." The group agreed. As the tour came to a close, they were lead back out to the vehicle. "I hope this was a wonderful experience for all of you, because it surely was for me. Be safe and God bless." she said to the group. Sis. Cook reached in her pocket and handed her a church information card. She took it and watched them load up and pull out.

Soon they were at the front gate and they were ready to go, especially Nurse. They all had been so wrapped up in the zoo experience that they had all but forgotten to go by the gift shop and get their gift bags. Since they were on their way out, they decided to bless whoever walked by first. Each one was able to be a blessing to someone. Brother wanted his to be something special, so he looked for someone in particular and he found them.

A guy with a nice sized family was unloading his family when he walked up to him. "It was placed on my heart to bless you and your family. Before you say it, it doesn't cost you a thing. My girl and I want to be a blessing to you and yours. We have these food vouchers, gift certificates and wristbands that allow you to go to the paid exhibits for free. In other words, see the zoo on us." The other four in their group handed over their bands as well. The man began to tear up,"I told God this morning in prayer that I, rather we needed a miracle. And He has answered my prayer. Thank you all so very much." "Here's my number, if you need to talk to someone, get at me." Brother said as he shook the man's hand.

Grabbing his girl by the waist and jumping into the van, he felt more alive than he had in years. God was communicating with him and he was listening! The group pulled off and left the zoo. It was a good day, yes it was.

CHAPTER 24
My Brother's Keeper

"You know that dung beetle really reminded me of this cat I used to work with. He had been there for years and only could get a 30/89 day job filling in for bosses that were off and such. But whenever he was called to fill in, he always went too damn far. You know, one of those old uncle tom niggers. All that lying and tricking on folks got him no where. Damn near thirty years there and he still crap cleaning for the farm. The thing about this uncle tom, was at one point we were cool. He turned on me and my girl. Laugh in your face one minute then write a letter on you the next. Him and Uncle Remus' bear, that other black sambo, should be taken out and castrated then gutted and left for the maggots. Baby, I see how you looking at me but if we were soldiers at war, I probably would have killed one of them if not both of 'em. Real talk. I have never hated someone like I hate those two cocksuckers."

As Brother and Nurse sat on the porch talking, his phone rang. He was so worked up that he wouldn't answer his phone. "It's been a while and this still agitates me as if it was last night. I have hated this group of people far too long and I'm cool with it. If I saw them in a burning building I'd see what else I could throw in to make the fire even hotter!"

She had seen him angry before and this was of epic proportion. She tried to defuse the situation but she knew it was best to let him vent. She got up and went inside and put on Loose Ends. Jane Eugene always seemed to calm him down. When his favorite song by them, Mr. Bachelor, didn't work she played Slow Down. With that playing, she did her little snake dance, if that didn't work nothing would. Bless the heavens, because it did work. Pinning him down, she buried her face in his chest. He loved when she did that, oh yes he did.

"Please stop thinking about that kind of stuff. Think about me, us, our future together. We do have a wedding to plan, don't we?" she inquired. He nodded in agreement. As they were getting more into each other, his phone rang again. This time he answered it. "What's good?" Sitting up, his facial expressions changed. She backed off and let him take the call. "Yes, I remember you, it was only a couple of months ago, right? Yeah, I'm free, where you want to meet? Cool. I'll see you in an hour," turning to Nurse, he said, "That was old boy from the zoo that we blessed. He wants to talk. He sounded kind of strange. Sounds like he has a lot on his mind." He kissed her and set off to meet Old Boy.

Wondering what was going on, he drove on to the meeting place. When he arrived, he was about fifteen minutes early. He sat in his car for a few minutes then stepped outside. Leaning against his car, he looked at the people that were milling around. As he watched, out of no where, Old Boy walked up to him. "Thanks for meeting with me. Man, I need someone to talk to. I usually don't go around telling my business but it was something about you that I connected with. First, thanks for being a blessing to me and mine. My girlfriend and I have really been struggling lately. I mean in every area. Those kids are hers. She was pregnant with our child but she lost it a few months ago. Sometimes I want to walk away, but something keeps me put. Our biggest thing is the kids. Don't get me wrong, I dig all of them. But she puts them ahead of me, all of the time. It's like when we have things planned, she has to revolve everything around them. Even when they are gone she fidgets and fumbles about them being gone. We even discussed scriptures that dealt with the family and its structure. She believes that that was written for a husband and wife that shares children. What should I do?" "Do you love her? "Yes. With all my heart." "Well, you have a couple of choices. You can either stay and try a little harder or cut your loses."

"I was once involved with someone that constantly ran behind her kids, and we're talking adult age. She was so close to one of them that she would still cut up his pancakes and stuff. He was well over 21 and as she did this, he sat back with a big dumb grin on his face. I could have slapped him so hard that I had to just shake my head. Then there was this other one that I had met in the club. Now this one was real cool. We got along real well. One day I realized that she had a horrible sense of time, especially when it came to things we had planned. We were going to meet some friends for a 4th of July event. This was planned weeks in advance, so the 4th comes, she calls from work to let me know she'll be off in time. Cool. A few hours pass and still she isn't around. I call, no answer. So I call my peeps to tell them I'm on my way. As I finish putting the things in the car, my phone rings and its her. She tells me that she had to go home to check on her kids and sister. I was furious! Because her kids and sister were in over thirty. When I told her that I was still going on without her she was pissed. I hung up and called Plan B. So my brother, I know what you are going through. But if its love, my advice to you is to hang in there. Especially if your hearts in it."

"Its more to it than that. I have no idea why I am sharing all of this with you. I know my boys are tired of hearing it. But our other thing is church. We go to separate houses of faith. We go together occasionally if there is something special going on. We discussed where we would fellowship if we were to marry. She is very active in her church. She attends every service, bible class and whatever else is going on, she's there. I told her that I believe that we should fellowship together. But I don't want to be in church all day. I love my church, we have one service on Sunday, mid week bible class and a service on Thursday night once a month. If she ain't talking about those kids she's rambling on and on about her pastor. I told her that I wasn't going to compete with her pastor or anyone else. She has been by herself so long that she lives vicariously through them. What am I to do? She is fun and I care deeply for her, but sometimes I think of taking my ball and leaving." he said as he summoned the waitress over. They placed their orders and continued to talk.

Hours passed and soon it was closing time. As they walked towards the parking lot, they stopped and agreed that their chance meeting was what both of them needed. For some strange reason, Brother felt close to this guy. They agreed to hook up for a round of paintball and golf in a couple of days. Sometimes it felt good to breakaway from the norm because lately things had become complacent in his life.

When they hooked up for paintball they sat in the parking lot talking. They loved the art of war that this game provided. It gave them a chance to take on challenges and assault others without having to go to jail. They even gave it a name, War Games: The Match Beyond. Old Boy was black using white paint balls and Brother chose black with red paint balls. As they finished gearing up, they went their separate ways into the woods. For Brother, this was a chance to get back into something that he loved. Although he had left the slaughterhouse behind, he still had the primal desire to hunt and slay. As he went deeper into the woods, his senses heightened, almost to a calm frenzied state. This was his first time playing against Old Boy so there was a sense of urgency to succeed.

He found an abandoned tree stand that was well camouflaged. He decided to mark a perimeter and to make some obvious tracks for his opponent. As he began to do this, he stopped as he heard footsteps in the distance. He took refuge behind a wall of brush. After a few minutes a deer came into his focus. Not what he was looking for, he went back into setting up the trap. While doing this, he had an epiphany. That what was missing from him and Nurse's relationship, the thrill of the hunt! Maybe just maybe, this could help

The Junky Chronicles Present: The Church of the Poisened Minds

him to really get back into their relationship. As he was standing up he heard something whiz past his ear. Somehow Old Boy had gotten the drop on him. He was always so careful when he played the game and had a personal record of success to uphold. He ducked into the underbrush and crawled on his belly to get to safety.

Cursing under his breath, Old Boy kicked the foliage under his foot. He was very accomplished at hunting and tracking. How could he have missed such an easy target. Frustrated, he knelt down to pick up the tracks of his quarry. This was an outing that he really needed. He had been so consumed with trying to make things right on every hand that he had somehow lost his way. He began to talk to God in an instant from being flustered. As he knelt, something took hold of him. Everything around him seemed to go into slow motion. Before his face, he saw the words, 'Be still'. As he tried to get up he couldn't. It was as if a hand was holding him down. He wasn't a drinker or drug user so he wasn't under the influence. What was this mighty force that was taking hold of him? Giving in to the pull of the force, he submitted and he began to speak in tongues. For all of the years that he had been involved in his christian journey, he had never spoken in tongues before. He had wholly felt the rush of the Holy Spirit and other feelings but nothing like this!

From a distance, Brother focused on his fallen quarry. He had the perfect shot and as his began to squeeze the hammer, he couldn't pull the trigger. Something caught his eye. He watched Old Boy in fascination. Soon he was walking towards him. The closer that he got, the closer he was drawn. As he stood a few feet away, he put his gun away. Just as he did that Old Boy began to come to. Standing to his feet, he placed his hand on Brother's shoulder and a jolt shot through him. He stood there and a vision flashed before his eyes and soon he too began to speak in tongues. For him, that hadn't happened since his youth.

As he came out of his trance, he looked at Old Boy and the man looked different. "Today, we have seen the glory of God," agreed the men. They began to walk out of the woods and back to their cars without speaking a word to the other. Both lost deep in thought about what had just transpired. At their cars, they began to pull off their gear, still in silence. After a few minutes, Old Boy turned to Brother and said, "I am my brothers keeper. Today I was going to do harm to someone that I thought, I mean, I knew did me wrong. This outing was to help me get my skills back in sync. I have been putting in work for years and when I was told that I was going to be a grandfather soon, I decided

114

to retire. I went to the Old Man and explained to him that my life was going to change and that my son was going to be a father and I wanted to be available to assist him and his wife in every way that I could. His mother passed and I had to raise him and his sister the best way I knew. I was deep in the game and that was all that I knew, since I was a kid. My daddy sat on the counsel as did his daddy. But me, I'm a worker, not a king. I love the challenge of getting up close and personal to my victims. Seeing them take their last breath was a rush. I always thought that one day one of my victims would come back and haunt me. Sometimes I would see blood on the moon. I never had a drink or anything that wasn't natural. To a degree, I was brought up as a Nazarite with a killer twist. I was breed for this, born into this thing of ours. But on this day, I saw for myself that God was willing to forgive me and He showed me in a vivid and all too real vision and I believe you saw something as well. You saw the hand of God and the blood of Jesus Christ as He hung on the cross. But more importantly, you saw the two of us hanging from the crosses that were to His left and His right." "You're right, that is what I saw. I'll see you later." He got into his car.

As he pulled off, he watched his friend in the rear view mirror. He still looked different. What did all of this mean? Who could he talk to? Why did this revelation have to come his way? Was he his brothers keeper? So many questions came zipping through his mind. For the short amount of time that he had known Old Boy, each encounter drew them closer together. "Yes, Old Boy, I am my brothers keeper."

CHAPTER 25
Greg

With all that had been going on, Pastor was well pleased with the progress of First Lady's recovery. That rupture did more damage than what was immediately diagnosed. But the family kept vigil and worked around the clock. No one was more helpful than Top Notch and Girlfriend. He reminded everyone that they needed to keep their normal routines and just to help out when they had the time. This worked to an advantage, this way he wouldn't have to hurt anyone's feelings. He knew that everyone meant well, but he also knew that he had to have some time that they could be alone. Some nights one person would spend the night to help out. So far everything was working. She was progressing well. The doctors would come by for routine checkups but that was about it.

Soon she would be starting rehab and it would be good to get her outside. All week long he had been thinking about what to get her when he returned to work and to the pulpit. The time had gone a little longer than he had anticipated but everything in both places seemed to be thriving without them. When Girlfriend came later that afternoon he went on his quest for the perfect gift for his wife.

Every idea that he thought was a good idea seemed to fall by the wayside. Either he didn't like it or something just wasn't right with it. She had lost a little weight so that was a challenge in itself. She was resting a sleeping a lot so movies and things that required time and concentration was out. Although he was going back to the daily grind, she wasn't and he tried to keep that in mind. She loved board games, but he wanted something that she would really appreciate. All the gifts and dates that they shared they prided themselves on.

As evening was drawing nearer, he sat in his car still gift less. This bothered him and for the first time in years he wanted a cigarette. He followed behind a couple that had parked a few cars away, taking in the sweet tobacco aroma as they walked towards the fairly new strip mall. He had passed this place several times but had never stopped, but he was led there. Thinking about the cigarette took his mind off of the task at hand.

When the couple reached their destination he realized that it was a pet store. Without a game plan in place he walked inside. This place had every thing in it. He listened to the many animals making noise that filled the store. Then it was the smell of the animals that really awakened him. He stood in the middle of the store and closed his eyes trying to focus on what animal to go after. Realizing that fish and others don't make noise he decided to search the whole store. One thing about him was that if he had to go into a store he wanted to do his business and hit the bricks. That's what he loved about his wife, she would go to the store and get one orange as well as stay all day just shopping. She didn't pull on him and he didn't mind. If she asked him to go it had a reason that warranted it.

Thinking about his queen he didn't hear the announcement that the store was closing soon. "Excuse me sir we will be closing soon. Is there anything in particular that you are looking for? Maybe I can help you." he was asked. "I'm looking for a special companion for my wife. She recently went under the knife and she is home recovering and I will be returning to work soon. What ever I get, it has to be special. Price isn't an issue, I just want both of them to feel comfortable with each other." Before he could continue, the worker said, "We are closing in five minutes and it seems that you will need a little longer than that. Wait a minute, I'll be right back my manager is motioning for me."

After a few minutes the worker came back with the manager. "Hey Pastor, I was told that you are looking for a special gift for our first lady. Take your time and look around. We will be happy to help you." smiled Manager. "I can come back tomorrow when you first open. I don't want to impose on anyone. I know when its time for me to go home, that is exactly what I want to do." "No, you're good, we got you." He thanked them and they began to walk through the store. Now the store was basically empty except for the three of them and the animals had calmed down drastically.

Finally, they walked into the cat area. There was a wall full of cats and at once he knew that he was in the right place. Now his new problem was finding the right one. As he was thinking about this he asked, "Which of these has the hard knock life story?" "It's funny that you would ask that question. If you follow me, I would like to introduce you to my personal favorite" They walked past the rest of the cats into the area for employees only.

Manager opened the door and sitting in a chair was a fat gray, black and white cat. "Pastor, this is Greg, he is like our overall favorite animal in the store. We keep him back here because we don't want just anybody taking old Greg from us. We all agreed that we would only let people that we know and that's going to give him the love and attention that he needs, to see him. When we got him, he was shell shocked. He was jumpy and nervous about everything.

The family that had him treated him bad. We came to work one morning and someone had tied him up in a bag and left it tied to the door. We thought he was dead at first and that someone was playing a cruel joke on us. Believe it or not, it has happened before. At any rate, we got him his shots, neutered and everything else that he was in need of. He has spent all of one night in a cage here. We let him roam freely when we close. He has the run of the house and he seems to know it. Whoever gets him surely will be blessed for it. He is very easy to get along with and no trouble at all to have around. Should we leave you two alone for a few minutes?" "No, that won't be necessary. I like Greg and I am sure that my wife would love him. Back in the day she was a tree hugger and animal rights nut. But that's a story for another day."

As they opened the door, Greg jumped off of his seat and ran before them. When they got to the front of the store, Manager turned to Worker, "Try to get Greg in one of those large carriers, please. He is way too big for the regular size carriers. Pastor, if you give us a minute, we will get all of his paperwork together." Standing by the register, he asked, "How much is Greg? I saw the prices on some off the cages and I never would have thought that an animal could cost that much when there are so many running around loose and free." Smiling at him, Manager pushed his money away and answered, "We are blessing Greg with you. No amount could pay for that. We decided that whoever took a chance on Greg wouldn't have to pay for him. Just give our first lady and Greg our love and that will be payment enough. And keep the carrier. It was once the transporter for a cat that came from a very prominent and influential family. He deserves the best. Actually, he thinks its his anyway. He sleeps in it sometimes. Your wife ministered one time about how favor ain't fair and that went so deep. She said, 'We can't get blessed because we are so busy trying to turn people away from blessing us. Her subject was,'Too Blessed to Get Blessed' and I will never forget that one, because I was one of those people that she was talking about." By the time Manager finished recalling the sermon, Worker had a cart full of everything that was going to be needed.

"We all are going to leave out together. We want to see our favorite patron leave out of here." Manager unlocked the doors, hit the lights and turned the security alarm on. Since Greg had been there, they stopped turning it on because it was motion sensitive. With the store locked, they proceeded to the pastor's car. They loaded Greg and his stuff into the car. Pastor thanked them and they waved at Greg maybe for the last time. They knew that the store wouldn't be the same without him being there anymore, but they were happy that he was going somewhere that he would be wanted. Pastor waved goodbye and they were on their way home.

He thanked God for favor. One thing he tried to stay away from was using his position as a pastor for gain. He had seen many of his fellow laborers in the gospel use their influence to the fullest. He remembered an incident earlier in his pastoring when a minister checked the emcee for not calling him Dr. Pastor. And then the other time when a minister told a congregation that preaching the gospel was a very expensive job. But the coupe-DE-grau was when a minister insisted that his entire entourage be compensated outside of his stipend. He knew ministers that wouldn't preach the word of God to small congregations because they didn't have the finances to cover their expenses. He knew ministers that shunned smaller ministries that were under them, but still would be expecting monthly dues. Then their was the ones that always wanted to let EVERYBODY know how much they put in someone's offering tray. With every incident that he saw, he wrote down and shared with his wife and committee. "If I ever act like this or any other inappropriate way as the covering of this ministry, please hold me accountable for my actions. Seriously."

Snapping back into reality he thanked the Lord again. Soon he and Greg were home. Top Notch and Ma Dear was sitting with First Lady on the couch watching tv. He spoke and kissed his wife on the forehead."Honey, I have something for you." he said with a wink. Stepping out of the door he picked up the carrier and turned to her. When she saw what was inside she let out a squeal. "My Love, I present to you, Greg." He opened the cage and Greg took off running. The cat ran past everyone and down the hall. Pastor chased after him as the women laughed and laughed.

He began to search for Greg until he found him under a bed in the guest bedroom. He tried to coax him out, but the cat wouldn't budge. The closer he got, the further the cat would go under the bed. After a few more minutes he gave up and left the cat alone. Walking down the hall, he remembered that he still had to get the rest of the stuff out of the car. The ladies were still laughing and soon he too joined the laughter. To see his wife laughing was a blessing and he thanked God for that.

At his car, he started to really appreciate times like this. That darn cat jump started his wife and it was wonderful. He began to unload the car and bringing things inside. Top Notch met him at the door to give him a hand. "Do you think that's wise to bring that stuff in and that cat might run outside and never come back again. And where did you get him from anyway?" Before he could answer they all broke out laughing again and rehashing the last few minutes. He waved them off and finished bringing Greg's stuff inside.

After he settled down with the women, he told them about how he came to the conclusion to get her a pet. When he got to the part about the cigarettes they all looked at him funny. It had been years since he had had a 'puff' as he referred to it. Finishing the story, he sat back in his seat and sighed. First Lady looked over at him as did the other two women. They were very proud of him. Top Notch and Ma Dear prepared to leave. He got up to walk them out and held his mother's hand then he kissed her on the forehead. He walked them to the car and opened their doors. They waved and drove away.

Back inside he sat with his wife on the couch. He held her hand and caressed it. They sat there lovingly in the comfort of each other with nothing say. Soon they were sleepy and went to bed. As they prepared for bed he checked her vision, ear and head to make sure everything was fine. As they did the eye tests, he looked at this vision of loveliness. He took her chin and began to kiss her passionately. "You always make me feel like a woman and I love you for that. Thanks babe." she whispered. Getting back to the checkup before things got out of hand he removed her scarf to check her scars. Soon her hair would cover most of it but for now it had to stay short. He actually loved her short haired look. Few women could pull this look off but she did it well.

Now that the inspection was over, he kissed her scars and laid her on the bed. They both had been looking for this night to happen. They hadn't had any real intimacy since she took ill. But tonight was the night. One of the first non-medical questions they asked was regarding how long it would be before they could go to the killin' floor. As passion filled the air, the man and woman came together. Months of pent up tension was finally being released and it took most of the night to put a cap on it.

As the morning sun broke through their bedroom the lovers began to stir about. Sitting up, he looked at his wife and smiled at this vision of loveliness in her nakedness. "Man, go brush your teeth or something I haven't even had breakfast or my medication yet and you already to go, again." "That's the way love goes, baby" he responded and playfully squeezed one of her breast."You know I do have another one of those." She responded to his touch. And with that, they were back at it. This time it was all out war!

Finally, they were both satisfied and they went to their separate bathrooms. In his, he showered and did his manly stuff as she did her womanly business. As usual he was done way before her. It didn't matter if they were going out or not, the result were always the same. That's why they had to have multiple bathrooms in their house. Walking towards the kitchen, he stopped to check on Greg. He looked under the bed and the cat was still in the same spot!

In the kitchen he fixed Greg some food and placed it in his tray with some water. That was the easy part, now he had to find a place for the cat bed and litter box to go. Somewhere that the woman of the house would approve of. He washed his hands and pulled some food out for breakfast. She soon joined him and they waited for the water to boil so they could at least have coffee and tea. "Lets have some bagels and cheese this morning. There is some steak leftover from last night, hey, we can have steak bagels. What up?" They laughed and made small talk as they prepared their meal. "From day one I have always loved eating with you and its just as much fun when we hook up in our own kitchen." "True dat." They sat down to eat and to enjoy the moment.

After three days of being under the bed, they started to worry about Greg. He hadn't touched his food or litter box. When they got home from the therapist, he went looking for Greg. He wasn't under the bed, but he still hadn't eaten or used the box. They began to search for their elusive cat. She took one end of the house, he the other. When they met up neither had seen hide nor hair of Greg. They went out on the patio to enjoy some of the beautiful weather and worry about the crazy cat later. "Are you sure that was a cat and not a ghost or spirit that you brought here?" she teased. They spent the better part of the day outside so that she could really get some fresh air.

When they came in, they both noticed that the cat food was almost gone. At least now they knew that he was alive. So they went on with their night. Around 2:45 am. there was a commotion in their room. He turned on the light and the crazy cat was running around the room and trying to attack the cat that was in the mirror not realizing that the other cat was him. He turned the light out and soon they were asleep. When they woke up Greg was laying on the foot of their bed. "Hey Greg, its nice to finally meet you." Then she began to breakdown in tears. "I miss our son. What have we done to make him hate us so much?" He knew that no matter what answer he came up with, it wouldn't suffice so he climbed out of the bed and let her have her moment.

He went into the kitchen not really hungry and turned on the TV. He stared blankly at the program not even hearing what was being said. He had done good to put his son and emotions out of his mind and heart, especially after that stunt that he pulled at the hospital. He knew what he did was wrong and so it was what it was. He wouldn't shed another tear for him and his decision to walk away from them. As far as he was concerned it was good riddance to him. Like he yelled at him, "I'm a grown ass man and I do what I wanna do."

"Babe, I just noticed that Greg doesn't have on a flea collar. If he is going to be in our house, its a must that he gets one. Okay?" He was just happy that she didn't come in there talking about her son. "I'll run down there to get one. Is there any color you want in particular that you'd like?" he asked to break the tension. She shook her head and waved her hand in the air. Grabbing his keys he hurried out of the house and jumped in his car a jetted down the street. By the time he arrived at the pet store he realized that he had left his recovering wife home alone. He grabbed his phone to call someone to go over to sit with her until he got back home. As he scrolled through his phone he decided that he would be back in a little bit and that she would be alright.

Once he was inside of the pet store he went looking for the perfect flea collar for Greg. As usual, there were way too many to choose from. Thinking about his wife, he choose her favorite color and picked one that he thought that she would approve of. Standing in line he overheard a woman going completely off. She wanted to know why she had to go through all of the paperwork to adopt an animal. From her tone, he could tell that she was very pissed. Just as he was paying for his item she stormed out of the store.

As he walked out, she was standing by the door and she began to vent, "All I wanted to do, was get my little boy a puppy and they give me this run around just to get a mutt. I probably could get a damn baby without having to go through all of this mess. He placed second in a math contest and the kid that beat him was a grade higher. He wanted a bird but that wasn't going to happen and we both like dogs so I wanted to get him one and save a dog and give it a nice home but these, ooh, people are ridiculous. I mean these animal rights do-gooders make things difficult and they wear much leathers and furs. Probably eat more meat than the law allows. They probably would help an animal and walk right over a human that's in need." she vented. "If you are getting it for a kid then you should rethink it. Sometimes we have to sacrifice for our kids. They might not never know it, but as long as we do it because we love them, that's all that matters." he advised. She looked at him and said, "I know you. You're Baby Girl's brother, the preacher, right?" He nodded in agreement. "Damn, I just cussed at the preacher. Please forgive me, sir."

All he could do was laugh and soon she was laughing with him. "You know, one day I could walk away from the faith, but I will still be a human. So I don't go around criticizing people. You are mild compared to my baby sister." "I think I will go back inside and get that mutt for a great little guy. Thanks and we will see you on Sunday." With that, she went back into the store. Grateful to be heading home, he hopped into his car and drove away. When he walked inside their house, he was greeted with a big hug and a kiss. Greg sat on the arm of the sofa and purred as she placed the beautiful collar around his ample neck. All three seemed to be at peace in spite of the recent actions that happened to them.

CHAPTER 26
Uncertainty and Dirt Roads

Today was going to be something special for the Clean family. Their oldest son was coming home from prison. He had completed a fourteen year sentence and hopefully this would be the last time that they would have to endure such heartache and pain. "You know, this gets harder and harder every time that we have to go through this with him. He says all the right things and does all the right things until he hooks up with that mob of his. I suspect that from the way that he's been talking lately that all of that is in the past." she shared with her husband. He nodded in agreement. "Its like we have been taking care of him all our lives. Either in jail or out. When our friends gave up on their own flesh and blood, that inspired me to keep on believing in God and my son. I remember when he was first starting to break bad and we sat him down for a talk. We did it as a team, me and you, because we wanted him to know that we both loved him and that we were a unit of one. And I really thought that he would get it, but evidently he didn't. Maybe, by the grace of God, this time will be different. Well we better get going, his bus should be at the depot soon."

They left the house and was on their way to pick up their son. Usually they would pick him up from the prison, but this time they wanted him to have a long ride home to think about his future and not to dwell so much on the past. They knew he would be tired by the time his bus arrived. How ironic it was that the bus ride would be fourteen hours long after serving fourteen years. No matter what, he was still theirs and they loved him dearly. They loved him so much that when they met with the public defender they placed their son's life in her hands. They broke from the norm and did not go with their family lawyer but instead went in a new direction with the public defender.

This shocked everyone, themselves included. They wanted him to know that he was running on borrowed time and money and neither he attempted to make restitution on. They were too old to put up bond for him. "I remember telling him the last time, 'If you are going to still live that sort of life at least put money away so when something happens to you it won't fall on me and your mama.' And no sooner than those words were spoken they carted him away and the judge threw the book at him. What makes him and these others that grew up with him think that they can go to the city and do what they want to without no repercussions? I just don't get it. I know living only an hour of so from the big city and getting in trouble here is different from up there. At least they would get a break or two here, but that's not the case when they go up there and act like they are above the law. I don't believe that anyone was more shocked than he was when that public defender gal called his name. We know he thought Lawyer or someone from his firm would be there but it was not to be."

This type of dialog was good for them. They recently had begun talking about what ever was going on that involved them. They agreed that they would share and talk instead of prancing around like nothing was happening. When friends or family would ask about him, they had no problem sharing what they knew. "Can't nobody put us in heaven or hell because of the sins of the son. We did the best we could do and it was his decisions not to follow all that we showed him. One thing I can say about him is that he did his time and didn't try to have us to to it with him. I believe this time is going to be different." As they rode towards their destination the conversation became less and less. It seemed every mile closer, they became deeper in thought.

They had finally reached their destination and the bus still had a few minutes before it arrived. They got out of the car to stretch and look around. It had been years since either of them had been at this particular bus terminal. It almost seemed like an eternity to them both. As they waited they held hands and reminisced about the past and what this place meant to them. It was here that they met decades ago and how God placed them in each others path.

She was getting off the bus and couldn't find one of her bags. It was he that had accidentally picked up the wrong bag. He explained to her that this was his first time away from home and that he had never had a bag before and he barely remembered to grab it before going to look for his relatives that was suppose to pick him up. All the time apologizing constantly. "I thought that you were going to call the cops on me the way that you were carrying on." he said as she just smiled. "All I could hear in my heart was to stand still and watch the goodness of God. And I am glad that I listened to my heart because I got you out of all of that confusion. Just look at how far we have come since those days of uncertainty and dirt roads. I thank the blessed blood of Jesus that our first date was to church because if you wasn't a God fearing man or had a desire to be one, then we never could have been. We lived in such a chaotic time for our people and I had to have a man that was going to cover me not only in bed but as my protector naturally as well as spiritually. My virtue had been taken long before I met you but you didn't care. You said, 'The past is just that, the past. We are the present and we together are the future. You can always talk to me because I want to always talk to you about everything.' Some times I reach out for those words and hear your voice and what ever I am going through, it feels better to know that we are still one after all of these years. You are still my best friend." They were so caught up in the way back machine that they barely heard the bus arrival announcement or the bus pulling in. They were in their happy place and all was well.

As Jr departed the bus he saw his parents in an emotional embrace and it did his heart proud. He stood there and watched until he felt the pull to go over to them. Just as he began to walk to them she looked him in his eyes and left her husband to receive their son. The words were there but they wouldn't come out. Clean took his son into his arms with an embrace only a father could give to his namesake. "Where's your bags and stuff, son?" "I left everything behind me for a reason. I did my time and all those letters and pictures would just remind me of the failures in my life. Today is a brand new chapter in my life and I can thank you two for that. Before we get in the car can we do something? Can we pray, because I need that from my folks. I left every thing behind including my empty promises to you. Please pray for me and with me. Not just today but as much as possible."

They took each others hands and formed a mini prayer circle. As Clean opened in prayer a few more people joined in their prayer circle. By the time the prayer was over, there was about a dozen people in the circle and that included the bus driver!

When the circle broke, Bus Driver approached them,"Is this your son? If so he is one fine fellow. During our travel he kept the atmosphere loose and lively. At one point he even lead a little bible study and before long we were almost having church right there on my bus. I've seen a lot of peculiar things, but this was by far the most peculiar of them all. On one of our stops, he shared some of his testimony with me and it all revolved around you two, his parents. He is blessed to have you in his life and I told him that. Well, it was nice meeting you and you all be blessed." Looking back at this fine family, he got on his bus and pulled away looking forward to getting back to his own wife and children.

The ride home was full of chatter, highlighted with a stop to grab some groceries for the nights dinner. He snacked on a few chips because he was saving his appetite for his folks home cooking. When they got in the kitchen together, those two could really burn. Sometimes, it turned into an event without even trying. People would smell that food wafting through the air and would just stop by and they never turned anyone away, never. Then there were the times when the event was planned and the kitchen would be overrun with people making this dish and that dish. It was hectic but it was worth it in the end.

Normally when someone came home, especially from jail or the service, there would be a big celebration at the returnee's family home. The red carpet would be rolled out and the festivities could run into the next day. It was always a blast. Lots of food, fun and family. But this wasn't going to be one of those events. Jr. wanted no fanfare and nothing planned. He felt that he had let everyone down and he felt very undeserving. He often quoted the Apostle Paul counting everything that he had done as dung.

For a while, he was the man. He knew people and they knew him. From this region to the suburbs to the big city and everywhere in between he was known as 'the man'. He clawed his way up to the top and not only got there but he stayed there longer than many of his counterparts did. The only one to stay on top longer was 'thee man'. He was the major player of all the players in the game. If anyone was untouchable it surely was 'thee man'. He operated right in the open but he had so many layers that it would take a supernatural power to bring him down. He taught all that sat at his table that knowledge was the key to survival. Jr. did his time and did it well. After his parents backed away with their lawyers he didn't even try to fight it. He knew better than to rely on anyone other than himself. He took the fall because it was his to take.

Sitting in the kitchen, he watched his folks get down with the get down. He felt like a little boy all over again. He remembered all the family and cousins being around cramped in the old tiny kitchen. He remembered when his father took out a loan to upgrade the house and to expand the kitchen and how his mother was so excited about the coming changes. He really wanted to move but she stood her ground and said, "This is our house and I ain't willing to walk away from it just yet. At least wait for the kids to get out on their own, then we can talk about going somewhere else." After all these years, they were still here and they wouldn't have it any other way.

With the food cooking and the great anticipation of a home cook meal the three sat at the table and just talked. Over the past fourteen years their conversations were very limited to holidays and birthdays unless there was a death or something. This is the way that he wanted it because the more that he talked to them, the more homesick he became. He wasn't going to allow them to do 'his time' with him. When he explained this to them they understood that fourteen years was a long time for anyone to be away. They went back in time and talked about all of the love ones that had gone on ahead of them. Clean got out a big plastic container that held volumes of obituaries and passed them to his son. He wanted to go over every single one of them but when he came to one in particular he began to tremble. Without having to even look at who was on it, they already knew.

Before anyone could say anything the phone rang. Jr was closest so he answered the phone. It was Fixx and he was surprised to hear Jr's voice. Jr talked for a moment then passed his dad the phone. He and his mom left the kitchen and went to sit on the porch. "Its good to have you home, son." "It's good to be home. And thanks for keeping it quiet." Soon they were joined by Clean and they talked about the obituary and his fallen friend. As much as he had put the past behind him, the reality of his past life was more evident than ever, right now. "The Fixx family are coming over in a little bit. They really want to see you, my son." When he was locked up, he received cards and letters from family and friends. But the Fixx sent money for his books. Never sent a card or letter, just money and that was the way that it was, all the while he was on the inside. His folks went back inside to finish cooking and left their son to himself.

Within minutes, the Fixx family were there. He opened the door and embraced them. He was happy to see them and they stood there just looking at each other."Thank you both for the love that you have shown me while I was down. If there is any thing that I can do to repay you, just let me know." "Staying out of prison is all that we ask of you. We did what we did for a reason. We love you just like you are our own. Your folks would've done the same for us if the shoe was on the other foot." They went inside to the kitchen. "Oh yeah, the Cooks are coming in a bit. They were shocked to know that Jr was home and you two didn't say anything to anybody." Jr threw his hands up in the air in the 'I give up' gesture. At that point, he knew that he was home. At least for now, he was going to enjoy being around family and friends.

Soon their house was jam packed. The music was flowing and so was the food. So many well wishers showed up to show Jr love. The mood was lighthearted and festive. And then the bottles started flowing. He hadn't had a drink or smoke in years. As a matter of fact, he had lost the desire for getting 'bombed' before he even went back inside of the walls of prison. When he was offered a drink he just turned it down and kept it moving. No one tried to force any thing his way, but that didn't stop them from indulging. Many thought that he was probably on probation and had to take random drug drops. Once the word was out that he wasn't sipping, everything was everything. It was all good.

He was sitting on the hood of one of the homie's cars when a dark shadow appeared in the distant. As if it was old times, the homies surrounded 'the man'. Before the figure came into full focus he waved them off. He didn't have any problem with anyone and he had long turned over the keys to his turf. The figure was soon noticed as Professor. His longest tenured pal. They had been buds since grammar school. One went one way and the other went the other way, but they were always down with each other. The two brothers hugged each other and gave up the pound, a hood handshake that was almost as old as they were. Only a few O G's was privy to this shake and it wasn't taken lightly.

As the festivities progressed deeper into the night he made his rounds through the mass of humanity that was gathered to show him love. But when he got back with Professor he put his arm around his neck and the brothers walked away from everybody. Jr said, "Man, when we were kids I thought that you were a little soft. While we were out pulling capers, you stayed close to the titty. But now look at you, a big university professor, getting your teach on and stuff. Before you say anything, I want you to know just how proud I am of you and your successes." "First, I was never soft. Second, I learned from all of you other guys mistakes and at an early age I decided that jail or the service wasn't for me. Hell, I like to eat to much. I like to eat what I want and when I want. And I knew that wasn't happening in the justice. It wasn't that I was so good and perfect, it was just, when my old man walked out on us, I was left to grow up real fast. I had to go to school or else get kicked out of the house. After I got out of the game, I found Jesus. One day I fell on my knees and begged him to help me. Man, I was going crazy trying to fill the old mans abandoned shoes. Everyday that I went out to grind, I was scared crapless. Besides, no one knows my story better than you, my brother. Its good to have you back. I missed you more than you would ever know. Have you seen your kids yet?" Professor asked. Jr shook his head no and sighed. "Sorry man." The brothers walked back to the gathering in silence.

CHAPTER 27
Clothes That Don't Fit

It was finally Sunday and he was excited to be going to the house of worship. Being locked down for so many years he lost a lot of memories about certain things. The church was one of them because he walked away from God and the church well before he was locked away. He had never made any promises to God and he wouldn't start now. He had set in his mind that he was going to take his life one day at a time. It wasn't just living life in the fast lane but it was with every day that he knew that this could be the last day of his life.

He stood looking at his clothes that he had recently purchased and for the first time in years he had to make a decision about what to wear. The first few days out was relaxed wear, but today, he was going to church and he wanted to be as sharp as he could be. He had done his time and he was free to do or go where ever he choose to. All of a sudden he had a flash back to a time when he was married.

He and his ex-wife were watching a movie, she asked if he wanted a sandwich and he said yes. She went into the kitchen and wanted to know what kind of meat he wanted on his sandwich. He didn't care, he just wanted a sandwich. She began to yell and scream at him, she was having a mental meltdown. He rushed into the kitchen and tried to see what the problem was. She was sitting on the floor crying. "All I wanted was a sandwich, it didn't matter what kind of meat you put on it because I only buy the meat that I like." It was at that point that he noticed that something was wrong with her. Maybe it was there all the time and he just ignored it. Shaking the past out of his head, he finally made an 'executive decision' on what to wear.

After getting dressed, he went into the kitchen where his folks were having breakfast. His mom looked at her son and smiled with pride. "Looking good, son. Want something to eat before we head out?" He kissed her on the forehead and said, "No ma, I'm good." He was fasting for the day, because he wanted to hear from the Lord. Fasting was something that he had learned earlier in life and never forgot about it. Although, he hadn't practiced it much, or at all over the past two decades, he still knew its wonder working power. "I'll be outside." As he sat on the porch, he watched the people gearing up to go to church. The sky was a perfect gray and he was highly anticipating the service for one reason or another.

He pulled out his phone and just played with it to kill time. Although, he had had it for a very short period of time, he had amassed a nice amount of contacts. So far so good. Standing in the store waiting for an associate to help him, he remembered being the first one to have a bag phone and a car phone. He started to remember more things that he had suppressed over the years and it was okay with him. He didn't have to define or defend what his life had been up to this point and he felt great about that.

As he was deep in thought, O'landa Draper's, Got a feeling, banged out of the house across from him. "Yeah, yeah, yeah, yeah, gonna be gonna be alright every things gonna be alright. Jesus told me every things gonna alright," he sang as he banged his head to the crisp music. Clean tapped his son on the shoulder and motioned towards the car. The family got in and he just continued to beat that song into his memory.

Oblivious to all that was happening around him, he sunk deeper into thought. This was going to be his first time in the new, or what he would call the new church. It was like when he would take his family on family trips. It was the same excitement for him. Before he realized it, they were there pulling into the parking lot. He looked in awe at the great structure. He had seen pictures of it but the pictures didn't do this grand cathedral any justice. This ministry had come a very long way from its humble beginnings. He was glad that no one really had shared with him the inner workings of the service. He was ready for whatever God had for him. His mother and father flanked him on both sides. He reached out for their hands and they walked hand and hand inside.

As he walked inside he had to hold back the tears. Under his breath, he began to bless the Lord his God for keeping him all of the years that he had turned his back on Him. They found a set of seats and sat down. His mom held his hand tight as if to hold him from flying away. Clean excused himself. When he returned, the service had begun. He was so happy to see his son relaxed and not looking over his shoulder with worry. He had wrestled with his decision not to help his son the last time for a long time. But the results seemed to be worth it.

The atmosphere was so high that whatever burden was on someone it could be broken. Once the choir finished, Pastor approached the podium. "We honor the spirit of Christ and we greet one and all with the words 'Peace be multiplied'. Before I go any further, I want to recognize one of my friends that I have called a brother for a very long time. Jr would you please stand and come down?" Looking like a deer caught in headlights, Jr stood up and was lead by an usher to the pulpit. "Family, this brother has a powerful testimony and I hope that he will bless us with some of it. Is that alright?"

The congregation applauded and Pastor beckoned him to ascend into the pulpit. Jr motioned that he'd like to do it on the floor in front of the people and not in the pulpit. He was handed a mic and he began, "My name is Jr and I come to you through the penal system of our great state. Before I turned away from Christ, I was one of Pastor's closest friends. As he said we were like brothers. Yet, we took very different paths. I chose the game and he chose to be a game changer. I used to be over the youth ministry and the outreach program and then one day I was discontented with God and the way that He was doing things. It wasn't death or anything that was being held from me, I just lost my love and it seemed like it was overnight. I had a very good life and upbringing but something was missing. I tried everything that I could think of, but I just wasn't feeling it."

"After I left the ministry and got into the game full time, my life went into overdrive. Within a year I had more stuff than I could have ever dreamed of having. I had it all and for a while I was the 'the man'. People knew me every where that I went. At first it was cool being recognized, but soon I didn't recognize myself. I started carrying a gun or two and I was leery of everyone especially the ones that were closest to me. Then one day I got caught up in some emotional stuff and I beat a person into a coma. No one dared to rat on me, but in a few days the cops pulled me over and I was arrested."

"I beat the rap and I was back at it. The second time I was looking at doing some serious time but once again I beat the rap. Now at this point, I feel like I *am* invincible, so I do my thing with little regard to circumstances. So this last time I got pinched, I didn't beat the rap. My folks who had put up great sums of money and assets to keep me with the best lawyers that money could buy backed out on me. I had lost so much money tricking off and gambling that I didn't prepare for a rainy day, so to speak. Here's the catch, the judge threw the max at me and I couldn't do nothing but catch the time."

"When I went inside, I was looking at fourteen years of real time. I wasn't one of them cats who got locked up to know who God was. I knew Him before I was locked down. I just didn't give him the time that I should have before I went down and I wasn't going to go running to Him and start begging Him to get me out of a jam. People on the inside would ask me, 'What happened to you, that you got pinched?' All I could tell them was, 'I'm what happened to me. I'm to blame. Nobody but me.'

"There was this one incident where another inmate approached me and said, 'Me and you go tangle.' Not one to back down, I shared with him, 'Its gotta be to the death because if you don't kill me then I am going to have to kill you. That's the law.' That cat never approached me again. My rep was one thing, but the favor of God is another thing. When I got about ten years into my sentence, somehow I came up for parole. I denied myself the possibility of getting out early. I sent word that I wanted to do all of my time so I wouldn't have to answer to anybody once I got out. I wanted to be a free man, nothing less would do. I didn't want to have to report or check in to someone else, I had already done that while I was still locked up."

Today I came here to see my big brother and witness what God has done for him. I remember him when we were youths and we were going to some other old church and how at an early age he got the knack for this Jesus thing. The day that I walked out of prison and I turned in all of my state issued clothes I told the guard, 'These clothes never did fit me because they were intended for someone else.'

When he said that the church exploded into praise. People began to run the aisles and just praise God. Soon the musicians had hit their mark and a shout and dance went forth like it hadn't done in months. As Jr handed Pastor the mic, the two men clutched one another and began to cry. This went on for several minute. As they broke their embrace they too broke out into a Davidic dance. Soon the service began to come back to restorative order, yet, the spirit was high. His parents stood in the aisle crying and waiting for their son. As he approached them, there was a glow around him that had never been seen before. Several people reached out to touch him and as they touched him they began to either speak in tongues or fall out in the spirit of the Holy Spirit. "Mama, Daddy, God is real."

Back at home after service was over Baby Girl was ready to free herself of some things also. All she could talk about was Jr's awesome testimony. The words regarding clothes that didn't fit resonated in her spirit so strong that when she stood in front of her closet she couldn't wait to get rid of all the clothes that she had used in her former line of work. Sure, they were pretty and expensive but they had to go! She and Neighbor agreed that they would leave that lifestyle behind them and this was their second step in being delivered from the horror of prostituting themselves.

Ever since they had rejoined the ministry, they still were tempted. But somehow they wouldn't fall back into the pit. They kept each other lifted up in prayer.

They had agreed that when temptation set in, they would tell the other and it had worked so far. They knew that no one had the others back like each one did in this case. They had been too involved in the others life to allow any slip ups, because if one fell the other would surely soon follow.

"Once we get my clothes out, then we have to do the same with your stuff. Agreed?" she asked her best friend. "All for one and us for all!" agreed Neighbor as she sat on the bed watching her friend make critical decisions regarding her wardrobe. Soon the floor was full of exotic and provocative clothes and lingerie. Once she was finished in the closet she went to her dresser and began the same process of purging her clothes. Thousands of dollars were spent and made many times over with these clothes.

"You know what? It was hard being know as the 'ho sister of the pastor. But I learned to use that for my good. If someone came at me that knew me, I taxed that ass because I knew they were going to brag about 'banging the pastor's baby sister'. Now, I don't give a damn what they say or think about me. Because no matter how messed up I was, my brother proved to me that he loved me regardless. He would say, 'One day you will be in your rightful place and it will be only by the hand of God that you will be released from this hell you are in.' He'd kiss me on the forehead and leave. That's my big brother from the same mother." They high-fived and began to put the clothes in trash bags and it was off to Neighbor's place.

"We been dressing like 'hos for so long, we gonna to have to get some classy broad to help us with our wardrobe. I've been dressing to please who ever had the dollars and wanted to make sure that I was tight when they got with me that I forgot how to dress conservatively. Cleavage, nipples and booty been showing since grade school. I wonder how did Rahab dress when them fine Israelite spies came through there. Just think, it was a 'ho that helped them get away. You think they got a little something before they kicked bricks? All the good that we do and we still don't get the credit we deserve. Well, its time to purge. You blessed, your brother protected you as best as he could. Mine was like my first pimp. He didn't put me on the streets but he did put me up on game. In order to get in his sisters panties they had to pay up front. I used his place and when I was done, I'd leave him a cut. We both had habits and I felt safe at his place. Before he died, we were still angry with each other and he said, 'You a 'ho now and you go die a 'ho.' My mother slapped him and he slapped her back then he came at me. I grabbed a knife and you know the rest is history." Silence fell over the two women like never before. Although they had shared so much with each other, there were still secrets hidden deep inside their souls.

When she finished, she had just as much stuff to throw away. Before she placed the clothes in the bag she took her friend by the hand. "If we are going to go all the way with this Jesus thing we got to really free ourselves of every thing. When Jr talked about the clothes not fitting I began to think about our relationship. Neither one of us really could wear the clothes of that lifestyle again so I will keep my hands off of you and you have to keep your hands off of me. Agreed?" "Word." Baby Girl replied. They fist pumped with an explosion and began to laugh as they placed the garments in garbage bags.

Standing by the dumpster, the women prepared to toss the bags into the bin. "Should we really throw all of these good things in the trash when there are homeless women that can surely use them?" "Let's kill two birds with one stone. Since we need someone classy to help us clean up or rather soften our image, I'll call Top Notch. She knows where all of these clothes can go plus she can help us as well." "Top Notch is cool. She one of us, except her clientele is the upper crust. Girl, I thought at first you was going to suggest your sister the first lady. I can breathe easy now, because she would have been trying to get us to wear those gaudy hats. It's what first ladies do ain't it?" "You silly. My sister-in-law, rocks hard whatever she wears. She steps in the place and shuts it down! Besides that, my brother don't play that. Lets call my girl Top Notch."

When her phone rang she was surprised that it was Baby Girl. They had seen each other around but they had not done any hanging out. "What's up girl?" "Me and my girl are trashing some of our things and we need you to help us. You busy?" "Watching The Wire, you know Stringer Bell and that fine Avon." "Speaking of that, did you hear that awesome testimony Jr gave? Well that got us thinking about some things. We came home and started purging this part of our lives and that's where you come in. Come over and we'll talk." "Be there in a few." As they waited for Top Notch, they sat on the chairs in the backyard. Their lives had come a long way in such a short time.

Top Notch finally pulled up and joined the ladies in the backyard. "Want a beer or wine cooler?" Neighbor asked. "A cooler is fine." Neighbor went inside to grab them some drinks. When she returned and passed the drinks out she sat back down. The two women began to go a little more in depth about what had been going on within themselves and the transition that they were going through. They felt that if anybody could understand their plight, Top Notch was the one. "I am honored that you guys thought enough of me to help you with your transition. I would be glad to help a couple of sisters out. It seems like y'all serious. Many people are going to blessed by what y'all doing." The ladies began to high-five each other and toast to better days.

"In case y'all didn't know, there is going to be a big job fair next week. Resumes are going to be needed. I got the hook up, so all you have to do is show up and I'll handle it from there. Back to those clothes, I'll have someone pick them up and take them to get laundered. Once that's done, we'll go shopping. I'll call my favorite shop and we'll do it right. I'm doing this because I believe in y'all. Besides, I never forget where I came from." she said. Looking down, tears slowly streamed down her face. The ladies got up and comforted their sister. "Remember when we used to joke about unionizing? We could have been like Hoffa. Get me another cooler, please." They sat out for a while and talked until it was late.

On his way to pick up Nurse, Brother was happy to be able to spend some time with his girl. They had been looking forward to this midnight cruise for a long time. It was her families big event. When he got to her place, he went to the door instead of calling on the phone. She opened the door and he went inside. "I'll be ready in a few, fix yourself a drink. There's some other stuff you might like in the 'fridge." He opened the refrigerator and grabbed a couple of beers out. He went into her room and sat on her bed. Handing her a beer, he gave her the once over and whistled at her fineness. They clicked the bottle necks together and took a drink. He walked out of her room and went to sit on the couch. Sitting back enjoying his beer, he began to think about their relationship. He still hadn't given her the engagement ring back yet. He had pretty much given up on marrying her, but they were still good friends.

When she came out he stood up. She looked at him with a strange look as he took his bottle to the trash. By the time he had gotten to the kitchen he had pulled his pants up twice. "You got on a belt?" she asked. "Yeah, why you ask?" "Because it seems like your pants are too long and whats up with that jacket. Come here." He came over to her. "Look, before you start. I couldn't get to the cleaners before they closed so I borrowed a suit from one of my guys." "You have to be kidding me, man." "Whats the big deal. You wanted me in brown and I am in brown, okay." She huffed and walked out of the door. He locked up and followed her out. She may have been pissed, but she still waited for him to open her door for her.

On the way to pick up her folks to save time he jumped on the freeway. They argued vehemently. "It's like I can't please you in what ever I try to do. You don't even respect the fact that I try and I try hard to please you. But you hold on hope to be with someone that stepped out on you years and tears ago. That's cool, ya dig, because this night is our last night. So you can still sit by the phone waiting for your baby daddy to decide that he's ready to come back. I'm a fool no more for you. Chicks like you, I just don't get. Why is it that you tell this great big lie that you wished or prayed for someone that's good and kind but when you get someone like that you piss all over him. But a cat that goes upside your head or cheats on you behind your back and in your face, lay up on your couch while you go to work, drive his other body buddies around in your car and eat up your food, you give him your all. This is the last ride for us. You can kiss my.... forget it, you ain't worth the pressure of my blood to rise." "Well, if you feel like that you can just let me out." she shrieked. Crossing over three lanes to get to the interior shoulder of the highway he hit his hazards and pulled onto the shoulder. With a look of absolute horror she asked him, "How am I suppose to get out?" "I guess with caution. What difference does it make to me if you get hit or the door gets knocked off, hell, its your car anyway. Either way, I'm still going because I paid for the tickets."

She backed down and released her seat belt. She took his hand and placed it on her thigh, high up. He pulled his hand away, "Not tonight, love. This can't be fixed with that or anything else. The way that you have treated me over the last year, if we are to ever get back together, you have to date me all over again. Other than that, I'm done." She said nothing as he pulled off of the shoulder. For the first time in months he wasn't thinking about what else he could possibly do to better their relationship. At this point, he cared less. No more dog and pony shows!

They rode in total silence. He turned the radio on and put a disk in. He turned to her slightly and looked at her. He wanted to slap the eyelashes off of her face. She had become a monster to him. All he wanted to do was love her and she to love him back in kind. He turned the volume up high and began to sing aloud. He didn't care if she was annoyed or whatever she was feeling. She had constantly trashed his feelings over and over again. He tried to rationalize his stupidity for her before, but now the writing was clearly on the wall.

"I'll try to do better. I promise," she muttered. With the music blaring, he could not hear her. She reached to lower the volume and repeated what she had said. He ignored her, but he did hear what she had said. Finally, they arrived at her folks place. Before the car came to a complete stop, she jumped out and ran inside. He slowly walked from the car and was met by her sister. "Got a smoke, brother-in-law?" He reached in his pocket and pulled out a couple of cigarettes. They made small talk and puffed away. When they were finished they went inside. Most of the family was there and they were waiting for a few others.

They complimented him on how sharp he looked and he laughed turning his back to her. "Want a drink, son?" her poppa asked. "Yes sir, thanks." Nurse got up and fixed him a drink and brought it to where he was sitting on the couch. As she handed him his drink she winked at him."Thanks." That was all that he could muster. "Are we that fractured that you won't talk or look at me?" He took his drink and went into the kitchen and took a seat at the table. "Oh wow, is lil' miss goody goody having man problems again? You should let me have him. I know what to do with that. Although he ain't much to look at, when that mf' fart, his fart smell like money. Come on, let me have him." teased her sister, Thickness. Nurse walked away from her before something ugly transpired. She stood in the vestibule not knowing what to do.

As she stood there thinking, the limo-bus pulled up. The family decided that since they would be drinking heavily to get a limo-bus. This was a new practice for them since a near fatal accident a few years earlier. Their father was a family man through and through so losing a family member would be devastating to him. Poppa and Mama spent years forming the perfect family with minimal counterproductive activity. Although all of their children were grown, they still treated them as if they were still children. Nurse felt so overprotected by them that she excelled in high school so she could graduate early just to get out of the house. The family began to board the limo and soon they were on their way to The Marina.

"Lets get through this night as best as we can. I know that we have been through a lot, can we try to enjoy the moment?" she asked him. Without looking at her, he nodded in agreement. One thing he did enjoy about her family was that they were a lot of fun. He got along well with all of them, and it was a lot of them. When ever they had family functions he was always welcome to come. He thought about the bonds that he had formed with her poppa, sister and son especially. While some of the family was stuffy, these two were somewhat like him. The trip to The Marina was loud and festive except for one couple.

They were to celebrate her parent's forty-fifth wedding anniversary. It felt like anything but exciting. Thickness came over to them and made small talk. Although she had a contemptuous relationship with her sister, she still liked Brother and she didn't want to have this night ruined by anyone, especially

138

by the golden girl, Nurse. "Man, we gonna get it in tonight, huh?" she asked. "Yes indeed, sister-in-law. It should be a blast. I know you have a lot of tricks up your sleeve." "And you know this, my stellar dude." She got up and danced in the aisle. This got the gang amped up and rowdy. Their family parties were the stuff of legend. One could only anticipate what was going to happen or who was going to show up.

At last, they reached the marina. It was their custom to be fashionable late and they didn't disappoint. Another special event happening tonight was that two more members of the clan was turning the legal age for drinking. It was a birthright of passage to be able to attend the 'grownup shows' upon turning legal. Entering into the massive cruise ship where the party was being held, they could hear the merriment as they got closer.

When they got to the door, the door man stepped inside and the photographer began to take their pictures. Next, both doors were slowly opened to the sound of Pomp and Circumstance. They were lead inside by exotic dancers and snake charmers. Her parents were shocked and amazed at the detail that their children went through and this was just the start. As they took their seats, DJ welcomed the grand hosts and the music was turned up to a deafening level. Once everyone was on board the ship pulled out of the marina.

So many family and friends were there and the tables were full, because everyone that was invited showed up. They had a seating chart for their guest, because some people just didn't need to sit near or around certain others. Yes, fights had broken out before while their party was still going on. Since they instituted assigned seating, there was very limited provocations. Free liquor and pent up hostilities are a very bad mix, especially for these people when they let their hair hang down. Nurse sat next to Brother and he was wishing that they had been separated like some others had the fortune to be. The only good thing was that her father was sitting next to him, at least he'd have someone to really talk to.

Sensing that he was still riled at her, she began to mingle with some of the other guests. He was relieved to see her go. At this stage in their relationship, she knew when to leave him alone. What he needed was a stiff drink. He walked to the bar and ordered three double whiskeys and three beer backs. Arriving at the table, he passed drinks to her poppa and sister. These were his drinking buddies as of late, and they always had a good time together. "Now, as a rule you know that I only have one libation before eating. But I'll attempt to hold myself to minimal conviction this evening." Poppa laughed. Soon he was back to the bar right before the meal came. They toasted to the merriment and much more.

The food was being served when the lights dimmed and a spotlight shun on the hosts table. Out from the shadows appeared Asst. Pastor. He was there to bless the food assumed Brother. What struck Brother odd though, was the fact that this family wasn't christian believers at all. Their vices were their gods, all of them! He sat back in astonishment, soaking this scene in.

"We are here tonight to celebrate the love of two wonderful people. We are also here to eat, drink and party hearty. On behalf of everyone here, we all thank you two for seeing fit too invite us tonight to be here with you on such a joyous occasion. Now lets get down!" exploded Asst. Pastor. The place went nuts and the music went back up as the food started to be consumed. There was salad, vegetables, three different steaks and rolls. For dessert there was ice cream in many flavors, strawberry cheesecake, chocolate chip cookies and chocolate anniversary cake. The champagne float and punch float were the drinks.

Within a hour or so, the dining was done and it was time to do a little dancing and drinking. DJ slowed it down and invited the honoring couple, Poppa and Mama, to the dance floor for a solo dance. He played their favorite song and the cameras went crazy. They looked like royalty dancing together. For a brief moment, Brother thought about his soon to be ex-girlfriend. Then as quickly as the thought came it left. He went back to the bar and reloaded. Instead of going back to the table, he set up shop by the bar. Right now all he wanted to do was to get hammered. Whenever he someone tried to engage him in conversation, he'd slide off to the side.

Soon he was at a level of intoxication that he was satisfied with. He sought out Thickness and when he found her, he lead her to the dance floor. They danced for a couple of songs and as they walked off of the floor he spoke to her, "Thanks sister-in-law." "That's whats up, I like that." she gushed. "Lets go smoke." They went outside to the deck of the ship and as the sat down she said, "My sister looks nice in that dress doesn't she? When she saw me in it last month, she begged me to let her wear it for this event. She claimed that she went looking for it at the store but couldn't find one. That's why its so tight on her. She has picked up a few pounds ever since you two started dating." Feeling a sense of vindication, he lit his cigarette and inhaled deeply.

140

CHAPTER 28
Boss Lady

After several months of recovery, First Lady was finally on her way back to work. She had attended a few church services and meetings just to get her feet wet. She was excited to sit behind her desk and to be able to interact with her staff and friends. She knew that it would take a little while to get back into the swing of things, but it was a start. She was only going to do a few hours a day for the first week or so and by then she should be totally cleared by her doctors to go full throttle.

"Okay, boss lady, are you ready?" asked Top Notch. "We have a meeting and a training session then lunch with your husband. That's whats going on today for your first day back. The training session is for the new ordering system. If you remember, you had already approved the new software to be installed." First Lady nodded in agreement as they walked out to her car. "I'm driving you this week and your husband is going to bring you home. As a matter of fact, you will be through with your day at 11 am all this week. Before you put up a fight, that's doctors orders."

The ride to her business was exceptionally beautiful. She had really appreciated God for all that he had done for her throughout her illness. She began to worship Him aloud. With tears streaming down her face, she blessed Him for the blood of Jesus her Christ that had washed her clean and had healed her. "Father, I bless you for the change. Thank you Lord for everything. Not just for this healing, but for all that you have done for me and mine. Where ever my child is, please keep him covered in the blood." She cried out louder and louder unto her heavenly father until she felt a release in her spirit. Top Notch handed her a tissue and continued to drive toward work. She knew that her godmother needed that breakthrough and she was blessed to be there to witness it with her.

Arriving at the building, she proudly looked at the logo and name, CORNERSTONE of GRACE, Inc., towering on the roof and over the doorway's entrance as Top Notch pulled into First Lady's parking spot. Looking at the three story building for the first time in months she was ready. As they entered, Security came from behind his desk and hugged his boss. "It's good to have you back, Boss Lady." He walked them to the elevator and pressed the button. "I think we are going to take the stairs today." He opened the door to the stairwell and went back to his desk. He picked up his walkie talkie and spoke. Climbing the stairs had always been one of her pleasures while she was at work. it was therapeutic and it helped to keep her legs in shape. She rarely used the elevators.

As they entered the floor where her office was located, she noticed how quite the place was. She had noticed the cars outside and it was close to starting time. Maybe they were out on the veranda having a last minute talk or whatever. Either way, she was just happy to be back. Stepping into the office, they were bombarded with revelry. Then as if everyone collectively remembered that it was her eardrum that had ruptured, they covered their mouths as if to take back what had just happened. "Thank you all so much. Well, when I talk to my doctor, I can let him know I survived a sonic boom." They began to laugh and surround her. She hugged and thanked each and everyone.

Finally ready to go to her office, she noticed that her door was decorated. Again, she began to cry as she unlocked her door. Behind her desk was a brand new master executive's chair. It had all of the bells and whistles and only two people on this earth even knew that she had lusted for that particular chair. Setting her purse down, she took her seat. It was adjusted perfectly and she knew that Top Notch was behind this one because they were similarly built.

Technical Support came in and hooked her computer up. It was policy, for staff that was going to be out for a period of time to have their computer placed in a secure location. As he left she thanked and hugged her."Good to see you back on the throne, Boss Lady. We had been praying hard for you to get well and get back as soon as possible." She closed her door as TS left. Clasping her hands together, she began to pray and thank God for a wonderful bunch of people to work with.

After a few minutes she emerged from her office. She knew it was close to the meeting time and started walking to the boardroom. "The meeting is going to be held in the conference area." reminded Top Notch. She joined her boss as they and others made there way to the conference area. Inside, most employees were present and seated. She took her seat and the meeting began. Vice President began, "Good morning all. As everyone knows by now, our founder and CEO is back in her rightful place. It has been a pleasure to serve in her stead. But it is also good to have her back. Lets welcome her back with an applause."

Standing to her feet, she waved to them to stop. "I want to thank you all for being so supportive in my absence. Over the last two weeks I have been closely monitoring each division and as I shared with VP that I am well pleased with productivity around here. In the next year or so I may be stepping down. I have been looking into several options for the company. Before anyone goes into panic mode, this is solely based on my physical capabilities. No one will be blindsided or cut loose. You all know how I get down. If you leave here its because you have found something better or you have done something unacceptable or you just don't want to be here. We have people who started out with me from the beginning and look at them now. VP was one of them. He started off in security then started applying for jobs and moved up along the way. We hire and promote from our own. Speaking of which, we have two new hires. They were hired on while I was away. And for all of you who don't know already, one of them is my sister-in-law and the other is a very good friend of the family. Ladies please stand, and lets show them some love as we do with all new hires."

When that was finished, she continued,"This will probably be one of our shortest all hands meeting because a few of us have training to do. Once again, thank you all and keep up the good work. Oh yeah, each department gets an upcoming half day off. Before the end of business today, the days and what department will be posted. If that's all lets get back at it."

Soon everyone was gone except VP. "That's why we work hard for you, girl. How you feeling on your first day back?" "I'm good. Its that training that I ain't quite looking forward too. Whats going on with the son, heard any thing yet?" "Nope, still just hanging in the wind. VP, I owe you big time for handling business while I was down. Come on, I got training and I hate it." "Leading by example is what that's called."

He walked with her to the computer training room, once there he left. Waiting for Tech Support to get there, she talked with the two new hires. She listened to them talk about some of the interesting features around the office. One in particular, the scream room was at the top of their list. It was an old telephone booth placed on the the third floor where one could go and let out their frustrations. The sign on the door read, 'Instead of going postal, go screaming. Its better for all of us!' The other was the room that was converted into a golf ball hitting area. It was put in place for stress relief not to improve ones game. She got the idea from her husband, one day he told her why he played golf. He said, "I don't care about my score or handicap. I just like to hit that little white ball as hard as I can. When I get frustrated I take it out on the balls. Whatever is bothering me I call it as I'm swinging." She shared with them as an inside joke. But in reality, she found that it really works. As a matter of fact, both have been priceless additions to the company. Finally, Tech Support arrived and the training session began.

When it was over, she realized that it wasn't as bad as she thought that it would be. She was also relieved that it was close to her getting off. Since it was her first day back at work, she didn't even get a chance to really hang out in her office and enjoy her well wishes. She would spend more time in her sanctuary tomorrow, but for now the day was over. She turned her lights off and locked her door. She waved goodbye and blew kisses as she left.

Her husband was parked by the door as she came out. He got out and opened her door with a kiss. "How was your first day back, love?" "Better than expected. They really went out of their way to make it as comfortable as possible. The meeting was fun and the computer training wasn't so bad. Now don't get me wrong, I ain't rushing to sign up for all new things, but I also do it to show the others that upper management is as committed as we ask them to be. I also shared with them about the future of the business. Enough about that, how is that greedy Greg doing?" "Well, he chewed up another shoe and I whacked him with a newspaper." "Don't say that to loud because the animal lawyers will be beating on our door with their petitions for removal, ha." They laughed and drove away. The rest of the week was very uneventful.

The following week was anything but that. It all started with an email that was sent out accidentally. It was intended for one recipient but was sent to a couple of other employees by mistake. The email was bad mouthing VP and how he was like the 'chosen one' by the queen and that he couldn't do any wrong in the queen's eyes and that he must be more than just a trusted foot soldier. One of them forwarded it to Top Notch who sent it to VP who in turn forwarded it to Boss Lady.

When she opened it she had to read it twice. After reading it, she sent out a mass email for an emergency all hands meeting at noon. That was lunch time for the whole building, but she didn't care. It was time for this to be dealt with and also to take care of some unfinished business that had been brewing for some time now.

After everyone was assembled she went in for the kill. "I am under the impression that there is favoritism running rampant here. Well I am here to tell you that that is absolutely correct. I have never kept it a secret that I reward faithfulness, loyalty and achievement around here. Not only do I encourage my managers to do the same, I insist on it. Now, VP, is my right hand man and I don't make any bones about it. If you don't mind, I want to share some inside information with you all about his and my relationship."

"We started out together many years back at the same job. He was there a few years before me. I was his understudy. Instead of him limiting me, he challenged me to be the best that I could be. We worked well together for years. Then I was promoted and he was one of my biggest supporters. Although I was in a different department, we still remained close. After a couple of years, I was given the opportunity to hand pick a group for a special project. He was one of my first picks. At first it was kind of awkward, then I had a meeting with him and the others to remind them that we work together as a group. I had arranged for us to have unlimited overtime with this project. The group that I had selected was supposed to be the best of the best. And for a while it was good. Then one day I fell ill and was off work for a few months and when I got back, my team was divided. I tried to get to the bottom of it, but kept running into a lot of bullshiggitty."

"One day I was in my office when VP came in to talk. He said, 'Look, right now, I don't know whats going on inside of that head of yours but those backstabbing s.o.b's are out to get you. That cocksucker who covered for you while you was out has been conspiring to get you gone so he can take your place. He been kissing all of the big bosses asses and taking notes on everything that you did. He even has one of the other bosses who was real cool with you in on this. That's why your team is trying to sink you.'

"While he was talking, two of the conspirators came to my door and asked me could they leave early. Even though company policy stated that they needed to give me at least three days notice, I agreed and let them off. VP went crazy. I let him know that because they are doing me dirty, I can't do them the same way. He was livid and left my office. He wouldn't speak to me for a couple of days."

"That Monday, we were having a meeting when someone form upper management and a quality control manager popped in our meeting. Everything was going good until the big boss asked was there anything that needed to be addressed. That's when one of the group looked him in the eye and asked for a transfer based on the fact that he didn't like my attitude. He went as far as to say, 'I don't do what she tells me to because I like her attitude. By the way, when it comes to our work, which way are we suppose to do it? The company's way, the bosses way or our own way?' And before either one of us could answer, the other one said, 'I have an issue with her as well. Even though she had been reminding me to get my certifications updated and that time was about to expire, I felt that what I was working on was more important.'

"Upper management tried to ease the situation so that he wouldn't have to deal with it. Before he left, he listened to what I had to say. 'The book says that what they just said in this meeting was insubordination and it should be dealt with immediately. We have a union steward in our midst. So whats the problem? You and QC just heard them admit to not doing what I have asked of them.' He stood there and tried to pacify me and when I looked at VP, he was furious. After the chance meeting was over, he and I went to my office. As we walked I could feel his tension. Before we walked into my office, we watched as management and the conspirators walk into the stairwell. In my office, I began to cry when VP said, 'The hell you crying for. I told your (bleep) that they were snakes and stool pigeons, but no, you couldn't do them wrong. Now look at you.' After we both calmed down, we mapped out a plan. And it worked."

"I shared all of this with you all because he and I are a team and we have been very good friends for a very long time. As I have always shared, if there is a problem with management, my door is always open. We will handle it together. This is not a q and a session, so with that being said, this meeting is over. Take lunch in fifteen minutes and we will see you all back in an hour."

Once again, it was just the two of them. "That's some top level gangster shiggitty right there, my friend. You told the truth and I appreciate that. Give a brother a pound." "We all we got. Ain't that what we been saying in times like this? I got your back 'cause I know you got mine. Well my day is done. Less than two weeks in, and I have yet to be able to retire to my office like I want to. Tomorrow is going to be a better day. I know it because I claim it in the name of Jesus that it will be." They hugged and that was that.

As she was leaving, Baby Girl and Neighbor was in the parking lot having a smoke. VP had joined them but was on his phone. She walked up to them. "I thought that we were going to lose our jobs today. Because when we saw that email, we was going to get that heifer for putting the mouth on you and VP. But you handled your business, Boss Lady, so we ain't gonna lay hands on her. Unless you say so." They looked at her as if waiting for a signal. "By the way, what was that plan that you and VP had and how did it play out?" "A few years later the business went up for sale. I bought it and fired all of their no good arses." She smiled and walked to her husbands car. In the car, she told him about her day and he told her about Greg.

CHAPTER 29
Schwinns, Cabbage Patch Dolls & Atari

It was time for the Festivals of Fathers fund raiser at the church. This was a time to celebrate the life and legacies of the great men that were in the midst. It celebrated their accomplishments inside and out of the home. Every year this event was a must see. People were able to hear about some of the men that helped to settle this part of the state. Pastor had long believed that when a man does a good thing it should be shared, because the men throughout their history had taken a beating down through the years. It wasn't limited to a select race just as long as the man had either strong ties to the ministry, region or was on his way up.

He had become tired of hearing about how the men were using and abusing those around them. So to help the men in this region regain their places at the head of the table, he came up with the idea to celebrate their success from the mouths of their offspring. He felt that no one could really tell a story about their father like a child could. The only real criteria needed was for the reflector to be at least adolescent age. He felt that just because someone was young, they shouldn't have that held against them.

The theme this year was '24/7/365'. This represented the time that the man influenced those that were around him. In some peoples eyes, their father couldn't do any wrong while others felt that he did the best that he could with what he had. But for Pastor, this would be a bittersweet occasion because he would be presenting his father, yet, his own offspring would not be there. Over the years he learned that whatever the situation was, he still had to press on.

As the people began to arrive, he and the staff greeted and took tickets. He believed in the smaller details as well as the big details. It was going to be a fun and exciting evening for all. He loved God and all of God's people. This year they were going to have around twenty reflectors. This was by far the greatest number for this event. With so many reflectors, this came with a new challenge. Some things would have to be modified or eliminated. This was usually met with opposition. But when he shared his concerns with the committee, they agreed with him. They felt that all that he had been going through, the last thing that he needed to deal with was a confrontation with them.

Now that the time for the service to start was upon them, he made his way to the pulpit. He opened in prayer and in turn called on the music ministry. He looked out at the people as they joined in with the musicians. He still believed in miracles and that maybe just maybe his son would walk through the doors. He didn't believe in fairy tales, he believed in God! And if his son never graced his presence again, he would never abandon God or his calling. When many gave up, he stayed. Of course, he had his doubts, but he remained faithful. No one could take that from him. Even when he and his predecessor would get into it, he knew his place. Only a select few knew all of the facts, but he swore that if he ever led a congregation it would always be about God and His people.

The reflectors were selected randomly by drawing numbers as they came to check in. This was designed so that no one could claim that the first or the last spot was given out favorably. The committee had that thrown in their face several times. When they presented this lottery system to Pastor he was shocked to hear that this had happened before. He gave them their blessing and it had been like that ever since. Soon it was time for the first reflector to represent. Not only was she going to be a reflector, she was also going to be the emcee. Pastor introduced her and the show was underway.

"I stand before you as a presenter and the emcee and I must say that I am overjoyed. Not knowing that I was in line for a double portion I will humbly ask Pastor if I could just do bits and pieces of my reflection throughout the night since I will be emceeing?" As he nodded in agreement, the audience clapped in approval. They knew that she was the real deal. She often ministered on behalf of the Leaders and when she became Chief of Staff, she took a lot of pressure off of the Leaders. She did a portion of her reflection about her dad and soon called on the next reflector.

Reflector #2 delivered a very rousing reflection about his dad. "In my closing, my dad shared with me something that I had to share with my kids. He once shared with me and my siblings,'I don't have all the answers, so I can't give you what I don't have.' I thought that was big of him, and dad, that blessed me to look up to you even more. I salute you as my hero, thank you. And he began to cry. His father made his way to his son and the two men embraced. The stage had been set.

Reflector #5 stated, "My dad is a mans man. He is the best of the best. There is no greater love for a son like the love of his father. He taught me how to love and to let go. When he lost out on love, he embraced his love even the more. He made us go to church and not just attend but to be attentive. He would say, 'If you can't sleep in court or school, you won't be sleeping in the house of God.' He would sing to us a song by Paul McCartney and Wings, 'With a Luck' but I would sing 'with a little love' and soon he was singing it that way. Just like those of us coming up to reflect on our dads, I love my dad with all that love plus some. Pop, you aren't just my dad but you are my champion. He stepped back from the podium and opened his suit jacket to reveal a NWA World Heavyweight Championship belt. The place went nuts when he walked over to his father and placed the belt over his shoulder as his dads wrestling idols of yesteryear had done for decades. When his father saw his own name stenciled on the belt he cried and smothered his boy with arms of love.

Wiping back the tears, COS, called for the intermission to prepare for the dining part of the service. Taking her seat next to the pastor and first lady she fought back the tears when looking at her father. He just sat there looking straight ahead. Within a few months he went from being a robust and fervent elder of the church to a shell of himself, speaking and eating very little.

The night was off to a very good start and there was an amazing buzz in the air. It could only get better and the ministry needed such a refreshing. Lately, it had become a little stagnant. Although they tried to keep the ministry fresh and exciting, every once in a while a lull would come in and they realized that that was the way it was. The only thing for them to do was to keep praying and pressing.

Soon the dinner was over, it was time to get back into the service. Up next was Superstar, she had come back from college to lift up her uncle. When she took her place behind the podium, the room fell quite. She hadn't been at the church for a while and many were so happy yo see her. She went from being an ultra active member to an absentee. "First, I want to let you all know that I miss you all very much. I am here to celebrate the men of this ministry and my uncle. Not only is he my pastor but he is also my father. When mommy wasn't around he and auntie helped us out a great deal. Believe it or not, your pastor disciplined me and my siblings. And when he did, he didn't give us that, 'this is gonna hurt me as much as its going to hurt you.' What he would ask was, 'Did it hurt?' and if you had any sense you'd nod yes. And then he'd say, 'Good'. But he only whipped us after he had all of the facts. Enough about that. Most of the men in this ministry know me and my love for sports. It was at the picnics and camps that they pushed me to work harder and harder. You all pitched in to help me and my family and I appreciate that. I can't stay all night because I have a curfew because we are in the championship round in our division. One more win and its the state and possibly on to the big dance. So please keep us in your prayers and remember that when we win, and yes I am proclaiming victory! We will be back to celebrate with all of you. Uncle and men, thanks for the biggest assist in my life. This alley-oop is for you"! She received a rousing standing ovation as went to hug her uncle and some of the other men.

"The word teaches us that it takes a village to raise a child. And all that this one, right here, has overcome, we should all be proud because she is one of ours. So far, all I can say is wow. We still have a ways to go but this is off the grid. Imagine if we were giving out awards, it would be chaos. Lets bring our next reflector up".

Sr Deacon stood up and made his way to the podium. He wasn't his usual boisterous self. In fact, he seemed almost normal. "Let me tell you all something. This has been a blessing for me to hear so many wonderful thoughts about the men around here. I would like to salute the man who helped me come into this world. Many of you know him as your doctor. I have always known him as my father. What many of you don't know about this wonderful man is the fact that when something goes wrong at the hospital he takes it harder than anyone. He suffered through many losses over the years but he would be there through it with the family. My mother used to get on him, but he stood on his laurels. So on this night, I want to share something with our family and friends. Next month, Father is retiring for good. His doctor, my mother, told him it was time and that she needs him now to enjoy his life. As many of you know, my mother passed years ago, but he still listens to her. Not only is he retiring but the hospital is naming the new modern arts of medicine medical building after him."

He stepped back and pulled out a replica of the new building and a plaque bearing his fathers name. The ovation was so thunderous when the picture was put on the monitor that he couldn't finish. He went to where his father sat and presented the items to him. The old doctor stood up and hushed the crowd. But it was to no avail, they loved him deeply. He was a big part of the community and their lives. He assisted in countless births and was the one to do a lot of the death certificates. As he put it,"Way too many deaths for my liking. But the Lord giveth and taketh away."

By the time order was restored, the next reflector was already up. Then a more came and it was all good. Some had done video tributes, spoken word tributes and some sang.

Reflector #14 was midway through his presentation when he began to breakdown. "For years, decades even, I was angry with my dad for not helping me to get a job when I was becoming a young adult. I saw how my friends were following in their fathers paths, some good and some bad, yet they followed. And to me it seemed that a father was happy to show his son the ropes. Well I didn't get that from my dad but what I did get was a good life and my provisions were well met. I learned how to become a man and make it on my own. Lots of times I failed but I kept trying so that one day I could rub my success in his face. And then I was talking to a friend who had just lost her dad and right then I repented for my hostilities toward the only man that did his best to be the best for me. He took his time to raise me as a single parent. When I graduated with my degrees, he was there cheering me on. Looking back in retrospect, this was how it suppose to be for us, me and him. Dad said to me, 'I'm proud of you my son.' And he showed it. He began to tell every one about my successes. I love you and thank you for the many sacrifices that you made. Those that I know of as well as the ones that I am not aware of. You are one in a million. So I want to share with you my first patent royalty check of one million dollars." There was an audible stunned silence. Then the applause began.

"Ladies and gentleman, we have just witnessed history. We have one of our very own as a licensed, patented and certified millionaire. This proves that hard work and a good support system can work wonders. All I can say is wow and wow again. We remember when he was in the junior choir and plays, now look at him. A certified millionaire. Whats next? Only time can tell, its time for our last ten minute break then we are going to finish up, wow."

After the intermission it was Reflector #15's turn. She and her family did a 'This is Your Life' tribute to their father who had over the years won the award for most family and friends invited that it was named in his honor. This was followed by the handful that was left with COS tightening the event up.

"As we close out on this historic evening, my last reflection of my father is that of Atari, Cabbage Patch Dolls and Schwinns. I was the first girl to have one. My brothers started a bike club and I wanted in, my daddy tried to keep me from being tomboyish so he and I made a deal. The deal was, if I ever started acting like a boy or boyish I would have my bike taken away. My daddy said to me, 'You are my only girl and I want to keep you that way.' Later on in life when my brothers started a car club, again, I wanted in. My daddy said to me after I got my drivers license that I could have his old '77 Cutlass Supreme. Not only was I the first girl in the club, but I had the fliest car of them all. Although we don't ride anymore, cameraman, please go to our live feed."

From the parking lot there was a collection of classic cars assembled and front and center was her daddy's classic '77 that was fully restored! "This was my first car and it was the first one of five of your cars that I either totaled or had accidents in. I would often tease at you and mommy and ask why would you keep letting me drive your cars? Mommy would say, 'Because we have the best insurance possible, ha.' I mean if it were me, I wouldn't let me get on a skateboard, insured or not. But daddy, you were different, thanks." A tear rolled down his face and he sort of smiled. She cried as she closed and looked at her father. How she missed him sharing his wisdom with her and for a brief moment it all seemed okay with her.

And with that, the evening was over. As customary all participants took pictures and the like. This was really a treat when they took the all hands picture, because it would be proudly displayed as a portrait and hung in the Great Room. Once again, the event was a success.

Making their way to the parking lot, COS and her daddy approached the vintage car. The closer that they got, he began to sit up straighter. She and her husband noticed this and he pushed him a little slower. By the time they reached the car he was sitting erect in his wheelchair. He reached out to touch the drivers window. As he touched it, he began to mumble something. They leaned down to hear what the patriarch of the family was saying. "Cut-dogg. I want to ride in my cutlass.." They stood there in awe of this miracle. This man had only used head nods, grunts and groans for the past years to communicate. They helped him in the car and off they went.

CHAPTER 30
Restored!!

Many months had passed and Elder had recovered by leaps and bounds. The miracle of the '24/7/365' event was still manifesting itself in his family. God had restored this once mighty warrior to his former glory with the use of an old car. He had been testifying to the goodness of God, that he was going to be the keynote speaker at the men fellowship and retreat.

COS was so proud of her father for his achievements. That night that they got home, he sat at the kitchen table and held mini-court. She and her husband sat and listened to him as he talked. For the first time in years there wasn't a tv or radio on. The only audible sound was his voice and her sobs. "When I first saw that car, all I could think about was when you were hit and left for dead. We didn't know what to do. As I approached your car, all I could see was your hair that was embedded in the windshield. I saw that before I saw you and I didn't know what condition you were in. The irony was that this happened less than a half mile from here and we had to go that way to get to the hospital. Your mother was a basket case just from the looks of everything. We only had one car so I sent her ahead and stayed at the scene with Chief and Deputy. I wanted to assist them in any way possible. Maybe it was the old bulldog in me." He went on for a little while, then he was ready for bed. The next morning he began to call certain family and friends to share his testimony.

People were being blessed by his testimony about God's goodness and mercy. When he walked into the bank that following week, Sr Teller rushed out from behind the counter and hugged him. She stood there in unbelief. He was always one of her favorites. He used to stand in line and let others go ahead of him until she was available. He would often say, "When I come to the bank I ain't in a rush." This was the reaction throughout the region. One had to remember that for years he was one of the most recognized persons around.

He spent time outside in his yard and with his 'mistress' his beloved cutlass. He loved on that car and he would spend quality time listening to Bishop Paul Morton's 'Bow down and worship Him'. There, in his garage or driveway he would have praise and worship with his God. And he would sing, 'This is holy ground.' King David was his idol when it came to worship and he embodied David's practice of worship. Never had a recovery been so observed by all. Many nights one of his descendants would have to come outside and get him.

He began to hold neighborhood prayer and bible study for those that were too ashamed to go to church. He would provide food and drink for all who came by. One day during one of these sessions, some of the men from a neighboring church started to attend. After a few sessions they approached him. "Brother, we have not only heard about the good that you are doing, but we have witnessed for ourselves. We are having a men fellowship and retreat and we would like for you to be the keynote speaker."

He stood there hearing them but slowly processing what they were asking of him. "If its okay with you, I need to pray about this and I will get back to you expeditiously." One of the men chimed in,"Man, this gig pays pretty good." The other men looked at him and hung their heads in shame."Please charge it to his ignorance and nothing else. We'll be looking for your confirmation. God bless you man of God." With that, they left. His son-in-law who had observed the encounter approached him.

As Son-in-Law talked, COS came to the door and called her husband. Before Son-in-Law could finish what he was saying, he dropped his head and went to see what his wife wanted. "I told you that I was coming out here to see what was going on with your father before I left out the door, remember?" He cowered as she stood above him. He listened as his daughter unleashed a tongue-lashing of epic proportion unto her husband. With a sly as a fox grin, Elder not only had an answer for the men, but he had a topic for his message!

He closed the garage door and sat inside of his wonderful car and called the fellows to inform them of his decision. After getting their positive response, they thanked him again for getting involved. He placed his phone on the seat and opened the garage door. Not hearing, but still seeing his daughter dealing with her husband, he quietly pulled out of the garage.

This was the first time that he had driven in years and he wanted to ride like the wind. Over the years, others had done the driving for him. Now it was time for him to be liberated. No sooner had he gotten down the street, his phone rang. He picked it up and saw that it was his daughter. He tossed it back on the seat, turned up the volume and cruised on down the road. There wasn't a need to get frustrated or discouraged, so he went to the place where his set back started.

When he arrived at his destination, he sat in the car and looked around his surroundings. Never one for fear, he did feel a chill. It had been years but it only seemed like mere days. He got out of the car and walked a small distance.

With every step, he tightened up. Since his recovery he had been as loose as a goose, as he liked to call it. But this place was different and he knew why. He spent the next few hours there praying and reflecting on his life. It was here that he began to jot down his thoughts for this upcoming event. He decided that he would use his life lessons as a sounding board and tie it in with the word of God. He wanted to empower the men, and he decided to use Old Testament men, Noah and Joseph. He loved it when Holy Spirit imparted wisdom into him. This reminded him of the many years that he taught the scriptures in church as well as on the streets.

Finally, it was time for him to leave. The darkness was starting to envelope the area and he headed home. Pulling into the driveway, he noticed that all of the lights in the house were out. This was strange, because someone was always there. Then it dawned on him that he wasn't inside. He parked the car and got out. Not ready to go inside, he went for a walk. He was gone only for a little while when COS and Son-in-Law pulled along side of him. She began to call out to him and he walked over to her car. He told them that he was fine and he would be home shortly. She huffed and drove off.

Along his walk, he ran into a couple of old war buddies and they walked together. They reminisced about the good old days and when they all played in the last recognized Negro Leagues and the state of baseball today. He told them that he would be doing a message for the retreat and asked them to come along and they agreed. He called Organizer and requested lodging for three. Everything was taken care of and they sat in the yard and talked even longer.

As he was departing his buddies, he noticed a beautiful silver-haired lady sitting on her porch. He inquired and was given the scoop on her. War Veteran offered to make the introduction and they all walked over to her house. Elder removed his cap as he was being introduced. After a while, the men left. It was unbelievable how God had ordered his steps in such a short time. It was as if the past years had gone by like a blip on the screen. When he got home, he called the classy lady and they talked until the wee hours of the morning.

They made plans to get together later in the day. Hanging up was hard but had to be done. That night, he slept oh so peacefully. He had pleasant dreams and awoke late. He had slept so hard that he didn't hear the others leave. But it was nice to have the house all to himself. After fixing himself something to eat, he picked up the phone and called her. She too was having something to eat. They laughed because they were both getting ready to eat a bowl of cereal.

"After my husband passed and they kids were all out on their own, I started eating cereal because it was simple and not a lot of mess to clean up." "You know, I make a killer bowl of cereal. Maybe we could have breakfast together soon." "So what are you doing now? Have you poured the milk yet?" "Not yet, whats up." "Come over and we'll eat together." "I'll be there in a few. What do I need to bring?" "Only yourself. I'll be waiting." They hung up and he prepared to leave. Always an impeccable dresser, he decided to dress comfortable and casual.

Before long he was standing on her porch ringing the bell. She opened it and was greeted with a smile and a beautiful flower. "Thank you, sir." She let him in and took his cap. She gave him a tour of the house and it ended in the kitchen. They sat at the Island table and he was very impressed. She had two bowls out and opened the cabinet, "Pick your poison. I have all sorts of fun cereal for the kids and the boring cereal for the older ones. What will it be?" "Apple Jacks, please ma'am." "Ah ha, now that is a fine choice." She poured cereal for both of them and he looked at her in amazement. "What? You thought that I only would have bran cereal and stuff, right? Well mister, let me tell you something. Everything that is in my house to eat, is what I like. So when I want to eat something, my only concern is, what will it be?"

They sat and ate talking about cereal, old cereal commercials and how much they missed all of the sugary sweet cereals before the do-gooders did away with it. When they finished they took to the backyard. With every moment and movement they drew closer and closer.

Sitting on the swing, she said, "Okay. We have had a great almost twenty-four hours and neither one of us has discussed our current situations. So I will start. I was married to my husband for decades and one decade too long. We had six kids together and two outside of our marriage. One by him and one by me. Although we never divorced, we separated and did our own thing. Then two of our children were killed in the city and we got back together somehow. I moved into this region a few years ago after my old man passed and yes, he was an old man, and here I am. Now you."

"Well I was married for a very long time and we had three wonderful children. We both were born and raised here. Never venturing far except for vacations and such. Our oldest has been incarcerated for close too thirty five years now. He did a murder and was convicted for his crime. He refused to cop to a plea and they buried him. My wife took it hard and did the time with him until her passing. But I have some really good friends and family that surrounded me. That's my life in a nutshell." "So, if you have been here all the time, why have I never seen you before. That car of yours I have seen a few times but it was driven by a young lady..." Before she could go further, he stopped her. "That young lady is my daughter and up until a few months ago, she was my caregiver. I was incapacitated for a long while."

As he talked, War Hero came in the backyard. She invited him in to sit with them. The three sat under the awning because the sun had become a little too much for them."Hey, you two. Later we are going to that new seafood joint and want to know if you want to join us." They looked at each other and he asked,"Classy Lady, will you honor me by having dinner with me?" "By all means necessary, it will be my honor. Yes." War Hero told them what time to meet them at the restaurant. Elder looked at his watch and prepared to leave. "I have got to go. But I will be back an hour before we are due at the restaurant." He took his cap and left. As the two sat in the backyard, War Hero filled her in on some of the life of his old buddy.

On the way home he thought about what a wonderful human being she was. In no time, he felt more connected to her than he did in the many decades that he was married to his deceased wife. For the first time in decades, he felt alive and vibrant! He couldn't wait to see her again. The excitement was refreshing and restoring. At home, he began to work on his message for the retreat. Within a few hours he had everything noted, looked up and outlined. All he had to do now was place everything in its proper context. After that he prepared for his evening out with an angel.

While he was getting dressed COS and Son-in-law came home. They inquired about what he was up to and he told them. Looking at him, one would never had known that just a few short months ago this man was a lifeless shell. As he checked himself out, he turned to them and said, "Don't wait up for me. Something tells me that I will be out for a while." COS looked him over and gave him a thumbs up. He kissed her on the cheek and she watched her daddy walk out the door. She sat down and looked at her husband as he smiled. "What are you sitting there beaming about? What, you wish that that was you or something? Well buster, this is your life. Right here with me. You know, like, til death do us part." He looked down at his hands and mumbled, "I couldn't be so lucky."

Driving to the restaurant the two listened to music and talked. When they arrived he pulled up to the entrance and she looked at him as the valet approached the car. He got his ticket and opened her door and lead her out by the hand. As he did this, she thought about some of the things she was told about him. She took his hand and said, "You are wonderful." "Back at you times two. No, take the back. I speak multiplication into your life." Then they went inside. The other couples were already there having cocktails. Neither one of them drank so they ordered juice.

As they waited, everyone introduced themselves. It was like a who's who. Some people they knew others were from different regions. "We have been getting together for dinner twice a year and it gets bigger every time. Thank you both for joining us. We understand that this is a good way for us 'old folks' to network without having to use all that new age technology. The only criteria needed is that the person is retired. We do this so we can get better rates and discounts." They toasted and began to look at the menu. "The world is your oyster and everything that's in it is yours." he said to her. She squeezed his arm and winked at him.

While they waited for their food, the house band began to play. Some of them took to the dance floor in front of the band. They swayed to the music and watched as the others danced. Soon the food was served and the grace was spoken over the table and they began to fellowship in eating. After the meal was completed some went back to the dance floor. This time they joined them. The band was taking request and doing dedications. He requested a song and dedicated it to her. It would be a little later, after a few songs so they sat back down.

When it was time for the song, Lead Singer spoke, "This dedication goes out to a classy lady from a classic gentlemen. This will be our feature song that we call on all couples to participate. Soon the dance floor was overcrowded, but they didn't care. It seemed like it was only them two and no one else. He held her close and rocked her in his arms. She nuzzled in his chest as they slowly danced to the music. His heart was beating so fast that he thought it would knock her over. She pressed into him so close that she felt like she was a part of his being.

Even after the song was over they continued in this embrace of each other and time. Neither wanted this moment to end but soon they made their way back to the table. As they approached, the people at the table began to clap for them. One of the ladies asked Classy, "How long have you two been married?" "Funny that you would ask me that. I just met him yesterday. Seems like I have been knowing him all of my life." she beamed proudly. "Let's get out of here." he said squeezing her hand. They said their goodbyes and left.

Waiting for the valet to return, he looked into her eyes and swam deep inside of them. "If I don't kiss you now.." "Well, what are you waiting for. That should have been done long a.." Before she could finish he pulled her close and kissed her softly. "I was once a frog, now I am a king." This was going to be a very memorable night and it was off to a very good start.

CHAPTER 31
Henpecked

The retreat was in a couple of days and he was so excited. He was making the final draft when she walked into the room. They had grown leaps and bounds since the night they first met. He pulled her to him and handed her the final rough draft. She looked at him strangely. "Forgive me. In my former life, it was an automatic. I'd finish and she'd proof it." "Honey, I would be honored to help you in anyway that I can. All you have to do is just ask. As a matter-of-fact, try it on me first."

He stood and cleared his throat before speaking as he had done many, many times before. Before he started he said to her, "Before my setback, I really used to be someone." She shrugged him off and stood up. As she was standing she grabbed a remote control and said, "Gentlemen, it is our honor to present this esteemed man. Prepare your hearts and minds for a mighty move of God." With that he began to flow with his message of encouragement and exhortation. After he was finish she had a puzzled look on her face. Sensing her question he spoke, "I have to leave some things out until the day of the event. It's a habit that I had evolve from days gone by. But it will make sense when I deliver it." Still puzzled, he revealed much more to her and did it again.

Cradling his hand, she encouraged him, "Baby, you don't have to be afraid of me. I understand that we are fresh and new, but if I ever had anyone's back, it's yours. Not to long ago, I was out with some of the girls and we held a men bashing session. The question arose in regard to a good man. Would we know a good man if he fell in our laps? I doubted that I would because I have had so many losers, before, during and after my husband passed on. But, when I first laid eyes on you, I knew that you were different." Next she did something that was quite unexpected, she began to pray for him. It was at that point that he truly knew that she was the real.

The following days were very eventful for them. She treated him out to dinner because she was going to leave him to himself the day before the retreat was to began so that he could focus on the task at hand. As he was preparing to leave for the retreat, he phoned her. "Thanks for everything, I'll call you when I return." "Go get 'em tiger." she said and hung up.

On the way to the retreat, he listened to the other men as they talked about the importance of the man and walking in God's purpose and understanding one's roll in the kingdom. Soon he tuned them out and began to look out of the window. This was going to be the first time that he was going out of the region since his restoration, but he was excited to be out and about. "Its amazing how God picks and chooses what and who he wants to use." he said to no one in particular. This changed the course of the subject and for the rest of the way they rode in fellowship.

Arriving at the logging cabins, they looked at the great and marvelous trees, mountains and the surroundings. It was so beautiful. As they looked around they were soon greeted by Organizer and his team. "Prayerfully your ride here was pleasant." "Yes it was and I must admit that this is absolutely God's country. Beautiful." They talked as they made their way to the cabin that they would be staying in, as they entered all three men mouths dropped open. From the outside the place didn't look that big but it was huge. Organizer walked them through and ended at the master bedroom. Opening the door he said, "I wish it were me." Elder stepped inside and was engulfed at the size of the room. Feeling humbled and almost overwhelmed he shook the man's hand and patted him on the back.

After talking with the men for a while and going over the itinerary for the weekend, Organizer left. By today being the registration day, there were no activity and that was by design. This way, when one arrived and checked in, they would have the rest of the day to sight see and get ready for the weekend ahead. The only thing that was organized was the dinner because many would be arriving at different times but by dinnertime the majority would be accounted for.

At dinner the men met several esteemed members from different regions that surrounded the area. The meal was very informal and laid back. No one seemed to be walking around looking to be noticed. Great men walked alone without their 'teams' surrounding them. It was like getting back to one's humble beginnings. Besides, history had shown that so called 'great men' who were speaking had abused the accommodations that were provided for them because their 'team' was there. Soon they adopted a plan that only covered the speaker and two guest. So if a speaker wanted his 'team' with him, then he could provide for them to be there. Once a speaker was notified of the policy they were not so quick to bring in 'their team'.

During this weekend, men could fellowship and commune with nature. Every aspect of the event was well thought out and executed because Organizer and his team worked tirelessly to make every years event a success. They prayed and fasted relentlessly for God's blessings over the events. Not only that, as soon as one was over, within the next month they were 'reinventing the wheel'.

That evening after dinner, many of the men had fellowship by the waterfall. Soon they began to talk about pop culture, sports and and its many different categories. One subject that seemed to peak many of the men interest was sex symbols. Soon one of the men went and got some paper. Each man was required to choose three women and after everyone placed their paper in the basket the lots would be tallied. Thelma from 'Good Times' ran away with the top spot. This sparked spirited debate and soon it was on. Some of the topics that were discussed were: if you could rid the world of sports of one team, what team would that be?: the evil empire won hands down. If you could be a member of a singing group: there was a tie between the Temptations and New Edition. Best wrestling move: the lariat/clothesline. Fascinating serial killer: Maury Travis. Mary Anne or Elly Mae: Mary Anne. Serial killer that you'd personally kill: Charles Manson. Greatest creation by God: man. Second greatest: breasts. Breast size preference: the larger the better. Favorite porn magazine: Player. Favorite centerfold: Ola Ray.

This was the turning point of the conversation. One brother spoke out, "What we are doing is fun but if we are really going to get real, lets try something. If you could have met one woman from biblical days who would it be? For me it would have been Rahab. Think about it for a minute. She was real. She had guile, spunk, and was fearless, besides the skills of her profession. Whats there not to like about Rahab?"

Looking at the men he said, "So many of us have been jaded and henpecked that we don't know what we really want in a woman. We are not only henpecked by women but also by society. Think about this. When we were young bucks, who did we go after first? Was it the 'fast' girl or the 'square' girl? Lets be real. All for the 'squares' raise your hand. A few raised their hands. "Okay, now who went after the 'fast and loose' girl. Many hands went up. "Its no right or wrong. Its just our preference. Esther had to had been fine because the king was willing to part with half of his kingdom for her. Ruth was loyal and Boaz looked out for her. Elizabeth and Mary had an anointing on their lives that were unique to mankind. And there are so many more in the bible to choose from but give me sister Rahab any day." They began to laugh in agreement. They continued on for a little while longer then it began to break up.

On the way back towards the cabin, Elder stopped the young man that was leading their impromptu meeting. "Brother, I just want to thank you for loosening up with the questions that you made us openly address. You said things that we are almost ashamed of. Me in particular would have been after Rahab, for sho' Because I was engaged to a 'fast' girl but ended up marrying a 'square' girl and I paid greatly for my mistake." The two men laughed and continued on towards their cabins. Elder was pleased that there wasn't or rather that there seemed to be no cock and bull among the men. Usually, there would be at least a few men that would try to be the 'bull of the woods'.

He decided to call his girl, just to hear her voice. As he reached in his pocket to get his phone it rang. It was her and he was excited. He answered and she sighed in his ear. This was her hello to him. They talked briefly but it was refreshing. After that he turned his phone off. As he was entering into the cabin, out of the corner of his eye he noticed two men slowly disappear into the woods. Thinking nothing of it he went inside.

Making short conversation with his roommates he retired to his room. He sat at the desk and pulled out his notes. Within a few minutes he had a weird feeling that fell over him. What was going on? What's happening? He got up and and stood on the balcony to get some air. That's when he saw the shadows on the path leading to the woods. Although it was dark he could make out that some of the silhouettes were holding hands. Not wanting to jump to any conclusions he slipped out into the night and down the path. He noticed that it was very quite and for a moment he thought that maybe just maybe his mind was playing tricks on him. But soon the reality was as real as the scene that his eyes witnessed.

He went back to the cabin and got his bible. He began to search for scriptures that pertained to this particular situation. That's when he realized that he had never had to be familiar with the subject or the topic. He also got the circular and flier that was used to promote the event. 'The Essence of Man' was the theme. For minutes he sat there and thought about the title and the word essence. That word had virtually been synonymous with women. He thought that other words could better identify with man's being. He got on his knees and began to pray and then he went to bed. He tossed and turned for most of the night until he was compelled to get back on his knees and cry out to God. Finally, sleep feel on him and he drifted off. When he awoke, he was still in a kneeling position. Fearing that he would be stiff he braced himself to stand and when he did he felt no pain. Looking up he proclaimed, "Thank you Lord and good morning. Whatever it is that you have for me to do on your behalf I am willing to do it, even unto death."

He went downstairs and his buddies were sitting in the kitchen having coffee. They talked about the kickoff for today and the many different events and seminars. He didn't yet speak on the events of the night before. He knew what he saw but he wanted God to order his steps in this regard. As the men talked, he really thought about leaving. Maybe fake illness or something. Of course no one would know, but as he thought about this, the Spirit of the Lord shook him. In his spirit he felt compelled to stay. If this was the case, then he needed to be there. God sent the organizers to seek him out for a purpose and a reason.

This lead him to remember how debilitated he had been months earlier and how he had all but given up on life. "Its almost breakfast time over at the pavilion. Y'all going?" "Yes sir." They got themselves together and headed to the pavilion. Many men had gathered already. The gospel was playing on the PA system and the vibe was pleasant. Soon they were sitting and eating. Some faces were familiar while others were foreign to them. They saluted or acknowledged as many of them as possible.

When the meal was over they had a few hours to kill so they decided to do a little boating. When they got to the lake there was a few boats left on the dock. War Veteran suggested that they take the pontoon out. The others agreed. After doing a thorough inspection on the boat, they pulled out of the launch. The canopy was lowered to get maximum sun intake. Noticing that the boat was equipped with fishing gear and bait, they decided to cast a couple of lines. With the waters being calm, they ventured even further out of the cove.

After casting their lines, they began to talk about the times when they took their sons out to the old catfish stocked lake that was owned by an old friend. That started the conversation about why some sons follow the profession of their father while others didn't. He knew personally why his son didn't follow him. Fate didn't allow that to happen. Of course, his friends were all to familiar with his sons sins and crimes. One thing he and his wife never did was shy away from the wrong doings of their sons.

By the time it was time to get back they hadn't caught a thing. As a matter-of-fact, they still had the same bait on the lines. Going back in, they laughed at their failed fishing exploits. Once inside the cove and docked, they headed to the cabin to freshen up and head back to the pavilion where the days service was to be held. He admired the way that everything was planned. There was only one speaker and one service for each of the three days. That cut down on the clashing of time and service.

The speaker approached the podium and began his message. It was thought provoking as well as compelling. He gave a brief testimony followed by a powerful message that sent shock waves through the men in attendance. As he ended he said to them, "I never would imagine or dream that I would be standing here before not only man but before God a changed man. I am who God says I am and I am proud of who I am and what I am. Today, I can say that I am saved by God's grace and his mercy. I thank Him for my come to Jesus experience. Now if there is any one who is feeling compelled to come to Jesus, please make your way down to the front. Don't worry about what some one thinks or says about you because when your day comes to stand before the Almighty, they won't be there with you." After a few moments, one middle aged man came down the aisle. The others clapped their hands and encouraged him. After confessing Christ as his personal savior, he took his seat. Some of the men surrounded him and prayed with him. After the benediction was done the service broke up.

For the rest of the day and night the three men enjoyed the fellowship of college football. They even skipped dinner with the others because they wanted to catch the big game between unbeaten #1 and #2. It was close to one am before they got to bed and by that time they were bushed. Going to his room, War Veteran said, "You cats ain't as young as you think you are. I'll see you two in the morning." Half hour later it was War Hero's turn to bail out. He tipped his hat and went to his room. Elder sat in front of the tv and began to drift off. Catching himself, he woke up and headed to his room. Laying across the bed he drifted off to sleep.

Awaken by the sound of thunder claps he sat up in the bed. Looking out of the window he noticed how dark and gloomy it was outdoors. Stretching, he walked out on the balcony just as the rain began to fall. He stuck his hand out to feel the rain pelt into his palm. Although it had only been a couple of days, he still missed his girl. After a few minutes he went back inside and got a chair to sit on. He watched as the rain came down harder and harder. Hopefully the weather would be better by the time service was to start.

He returned to his bed after a while and lay there trying to go back to sleep. He couldn't so he went back out on the balcony. It was raining even harder than before. He let the mist hit him in the face and stood there as if to be getting refreshed. Hearing a knock on the door he went to answer it. It was War Veteran. "Get ready, we are going back out on the lake to do some more fishing." "But its raining as you can see." "You only live once man, get dressed."

Although the rain had lighten, it still made walking difficult. When they reach the dock, the pontoon was still there. Boarding the boat they noticed that they had left the poles in the water. Reeling them back in, both had fish on them. One was dead and the other alive. "Now if that don't beat you. We cast lines and don't get a nibble, but we forget to bring the lines in and get not just one but two hits." War Hero said pulling in the lines.

By the time they had reached the clearing, they decided to stay close because the weather was still bad. Why they decided to go out in such bad weather was beyond all of their comprehension. Observing a boat a few hundred yards away from them, he began to share with them what he had witnessed the first night that they were there. The two men looked at him puzzled. "We thought that you know what was going on. As a matter-of-fact we both were shocked that you agreed to be involved." They talked a little while longer on the subject before talking about other topics. Soon the other boat was only yards away and getting closer. Organizer and a half dozen others were on the boat. They greeted each other and headed back out on the lake. Hours later, they were ready to head back into the cove.

Walking to the cabin, the weather had cleared and the sun came out for a quick peek. Tomorrow would be his day to minister and he had a lot to digest. With that in mind he went back to do some more studying. He processed the last few days and the events that lead to the next day's events.

While in his room the other men stirred around while waiting for the days lunch and service to began. At some point, all three had gathered on his balcony and looked at what marvelous work of nature that God had done. Somewhere in the distance John P Kee's, I Won't Let Go, was playing. "Now that's my man, Reverend Kee. He been through some things and he didn't allow that to keep him down. That's what we as men have to do." They stood on the balcony and began to pray for the strength of mankind, everywhere.

After prayer, it was time to head to the woods where the meal would be served and the service would be held. The path to get there was full of men and they seemed to be filled with excitement. Since there wasn't any seating arrangements anyone could be sitting at the picnic table with you. This time, there were so many men there, that some had to sit on the ground. "To keep everything decent and in order, we are asking that we start serving from the back to the front. Is that alright? We want to make sure that everyone is served. And after everyone has been served we will begin the service for this afternoon. Let's cease from all walking and talking, while our speaker comes forward to bless the food and service. Let the church say amen." The speaker came forward and pronounced the prayer and the blessing.

All of the food was either grilled or smoked. The meats were beef, pork and fish. The vegetables were served raw or steamed. The smell that these foods permeated were just unreal. And the drink was water or wine, red and white that sat in carafe's on the tables. For dessert, each table had fruits and nuts. It had the look and the feel of biblical days. The meal was amazing and only added to the expectation for the ministered word to come.

As they stood to receive the speaker, Elder recognized the fellow who had brought the word the day previously. That was refreshing to see. One could always glean from the table of others.

He went into the word and began to set the groundwork for his sermon. "I was attending an event a while back and I met a couple of people that really blessed me. We were at a church that held a shut-in for the weekend. That weekend I met a couple that really seemed to love one another. But the key was, only one of them was there. The other one was incarcerated. After I talked to this individual, I realized just how much compassion we should have for others. Even if we don't agree with their lifestyle. That weekend I learned so much about myself. I always thought that I had it together, but I realized that I was just a peon. If I died, yes, a few would mourn but I would be forgotten in due time. Which brings me to my text. For a little while I want to share with you about David. Not as a king but as a boy. One day he was called away from his assignment to rush home because his father needed him. When he got to his father's house he was paraded before another man. This man was the prophet Samuel. Who looked the boy over, spoke to God and God in return told the prophet to shut-up and pour the oil over the boy's head. Brothers, sometimes we don't look like what others want us to look like but God knows what we are going to look like in the end. We go about the business of trying to look like what society tells us, but in reality, all we are doing is faking it and covering it up. Years ago a woman bared her soul before the Lord Almighty and proclaimed that 'they will see my scars'. Our wounds are so deep and great that sometimes we just go about life 'poise-end'. We look the part but we are not the part. We think the part but our minds don't process the part. That's how we end up in the 'church of the poise-end minds'. We look, smell

167

and attempt to operate in what we do, but the reality is that all we are doing is posing. David went from being a shepherd to being anointed to be king back to being a shepherd before God called him to the kingship. What I want us to take from David today is that there is a king in all of us. I mean a real K-I-N-G. That's what Thee King ordained us to be: Kings!"

By this time, almost every man was on his feet. "Before I finish I want to take this time, not for an alter call but for a call to the alter for kings. If you are a king, come down to the alter and get your crown and place it on your head. Then present yourself to Thee King. Go before Him and give Him glory for your kingship." Cameraman passed out the crowns and with his own crown on his head he gave God thanks. The spirit came through in a calm wind and fell upon the men that opened their hearts to The Holy Spirit. Men began to fall on their knees and others began to speak in divers tongues. The Fruit of the Spirit began to manifest itself. Cameraman spoke to the men as calm was being restored. "Just remember that God is not a respecter of person. He loves us, but he hates the sin in us. David, shepherd or king gives us a prime example. God bless you, kings." He was well spent and some of the men surrounded him and began to pray for his restoration.

The fellowship was so high and there was so much food that no one left. The fellowship continued on for a few hours before almost everyone was gone. Sitting among the last of the remnant, Cameraman shared even more with them. And two of the ones that were still there was the two from his testimony. He didn't know their future but he knew that a seed for kingship had surely been sown.

Back in the cabin the older three men collaborated on the events so far. "Man. I don't know what you have in store for us, but the bar has been raised considerably." "Well, my friend. It's a good thing that I am not in competition with with the others but I believe that The Lord will make due." They sat watching sports for a spell then they heard a loud commotion outside.

They went to investigate and there was a gathering of men fighting off a bear. The bear had somehow gotten into the area where they had put the left over food. They had started to throw things at it and that only seemed to agitate the beast even more. When he stood on his hind legs, the enormity of its mass became very evident. One look at the bear in that posture, the men took off running. Finally, Park Ranger showed up. He hit it with a tranquilizer dart and waited for it to take effect. It seemed like the bear had a tolerance for the tranquilizer. Getting ready to pump another dart into the bear some one yelled out 'Jesus' and the bear lumbered off. Many of the men followed the bear out to the clearing and the excitement was over.

Soon the men were sharing video and pictures with their people back home. It wasn't everyday that one gets too see a bear in the wild and not at the zoo. No one was hurt and that was a good thing. Someone chimed, "That's why we have to watch as well as pray." The men went back into their cabin and relaxed. They didn't really feel like venturing out especially with bear incident. Besides, he needed to rest for tomorrow. He had witnessed what the other two dynamic speakers brought to the men and he was the last for the event. He needed to leave a lasting impression on the men.

Turning in early, he went to his room and undressed. He showered and went before the throne in prayer. He prayed that what he gave out that the men would be able to receive. After prayer he began to meditate. He had some juice and fruit before studying. This would have to sustain him until he was finished bring the message. He hadn't fasted in years but he felt that it was required of him to do so. Not just for him but for the men that he would be ministering to. He studied late into the evening before turning in to bed.

Laying in the bed he looked up at the ceiling and began to think about his son. He missed him and promised himself that he would indeed go and see him very soon. He drifted off into a deep sleep and awoke early the next morning. He felt refreshed and rejuvenated. He heard birds chirping and he looked out of the window to find a pair of birds mating. He smiled and lay back down. He knew that breakfast would be served soon but he decided to go out with the others even though he was in fasting mode. He remembered what his old Bishop told them years and years ago, "Don't be like the Pharisees when you fast. Look like you look everyday and don't run around tellin' folk that you fastin'. That's between you and your God."

Soon they were out and about and the weather was conducive for the occasion. Sitting among the men he sipped on water and just observed the goings on. In a few hours everything would come to a close. This weekend had been unbelievable for him. Getting lost in his thoughts he reflected on the past years. He was ready to live life to the fullest. God had given him another chance and he wasn't going to squander this opportunity.

After breakfast they went to an medieval weaponry demonstration. They were amazed at the amount of weapons that were on hand. Two weapons that really caught their fancy was a maul and a mace. The instructors did a demonstration on some fruit and the medieval weapon did not disappoint. War Veteran joked, "Man, if they had let us use some of that stuff like that during my time, some of the wars wouldn't have went the way that they did. Those things are just barbaric. Hell, I want one of those." He went to talk to one of the demonstrators to get more info on the two wonderful pieces.

They found other things to do until it was lunchtime. The bear incident was still the talk of the day. After lunch they still had a few hours to kill so they decided to go back out on the boat. When they arrived at the dock, all of the boats were gone. Walking back to the cabin he decided that he needed to rest. Inside his room he went before the King in prayer. Being around all of that good smelling food had taken a toll on him and he didn't want to break his fast. He knew he needed strength beyond his own ability.

When it was time for dinner he got dressed and met up with his companions. They prayed and made their way to the lake. The closer they got, the more the rich smell of food overtook their senses. This time they had a steer, lamb, and hog all laid out for one to serve himself. He stood in awe of the amount of food that was there. While he was standing there thinking, Organizer approached them. He lead them to the speakers table. He was lead to the podium to open the ceremony in prayer. Looking out at the throng of men he began to weaken. His knees shook and he held tight to the horns of the alter. Holy Spirit ministered to him that He was his strength. And with a mighty cry he called on the heavens. Not just for himself but for all of the men. After he finished he sat back down and felt the strengthening power of faith.

Once dinner was over, Organizer approached the podium to bring him for the message. "Brothers, this weekend has been the best yet. When we started doing this years ago, our goal was to help and not to hinder. Before we go any further, I want to welcome a group of men. Brothers from the D.O.C. please stand." About twenty men of different ages stood up. "These brothers have successfully completed their time and after this weekend will be released from prison. They came unsupervised and when they return they will be done. This is a new program that we are involved with we call, Restored. Let's give this men a hand. Amen. And now without further ado, lets stand to our feet and receive this mighty man of God as he comes."

The ovation was thunderous. He began with a couple of songs. "My Bishop never gave a message without warming up the congregation. Lets do a little of 99 in half by Hezekiah Walker. The music began and they to sing along with him. With every word he powered up and by the time the song was done he was ready. "I want to talk with you this evening about being 'Henpecked'. I have personal experience as well as scripture to back this message up. We will look at the story of Ahab and Barak and myself. Not necessarily in that order, per say. Let us proceed." He gave them the passages of scripture and gave biblical account of how being henpecked can cause a man's downfall.

"I too was like Ahab and Barak. My wife ran my life. Every aspect of it. When I was a young lawyer with aspirations of helping brothers that had fallen by the wayside, she came into my life and changed the course of my career. I wanted to help people, she wanted me to aspire higher. And with that I climbed the ladder to judge then mayor of our region. She controlled my every move and she was always quick to remind me that she was the 'grease' behind the machine. And she was right. She wrote out my speeches and planned my social calender. All I was, was a mouthpiece. I was worse than that henpecked Herman Munster. With him it was 'Lily, Lily, Lily. Lily this and Lily that.' But because I loved her and no one else seemed to want me, I allowed this to continue on. All the way until her death a few years back.

"When she passed I had no direction because she did everything. I realized at her funeral that I didn't even have an original thought in my head. When I did think, all I would hear was her voice. She controlled my life so much that I went into a tailspin. I reverted inside of myself. I stopped going to work in my private practice. I stopped functioning altogether. But my daughter took me to a appreciation ceremony and that night reacquainted me with my old 1977 Cutlass Supreme and God has been restoring me ever since. For years I stopped speaking, I would communicate with grunts, groans and pointing. I was hopeless, but seeing my old friend jump, that same car that had almost claimed the life of mt daughter started my recovery."

"One of the first places that I went to was the cemetery to visit my wife. I stood over her grave and told her, 'I am back now. You don't control me any more. I am going to live life until I am besides you.' I left the graveside and felt empowered. She even controlled me from the grave. Just to show you all how good God is, I started to hold small bible classes in my home then it got so big we went into the backyard. Men and women, boys and girls started coming. That's when I knew that God had a plan and purpose for my life. Later on I ran into a couple of my good friends and they in turn introduced me to the new love of my life. She is everything that I needed in a woman. She is kind and gentle. Besides being easy on the eyes, I couldn't have asked for a finer woman. After I met Classy, I went back to the cemetery and told my deceased wife, 'I will not be by your side. I will be by the side of some who truly loves me. Goodbye.'

"What I am saying to us all is the fact that God has the final say so in our lives. He created us to be the head and not the tail. We are suppose to lead, not pull up the rear. We have a tendency to run away when things don't go our way. Sometimes we run to other women when our woman ain't acting right. But as I close out, think about this: if you are going to cheat on someone. Try cheating with Jesus, because he died for you. No one else can make that claim. God bless you all."

War Veteran and War Hero assisted this great man back to his seat. He was emotionally and spiritually spent. But he was mostly hungry. "I'm fine. I just want something to eat."

After everything was done, Organizer told every one to get as much food as humanly possible because the rest was going into the forest preserve as well as the woods. Everyone did as commanded and there was still a generous amount of food left. They headed for their cabin carrying all of their food when a familiar face approached him. "That was a very nice message that you delivered. I won't hold you long. Here's my card. Give me a call, would you? We have lots to discuss."

To tired to think, he shook the man's hand and went inside of his cabin. Wanting only to rest and to hear the sweet sound of his woman's voice he sat on the sofa. Before he could call, he rest his head on the back of the couch and within minutes he was asleep. Not wanting to disturb him, his friends covered him and turned off the lights. They went to their rooms to pack and get ready for the ride home in the morning. They knew that they were watching God's hand at work and they marveled at what they were witnessing.

In the middle of the night Elder awoke to use the bathroom. As he pulled the cover off of him he stood to his feet. Unaware that he was standing on a part of the cover he tripped. Laying on the floor he called out to his friends. They came rushing to his side and assisted him to his room. With the lights on, they were able to tell that he was okay. Just a little shaken.

He noticed an envelop on the floor and pointed to it. "While you were asleep, the committee came over to thank you and to bless you for your time and effort. Open it." they insisted. He opened it and inside was ten one hundred dollar bills and a one thousand dollar debit gift card. He took two of the bills out and handed each of his companions one. "I didn't do that much work to receive this much." "You never know when you give something away how the ones that receive it will respond. It looks like you was well received. You gave a lot and we believe that." War Veteran said to his friend. They thanked him for the money and went to their rooms. In his room he called Classy and they talked for a while before she let him go. Soon he'd be back in her presence and he couldn't wait.

The months following the retreat had a lot of positive fall out. Men began to take some of their rightful places back. That came with mixed emotions. Somehow some way, the men were being empowered to want to do better.

At the big mansion, Brother had begun a transformation that was out of this world. Everything about him was different, from his appearance to his mannerisms. He had seen very little of Nurse since attending the retreat. She had urged him to attend. She wanted him to go so bad that she paid for him to attend the event. Even his sisters, Daughter and Sista noticed the change in him. They had heard the buzz that surrounded the event because it was well documented. The bear scare went viral and had caused quite a stir.

Today he decided that he would address the situation with Nurse. He had breakfast and took care of some business before calling her. He invited her over and she would be there soon.

Waiting for her, he sat on the porch thinking about what he was going to share with her. Soon she was pulling into the driveway. He watched her as she approached the porch. Even though it was early, the humidity was already taking effect. He knew that she didn't particularly care for the heat, but he didn't care. He was not going to allow her inside of his home.

"I called you here today to talk to you. First, I want to thank you for sending me on that wonderful retreat. Although, I had never been on one before, I am looking forward to going more often. Everyone that knows me, know that I can't stand being around a bunch of testosterone filled men for long. Next, I want to talk about us. We have had good days and we have had some really bad days. Our bad seems to outweigh the good. When we first started dating, we wanted what was best for the other. Well, because I want the best for you, I am letting you go."

"I realize that things change and people change, but I want better. We have tried, but there isn't any fruit. Think about all that we have been through, especially as of late. What I am saying is, I want someone that appreciates me. And you don't. I tried to convince myself, but I had to look myself in the mirror of my heart to see exactly where we are."

"From the holding on to your ex's last name, the arguing about the wedding plans, giving me back things that I gave you every time you were 'done' and when you canceled our wedding before we even got to tell people about it was the final straw. I'm not mad at you at all. As a matter-of-fact, I thank you for showing me the light. This way, I wouldn't have to be miserable for years regretting my decision."

"You used to burn me up when you'd come back from your women retreat. You'd come back with a different outlook on what 'we' are suppose to be, oppose to what we really were. The 'no touching' then 'touching' thing just wore on me. But, after that weekend, I must admit, in some aspects you were right."

"We had an informal gathering talking about some things. And we came to a discussion about the 'touching thing'. I was shocked to listen to how so many brothers were going through the same thing that I was going through with you. Not just the younger cats, but the older men talked about the temptations of being with someone that peaked one's interest."

"One brother admitted that he was almost incarcerated because the girl he was with got him so worked and at the height of their encounter, she went all angelic on him and stopped what they were doing. He said that he got himself together and got out of there because he was so jacked up. He felt that she had wronged him and his cock. When he finally talked to her after a while he told her that the prison has its share of guys who took what didn't belong to them and he wasn't going to be one of them. Then later on, he found out that she was putting out for everyone but him! I knew what he was feeling like. As a result of this encounter, we have become like brothers."

"At any rate, I wish you the best. Oh yeah, if there is anything that's left for you to give me back, just toss it on the porch whenever you get around to it." He finished as he sipped on his drink.

Sitting back as a deer caught in the headlights, Nurse tried to compose herself. "Well now." was all that she could muster. He stood up and before he knew it, she had draped herself around him. "Why don't you love me no more?" she pleaded with him. Prying her hands, arms and legs from around his body, he said to her, "The Teddy Bear said 'It don't hurt now' and he was right. Love ain't suppose to hurt but you have proved that theory wrong. I can let you go now. I know that I can make it without you. I fought for us because I thought that God had placed us together. But even a fool knows when its time to stop banging his head against the wall because its either result in a concussion or a hole. I chose neither."

He went inside and closed the door behind him, leaving her standing there. She thought that he was joking. Surely he was joking, right? After a few minutes she realized the gravity of it all. He *was* serious. Feeling defeated, she got in her car and left. He watched her drive away from the window. After her car disappeared he sat down in front of the tv. Sista had witnessed the whole thing. "You okay, bro?" "As best as I can be. I ain't gonna act like its going to be easy, but I need o allow the healing process to begin. You know, sis. I almost messed up. I know that love is real and I know that God is real. But we have to work together. Momma taught us to never settle. And I used to think that she could say that because Pop always provided for us very well. I never thought that she had ever struggled in her life until she and I had that heart to heart talk. I won't settle, ever again. I can do me until my change comes."

"That sounds good. I have watched your transformation since ma passed. You used to only care about you, your swag and your gangsta, but look at you now. I am proud of you. If you can change, anybody can. Remember this, I got your back." Sista said comforting her brother. "And so do I." Daughter yelled from down the hallway.

CHAPTER 32
The Band of the Hand

Sitting on the aisle seat at church he constantly looked at his watch. Service should have been over by now but it was running into overtime. He couldn't leave before the benediction. That was a no-no. But he also knew that the meeting was soon to start and being late was not tolerated. To him that showed a lack of commitment, especially since the meeting had been set months in advance.

After a few more minutes they were standing on their feet listening to the benediction. The amen wasn't in the air good before he was in his car speeding toward his destination. Fortunately for him, this meeting was being held on his side and it wouldn't look good for him to be the host and be late.

When he arrived at the destination he breathed a sigh of relief. He was the first one there. He rushed inside and made sure that everything was in position. These men were expecting a good time and he wasn't going to disappoint them. He took his place at the table as he waited for esteemed guest to arrive.

Soon his first guest arrived. Followed by the others. Within an half hour all six men were accounted for. After they had greeted each other he stood up. "Brothers, I thank you all for being here on today. I thought that I was going to be late because service ran a little longer, but how be ever, we are here." "Wow. So I wasn't alone, because we had a guest speaker at our church and she ripped it up." The men spent the next hour or so talking about church and what was happening at their ministries.

"Now that we have that done, it's time to get to business. Business has never been better. Not only that, we haven't had any unpleasantness between the families as of late. I have called this meeting today for a couple of reasons, which I will get to expeditiously. First, is there any business that we need to deal with?" No one seemed to have anything that was a pressing issue. They were very interested in this meeting and what it meant for the organization.

"Now as you know when we began this thing of ours, we agreed that no one was going to sit as a head figure. We learned that from the Commission. But what we did agree upon was that instead of having heads of regions, we'd form the Band of the Hand. Each finger on the hand has its own function. So instead of dividing regions, we divided businesses. This way, one wouldn't be tempted to breach areas that didn't belong to them. So to eliminate that, we decided what was to be done was being bosses over set entities. One would be over cocaine. One would be over heroin. One would be over marijuana and pills. One would be over crystal meth. One would be over the guns and contracts. We also agreed that we would shop only with each other. This was and is, what was best for business."

"As you all know, I am the last of the Rare Breed group that followed after The League of The Free Birds, who in turn followed our founding fathers, The Legion of Doom. I am about to become a great grandfather and its time for me to sit down. We have built upon a legacy that has transcended our regions by leaps and bounds. We haven't had to bury any of our own in years. I have talked with each one of you about my decision."

"We never allowed anyone to sit at our table that wasn't a One. But on today, I am pushing away from the table to allow one of my own to take my place. He has worked with all of us. Not only that, he did something for all of us. He sacrificed himself for the good of us all. If its okay with The Ones, I would like a show of hands that agree to my request."

As he sat, the four others came over to him and shook his right hand. Had anyone shaken his left hand, the request would have been denied. Every request had to be unanimous. After taking their seat, he stood up and went to the door. As he opened it, he beckoned the man inside. When he came in, he went to each man and kissed their right hand as an act of respect. As he approached the empty chair, he knew when he took that seat that life as he had known was going to be changed forever.

As he sat down, the host began again. "Son, you are now a One. I will stand by your side for a year as your counselor. After that I will be officially retired from every aspect of this life of ours. We will no longer refer to you as Jr, your new title is The Grimm Reaper. I in turn will no longer have the moniker of The Grim Reaper. When any of these men call on you, it is your duty to hear out the case and then carry out their request. You have been in the game a very long time and have paid your dues. You will have a crew that will be under you. Each man at this table has a man that was hand picked by them to be a part of your team. Your group is call The Grim Reapers. You will meet them later. Men, if you can show your tributes to The Grimm Reaper at this time."

He was given $100,000.00 in cash. With every tribute he received, his hand was kissed. The rest would be delivered later. "This is just a small token of our appreciation for what you did for us. By tomorrow, you'll be a very wealthy and powerful man." They finished the ceremony and soon everyone was gone except the Reapers. "I gotta go. We have a second service tonight, but I will be back afterward. That's when you'll meet the rest of the crew. So sit tight and I'll see you around early evening."

For the next few hours he replayed the events that led up to this day. He knew that he had put in much work for the league but he had never foresaw any of this. He recalled the day that he was contacted and he knew that his life would never be the same. He didn't have much, but he only knew what he knew. And that was the grind. He tried to square up, but he knew he was only fooling himself. Looking at the envelops full of cash he looked outside up in the sky and said, "I tried." He sat down and then the realization came upon him that just like before, he couldn't share this with anyone. At least, not yet.

Finally, Grim Reaper returned. He had some steak sandwiches with him. As they ate, Grim Reaper began to talk. "For the next few hours I am going to tell you all that you need to know. We will start at the beginning and finish at right here. Our forefathers were runaway slaves. There were five of them. One was the house nigga. He had this elaborate plan after he heard about the exploits of Nat Turner. But the night that they were to go on the massacre, he decided to escape. He was trusted by the owner. Although he was a house nigga, he wasn't allowed to sleep in the house. He slept in a cramped quarter slightly detached from the big house. He was given charge of keeping the 'boys' in line, if you know what I mean? But, he wasn't a task master. What he would do was take them away and teach them little things. Soon he had them learning different trades to 'help' the landowner. Within time, he was given full charge over them.

Then, when he knew that they were ready, he made his move. They crept out under the cover of darkness, stealing five of the landowners best saddles and horses. They made there way to the outskirts of a mining town, after three days of hard riding, where they settled down." He went on about the early stages of The League.

So when the last League of Overachievers member retired, we became the R B's. We decided to do things a little different than what the old guards had done. We started a co-op. We laid down laws for all of us to abide by. We saw what the old guard went through. So, for the sake of ill feelings and bloodshed, the co-op was a perfect way for us to not only survive, but for us to strive."

He continued to give the history lesson until there was a knock on the door. He went to answer it and returned with a group of men.

"Mr. Grimm Reaper, these are the Eliminators; Maul and Mace. Then we have The Gorillas in the Midst; Murder, Mystery and Mayhem. They have your other tributes from The Ones and will introduce themselves shortly. Collectively, we refer to them as The Grim Reapers. Gentlemen, lets get down to business." instructed Grim Reaper.

First was Mace. He approached his new boss by kissing his hand then handing him a briefcase. The contents were a couple kilos of heroin. As Mace closed the briefcase he spoke, "My name is Mace. I have a special infinity for getting up close and personal with my victims. Which normally would be women. I lack apathy and I sleep very well whenI go to sleep. I believe that bludgeoning is as primal as it gets. Plus, in our business, we have to be 100% certain that the victim is offline, forever." He left the briefcase and took his seat.

Next was Maul. His briefcase contained crystal meth. "I am Maul. I too like to get close to my victims. There is no greater feeling like the last pulverizing smash of my tools of the trade. Along with my brother, we have been successful on every one of our kills. That's why we are called The Eliminators." Leaving his briefcase, he took his seat.

Murder approached next with a cache' of firearms, ammunition and clips. "My name is Murder and that says it all. I'm your marksman. Trained by the very best that this region has ever known. I prefer long range targets because one has to be accurate within millimeters. My targets never know what hit 'em."

When Mystery approached he had two brief cases. One held marijuana and the other held pills of every illegal market. "Sir Grimm. My name is Mystery. I am the one that goes in and get the snitches and stool pigeons before they talk or talk too much. My tools of choice are knives and poison. I figure, if they wanna talk to someone, why not talk to me."

Mayhem approached with a briefcase of cocaine. "I'm Mayhem. I'm the longest tenured of the group. I specialize in garrotes. Although, my method is a little messy, it has its advantages. And on behalf of us all. We are proud to be Grim's Reapers. Sir, we will follow your lead until the death as we have your predecessor. All of us are blooded in and will be blooded out."

After he took his seat, Grim Reaper handed each man a pair of red gloves. "We don't do the old finger pricking thing no more. Please put on your gloves, gentlemen. And Mr. Grimm please follow me. He went to every man and shook his red gloved hands. When he finished, Grim Reaper took the gloves. He put them in a canister and set them on fire. As the smoke filled the air, he said, "If anyone here betrays his oath, may his life, memory and spirit be like these burning gloves. Just smoke in the wind." He took the burning canister and set it out on the patio.

And just like that, it was done. They sat around getting acquainted and eating. After dinner, he stood up and he raised his glass to make a toast. "To Grimm's Reapers, may we fulfill our destinies together." This was the things of legend and it was happening to him. He knew the work that he had put in over the years but he also felt that sooner or later some things would come to a head. Traditionally, when a One was replaced, it would be by a Second. He wasn't a Second, because when he went to prison he had to release his rank. That was the law of The League. No one could hold any rank or status while doing a stretch. A One had to be in the stream of life. Doing business behind bars was always bad for business.

After a few more hours had passed, the party broke up. "You know I hand picked you because of your loyalty and the others agreed. We knew that you were the most qualified to replace me."

"I thank you for your confidence in me and I won't let you or the other Ones down. Sir, I appreciate all of your help over the years especially when I was down. I tried to be like my father, but when he made it a point that he wouldn't open the doors of success for me, I had to sink or swim. Man, I was so angry with him. I always thought that a father would be proud to have his son follow the paths that he lead. But you took a chance on me and I didn't see that coming. You took me under your wings and made a way for me. When I had my first kid, I wanted to name him after you because of the influence that you had in my life. But I also knew that that would bring unwanted attention to us. So when I had my second son, I gave him your name to show my respect for you. Another thing, I never imagined that I would be sitting here as a One. Never."

As Grim listened he thought about some conversations that he had had with the other Ones when Jr was first sentenced. He decided not to share those conversations with him at least not right now. He also knew that eventually Grimm would find out one way or the other.

"Look, I gotta get out of here. My wife will be beside herself although I told her that I would be out late. Get some rest because tomorrow we go to work." "Well, I guess I'll leave with you. You can drop me off at home, if you don't mind." "Why would I mind, you are at home." "But this is your house." "It *was* my house but I am no longer a One." Grim reached in his pocket and handed him two sets of keys. "The cars are in the garage. Keep 'em if you want or trade 'em in. I'll see you in the morning." He walked the aging gangster to his car. As Grim left, he reflected on how many times he had accompanied Grim as his driver back in the day.

As the taillights faded into the darkness he went back inside. He had been here gazillions of times but now it was his. He locked up and set the alarms then he went to the bedroom. On the bed was the deed to the house and the land. Dumbstruck, he sat on the bed and began to laugh hysterically. Then in a moment of clarity he rushed downstairs and began to bring the envelops and briefcases upstairs. He put the cases in the closet and the money in the drawers. It had been years since he had this much stuff at his disposal. It was almost frightening. As a matter-of-fact, it was because he was protecting his stuff that landed him in jail. Soon he jumped in the bed and went to sleep.

He was awaken by a crook in his neck. As he sat up, he looked at the giant clock that was on the wall. It was close to noon. He picked up his phone and noticed that he had missed a couple of calls. He pressed one of the numbers and waited for an answer. "Good morning son." "Hey ma. Whats up?" "Just hadn't heard from you in a few days. Hows everything?" They talked for a little while before hanging up. He had agreed to come by soon for dinner. One thing he hated doing was lying to his folks. He made coffee and jumped in the shower. Soon he was dressed and waiting for his mentor to arrive.

Within the next hour his doorbell finally rang. Two men entered and they greeted one another. Sitting at the table the three men began to talk over coffee. "I have briefed Second. In light of everything, I felt that it was best that the three of us sat down and talked it out once and for all. In the history of our business this is only the second time that a second was passed over. Our forefathers paid a steep price for that one. It almost destroyed the business and friendship. So what I propose today is two things.

First, Second although we have placed Grimm in my seat. You have an option to head your own family. If you choose this, you will be over the gambling operations. All of the Ones agreed to turn over the operation to you.

Your other option is to maintain your status as Second to Grimm in his Grimm's Reapers family. You know my operation better than I do. We understand the nature of the beast, but these are the only beneficial options for all involved." Second sat back and took a drag on his blunt. "Let me think for a minute." "You got fifteen minutes." said Grim and the other two men walked to the study.

In the study, they sat in silence. One thing history had taught them was never to believe that you knew everything that's inside of a person's head. In less than the time allotted, he walked into the study and sat down. "At first, I thought that it was a bunch of bullshiggity that all the work I had put in for the family I would be rewarded one day to sit at the table of Ones. I mean, we the ones really putting in the work. We out there doing all the diabolical shiggity that only a few men could do. And then to be passed over, was like wow. Grim, we out there like them cats in The Wire. Not like the Sopranos or that Boardwalk Empire jazz. We down in the gutter, cutting and clawing to keep the family business afloat. Grimm, I'm like Avon Barksdale and you like Stringer Bell. I like getting after them cats who think that they Omar or Marlo."

"I decline to be over the gambling outfit. I'll stick to what I know and that's being a gangsta. As a One you have to hide in public, but as a gangsta everyone knows that you are what you are." He stood up and opened his arms. Grimm stood and the two men embraced. "Sir Grimm Reaper, I humbly submit my life to being one of Grimm's Reapers. He was given a pair of red gloves and went through the ritual. Grim watched his men carry on like times of old.

As he was thinking this, Grimm said. "Do you guys remember when we went to see the Griffeys when they came to town. Sir, you showed us way back then what a father and son duo could do together. The Kid played on the same team with his Old Man and we got to see that first hand. Now I really know what that feels like." "Knock it off. We got places to go and people to see." Grim responded.

The men took a short drive to the lawyers office. When they went in, they were immediately taken to a conference room. Esquire stood to greet them. Each man took a seat and the meeting began. "It comes to my attention that a friend of yours won a lottery a few years back. That friend has passed away and left you some land and money. As your lawyer I took the liberty to read over all of the necessary documents. All you need to do now is sign where there is an x." Grimm looked at Grim and he nodded his approval.

After glancing over the legal documents, he signed the papers. "Now you own everything on that property. It'll take the standard amount of time for everything to be transferred over to you. But as of this moment, you are as right as rain." Grim showed Grimm and Second to the door and closed the door to the conference room behind him. Silently they waited for the man to emerge. When the door opened, the two elderly men came out laughing. The three men left to take care of some other business before returning to the estate.

Before leaving, Grim stood in the hallway looking it over and taking some lasting memories with him. Although he always passed it off as a 'timeshare' to his family and friends it was way more than that to him. He spent the better part of four decades with the keys to the palatial Reaperland as he had nicknamed it. The only keepsake he wanted was his statue of the grim reaper with the death sword.

As Grimm walked the two men to the car, he noticed a tear well up in Grim's eye. Looking at his protege's, Grim spoke. "I never wanted this for either one of you. But we deal with the hand that we are dealt." Before he continue he stopped to fight back the tears. He reached out and hugged both men before getting into the car. Without saying a word the two men hugged each other.

Now it was his time and his turn to shine. He wished that somehow, someway he could have followed the footsteps of his father. He looked up in the sky and watched the birds fly overhead and felt the wind blow on his face. Before he made it to his door a car pulled up. It was the lieutenant. Putting the car in park he got out.

Grimm knew that this was bound to happen but he didn't think that it would be this fast. He bid Lieutenant to follow him inside. The men greeted one another before they went into the study. They made some small talk before getting down to business. "Before we began I must make a sweep of the place." He went out to his car and returned with his electronic sweeper. He covered every nook and cranny of the estate. When he was thoroughly satisfied that there wasn't any bugs or any other electronic devices, he packed up his stuff and returned it to his car.

This time he came back with a small briefcase. "Care for a drink or something?" "Maybe another time. This is official business so lets get to business. Inside of this case is a devise that debilitate sound waves. It not only scrambles, but it has the capacity to destroy the source. Although I didn't detect any thing, one can never be too sure. Every day when you get up, before you turn off your alarms, flip this switch and it'll send a pulse throughout the place. When the green light comes on it will start to blink. Once it goes solid green you can turn it off. Just in case you forget to cut it off, it has a smart switch and will shut down after a minute. So tomorrow cut it off, then the next day allow it to shutdown on its own. I'll be waiting your call to know that everything works perfectly." He demonstrated the device with Grimm. He was very impressed with the gadget. The men shook hands and Lieutenant left. He closed the briefcase and took it upstairs to his room. "Another f'n briefcase." he cursed under his voice. He called Grim but he didn't answer.

After a couple of hours, Grim returned his call. He told him everything that had transpired from the visit. "Good, that means that you are transitioning well. When he comes back, have something for him. It will be his squad that will be patrolling *your* neck of the woods. Make sure that its enough for the nestlings as well. They the ones that you'll be seeing. This was his way of introducing himself. One egg a month on the eight of the month will be picked up and taken to the farmer's market. The farmer will do the rest. Gotta go, I'll see you in a couple of weeks. Takin' a vacation with the wife. This will be a good time for you to get together with the guys. But if I were you, I'd go do some normal stuff, first. If you know what I mean." Grim hung up.

For the next year everything went smooth. His transition was coming to a close and he wanted to have a gathering with the entire league. When he talked it over with Grim, Grim shared something very important with him. "We learn from history and what happened in upper Appalachia. The only time that every one is in one place is if its a war. We been war less for a while now." "I get that, but that's the old way. And before you cut me down, let me say this. I have reached out to the other Ones and they thought that it would be a nice gesture. Besides, we want to unveil our new name as well."

Grim sat back in amazement at his protege's progress. In his heart he knew that he had done the right thing by picking Jr to succeed him over his own flesh and blood. He gave him his blessing and watched as he contacted each One and set up an appointment to meet with them. This too was groundbreaking, because Ones stayed out of the other regions unless it was an emergency. What Grimm was trying to do was build friendships not fences. It would be just him and his predecessor, that always was a sign of good faith. No muscle, no entourage.

The next week was built around getting out and putting the gathering together.

Finally, it was the night of the gathering. It was to be held at the Aquarium, as a black tie affair for the Aquatic Arts program that he had started. There was no way that there would be any interruptions or listening devises. They weren't worried about the local law enforcers, it was the feds that they had to stay ahead of. It was only forty of them but the dinner was held in the grand hall that held a couple of thousand. He and Thickness had worked tirelessly to make sure that this event came off without a hitch.

When they finished receiving all of their guests, the doors were closed and a couple of Reapers were posted outside as well as two by the interior door. The music played nice and softly. Many had gathered around the bar and talked. After a little while, Grimm stood in the center of the floor with his lovely companion. The gown that she wore cost a mini fortune and she could tell that all eyes were on her. And she loved it!!

"My fellow donors, we thank you all for coming out and supporting our function. We believe that this aquarium should be saved and with our help it will be. The goal is to raise awareness about the potential loss of one of our region's oldest landmarks. When we first heard that it was going to close its doors, we met with the board of directors and began to come up with a solution. Now, to tell you more, here is the director."

Director stood up among the fanfare and took his place in the middle of the floor and began to share with them about the state of the aquarium and the help that they needed to keep the doors open. He also mentioned the success of the walk at the zoo and the good that event did. After he finished, the music began again and dinner was served. While their guest ate, the couple went to each table and checked on their guest. "Why don't you two sit down and eat. Besides, it's y'all event." They took the advice and made their way to their table.

Looking at the festive faces, a calm came over him. He knew that what they were doing was potentially dangerous, but he also knew that it was important for business. As he looked around, she slid her hand under the table and rubbed his crotch. Within seconds of her touch, he was aroused. She fondled him playfully as she sucked on an ice cube. He in turn reached under the table and groped at her inner thigh. That was her hot spot. With his index finger, he drew an imaginary line towards her innards, stopping just short of the area desired.

She looked over at him with a look of excitement. And without warning she thrust her pelvis forward and slammed her legs closed, trapping his hand.

After a few seconds, she let his hand go. With both of their hands in front of them, they finished eating.

As dinner wound down, the lights dimmed and the music was soft and slow. He took her by the hand and lead her to the dance floor. Pulling her as close to him as humanly possible, they swayed to the melody of the music. They instantly became oblivious to their surroundings. It was one of the few times in the last year that he was honestly able to relax. Their intimate presence on the floor compelled other couples to join them.

When they came out of their love zone, they looked at the other couples that were enthralled around them. Instead of leaving the floor, they continued to dance. Getting back into the rhythm of the music, he looked around at his guest until his eyes settled on his mentor. For the first time he noticed just how frail the old gangster looked. Up until this point he had looked so strong. Obviously something was bothering him. When the song ended they left the floor. He made his way over to Grim. "You okay, old man?" "Yeah, young blood." "I'm about to get the others and we are going on a little tour. I'll be back in a sec."

He made his way to get the attention of the others and they prepared for the tour. Before leaving he took the mic, "Friends, we will be back in a bit. But until then, enjoy each other and you are in the hands of my beautiful hostess." He motioned for her to come and get the mic. He kissed her and joined his partners and they walked out.

Once outside of prying eyes he guided them on a silent tour. They ended up in a carnivorous underground section of the aquarium. "This my friends is why we are right here. Tonight, we end one chapter of The League and open a dawning of a new era. Grim, please come forward." When he stood next to Grimm, he put his arm around his predecessor. "On this night, we celebrate all that you have done for us. We didn't get you a watch or a rocking chair but we got you something that you can use." He handed him an envelop. They urged him to open it and he obliged.

He pulled out a card and had a puzzled look on his face. "That's the new way of payment. You have an account set up at this financial institution in a retirement fund. Every month, there will be monies deposited into this account." The old guy just hugged and shook their hands. "I'm the last of my breed. Only one other breed member is still alive and he may as well be dead because of his physical and mental state. When I made the decision not to have him 'extinguished' from fear of him psycho-babbling, I knew that it was a risk.

Before we became gangstas we were family. But had I ever thought that he would've compromised our thing, it would have been curtains for him. One year ago, I broke tradition with choosing my successor. And yes, there were grumbles, but as you can see, we had no problems. That in itself is a blessing. To be able to walk out of our thing alive is also a blessing. And I can truly say that I hardly miss the mental toughness that it requires." He stopped and said no more.

"Now that that is done, lets get to the next order of business. We retire the League of the Rare Breed and embark on the new world order of the League of the Horsemen of the Apocalypse. And our final piece of business is," he motioned for Second to come to him. "As the head of Grimm's Reapers we will refer to you as Ghost." Ghost smiled and shouted, "We them boys! The hell with forty acres and a mule! Let the ride of The Horsemen began!" Grimm and the others put their hands out and stacked them as a sign of solidarity. "Let's get back, oh yeah by the way of business, this area that we stand in will be an exhibit donated by the men in this room. As donors you will have fringe' benefits unlike any other." They walked back in silence just as they came.

The fundraiser raged on for hours. Seeing that it was very late, Grim and his date made their way over to Grimm. "Gotta go, I enjoyed the evening. This night I will treasure forever. But before I go I need to share something with you. I am not only retiring from this life, but I am retiring as the church's maintenance supervisor and they are giving me a banquet next month. I want you and your fox to be there with me. And there is one other order of business that I need taken care of." He handed Grimm an envelop. Ghost asked his father, "You ready to go, pop? I'll get Maul or Mace to drive you home. I can't leave the boss man by himself even though we are among 'friends'." "No, you take them and have Mayhem to cover for you." directed Grimm.

When Mayhem came over Grim patted him on the shoulder. Grimm opened the envelop and it was a picture of Grim's longtime girlfriend and date for the evening. "Follow me." They went to the other end of the room toward the kitchen. "Here, you take care of this personally. It has an expiration date on it." "This is what we do. Nothing personal, strictly business."

Making their way back to the festivities, Thickness reached out to him. He took her hand and held it tight. He knew that he would have to do something with her very soon. She was too hot and he didn't want to lose her and he definitely didn't want her harmed. That was the fate of Grim's longtime companion. She wasn't married to him so she could be touched. Besides that, he was wrapping up all of his loose ends so that he could retire in peace. She was just a liability to him although she had never shown any signs of being anything but loyal to Grim.

Regretting that he had even opened the envelop now instead of later he had to deal with it. "Come here, gorgeous." He pulled Thickness to him and planted a kiss for the ages on her! She was shocked and amazed at the sincerity of his kiss. "Let's party!! Everybody grab a glass and a body!" The music pumped and the revelry raged on into the early morning. By the time it was over, everyone was pooped and ready to go home. "Now that's how you throw a party, thank you baby. I couldn't have done it without you." He looked lovingly in her eyes as he reached into his pocket.

In the limo, he handed her a clip of cash. "This is for all of your hard work, and there is enough to give to your sister for recommending you. You really ought to think about turning this hobby into something for real. I got your back." She leaned forward and hit the button to raise the black panel to cover the widow behind the driver. After all these hours, she still looked incredible and she had never taken off her heels. He pulled the top of her dress down for her breast to pop out. He loved that and she knew.

They made love all the way home. When the car finally stopped and the motor was off, he hit the intercom. "Go ahead, Ghost. We gonna be here a minute." After the door closed he hit the locks and went back to work on his girl.

CHAPTER 33
Decisions, Decisions, Decisions

The basketball season was coming to a close and Local University was back in the finals for the third straight year. If they succeeded, they would be the first team to three-peat in their conference. But for Superstar, this championship would truly be special. This was the first year that she would be playing side by side with her baby sister. Baby Sister, had come a long way since she had her debilitating accident at the church picnic. Now she was standing side by side with her sister warming up for the big game. Warm ups had concluded when the coach called them to mid-court.

"Ladies, I have some big news for you all. I was going to share this with you earlier this season but I decided to wait until the most important game of the season to do so. Let's just call it a little motivation. Okay? Tonight, as well as for the most part of the year, there will be pro scouts in attendance. The difference is that they ain't from just big schools, there will be some from the new woman's league. That's why this week's practices were lighter than usual. I didn't want any of you to get hurt and miss out on a potential chance for major success. Well since I have gone this far, I will tell you everything. The basketball program is going to be disbanded next year if not earlier, men and women. The decision was made late last night and I have rarely kept important things from you, collectively or individually. No matter the outcome, the announcement will be made tomorrow. Since, I have shared that with you, there will be no phone privileges because if that got out all hell will break out. The doors will be open in an hour, so get your game faces on and get ready for the dawning of a new day!" The girls all sat down on the floor and were silent. This was a lot of information for them to process.

Captain shouted as she stood to her feet,"All of us here are on scholarship! Not one of us is a walk on! Where they do that at? At LU. We play multiple positions? Where they do that at? At LU! That's where we do that at! We them girls! Come on, rock with me! Bounce with me! We them girls!" They were up and doing their patented team bounce. She knew how to get them fired up. Coachette went into her office and closed the door. She had been the head coach for a long time and this group of girls were special. She knew so much about them and they were like her own daughters. Now this was coming to a close.

She picked up the phone to make a call when there was a knock on her window. "No phones, until after the game." Teased the girls as they made their way to the locker room. She put her phone down and waved them off. "Those are my girls. They them girls. Lord, what ever the outcome, please give us grace to remain ladies. Amen." Coachette sat in her office until it was almost time for the doors to be opened. Her tradition was not to let her girls hit the floor for warm ups until a half hour before tip off. The time leading up to that was used for going over last minute details and adjustments. Championship games were just another game, except there's a title on the line. That was her philosophy. She allowed them to figure it out and that put as little pressure on them as possible. Either way, they would be okay. That she knew for sure. She had never been around a group of girls that had the others best interest at heart.

It was incredible to watch them go from worse to first and it all started with love. They all seemed to love the game for what it was and less for what it shouldn't be. It was like they had fallen under a spell of maturity overnight. At one time, teams had them marked as an easy win but time turned that around. Then they were the hunters and not the hunted!

As game time neared, she went to the locker room to address the team. When she walked in, they were huddled around the radio listening intently. She looked at one of the trainers and the trainer came over to her. She explained to her what was going on. Some one had leaked the basketball programs cancellation to the media and a fire storm was brewing. "On the court in five minutes, girls." she called out to them before returning to her office. She began to curse social media and longed for the good old days when info took time to leak out. Now a days, everything processed so fast.

With the knowledge that it was going to be their last game as a team, they huddled up and began to pray. Not for a dumb title but that God would allow them to grow stronger in Him regardless to the outcome of the game. One of the girls spoke softly, "Let's do it again. They say that the third time is the charm. Because we them girls, lets put that theory to the test. Where they do that at? At LU! I can't hear you. Where they do they at! At LU, that's where we do that at!" They chanted and began to jog out to the gym.

The coaching staff was already on the bench when they came out for warm ups. Each girl thinking about one thing and one thing only, success. They could think about whatever else later. But the next forty minutes was going to be crucial.

Once the warm up was over, the captains met at center court and shook hands. Before they walked away the visiting captain said, "Call your girls over and I'll call mine over." They waved for their teams to come over. In a showing of solidarity, the women all hugged and shook hands. "May the best team win."

After that, they went back to their benches and removed their warm up suits. Coachette gave them their last second adjustments and waited for the lights to dim. The lights dimmed and the P A announcer began to call out the rosters. This got both teams hyped. Once that was done, it was time for the tip off and the game was finally underway. The last minute adjustments seemed to pay off early and it looked like LU was on their way to a comfortable lead. But then something strange happened, the lights began to flicker causing the referee to halt play.

After five minutes, the referee told each bench they could do light warm ups to keep loose. It took fifteen minutes to get the technical difficulties to be rectified. Each team did their best to stay loose before play resumed. LU had more riding on this game than their opponents did.

When play finally resumed, both teams came out swinging. They played tough and the refs allowed them to grind it out, only calling fouls that were well deserved. The crowd was rowdy and into the game. When halftime came, they went into the locker rooms tied. In both locker rooms, each team pretty much talked about the same things. Before they realized, it was time to head back to the court. Each time did their warm ups before it was time to return to center court. LU knew that whatever the outcome, this was it and the only thing standing in front of them was a team that had a future. Before breaking the huddle, Coachette did something that surprised all of her girls. Calling the young ladies in very close, she did the throat slashing motion and said, "Get blood." The way that she said it sent shivers up their spines. This was a far cry from her normal, "Always remember that you are a lady first and a baller second."

This time, there wasn't handshakes and mushy gestures. All those who were involved knew that this was for all the marbles. Even the crowd sensed that this was going to be a good one. Someone compared this half of basketball to Ali-Frazier. Another compared it to the Coliseum in Rome when the wild animals were turned loose on the humans that were condemned to death. And they played on as if they were listening to what was being said in the stands.

With three minutes left, LU called one of its last two timeouts with a one point lead and Superstar heading to the free throw line. "It don't matter what we win by, as long as we win." Coachette made one defensive move and sent her girls back out for the kill. "It took all of this to happen for her to finally act like what she used to be, ha. My uncle always talked about how she was a stone cold killa." Superstar headed to the free throw line and sank the first shot. Before she took the second shot the other team called a time out. As their captain walked past she said, "We ain't gonna be a goddamn footnote." Going back to their huddle, Superstar told them what she was just told and they knew that they had them on the ropes.

Before taking the shot, she leaned over to her adversary and said, "Not a footnote but footnotes." And like she had done over her career, she sank the free throw. Back peddling on defense, she pointed to her tattoo on the inside of her forearm that read 'ICE WATER'. Their opponents were doomed and within minutes the buzzer rang and it was *curtains* for another fallen foe. The arena went nuts and they mobbed each other. Soon the crowd poured onto the floor.

That's when they began to see their family and friends. One of the main reasons for Coachette to keep her team in the locker room late was she didn't want her team looking in the stands and getting disappointed if they didn't see certain family or friends. Well, that all ended today. They were champions again and no one could take that away from them.

In this region, they had turned the landscape of basketball upside down with their penchant for excellence and executions. But, even that could not stop the ax from falling on an albeit recent turn around in team success.

As the crowd was pushed back, the two teams sought one another out and shook hands. The commissioner of the region came to center court with the championship trophy to present to the victorious team. The team stood around him as he congratulated them and presented the coach and captain with the trophy. This was big for them because this was being televised on a broader scale than it had ever been before.

The side line reporter made her way to the team and held an interview with them. Coachette choose the whole team as MVP. "Not being cliche'd, every one of my girls went above and beyond their respective positions. I could never have had a bunch of sisters to play for one another like they have over the past three years.." As she was edifying her team, the reporter cut her off, "Coach, how do you feel about the future of sports here?" "My girls are champions and that's what's important here. Now, here is our captain and co captain." She stepped away so the team could get some well deserved airtime. She was also pissed that someone would take the focus off of her girls regarding a situation that none of them had any control over.

When the interview was over, their family and friends bombarded them with congratulations. They didn't let the big game atmosphere bother them. Superstar was greeted by her guy as she was hoisting the championship over her head. When she saw him she passed it on and jumped into his arms He held her close and kissed her on her sweaty forehead. Although he was the captain of a rival school's team, they were still a pair. They supported each other very well, except if their respective schools were waging battle against one another.

After cutting down the nets from the baskets, the team took it over to Coachette and presented one to her. The other, they would divide among themselves. This way everyone was to get a piece of history. That would be done when they got back to the locker room. And finally, they were making their way to the locker room and the cameras were still flashing as they whooped it up.

When they were in the locker room, there was a group of people with credential id's draped from their necks waiting for them. The team settled down as Coachette spoke, "My sisters, I would like you all to meet some of *my* friends. In a minute I'll introduce them to you. When I first was informed of the closing of the program, I reached out to some of them and they agreed to look at you all. As you know, the woman's pro league is expanding this year. The draft isn't the only big deal but they are adding a developmental league also. Each one of you are in a good position for success. We know that the papers have Captain and Co Captain ranked high in the top twenty. I wouldn't allow any scouts in the locker room because I wanted to do something special for my girls. No they ain't scouts, they are agents. And very successful agents at that. They are going to met each and every one of you and evaluate your future in basketball. I trust them because they are my friends and I believe that they will have *your* best interests at heart."

She began to introduce the three agents. Agent 1 was a heavyweight in the industry and dealt with 'the prima donnas in training' as she called her clients. Agent 2 was a lawyer turned agent and was well known for taking on mid-level talent and pitching the prospect of future returns from his clients. And Agent 3 was from the developmental league and was regarded as one of the all around best in her profession. They talked and set appointments for all of the teammates. "Thank the agents for coming out and get dressed so you all can go out there a celebrate with your well wishers."

Before they left the locker room, the captains thanked them and asked if they would stay for a second more. Forming a circle, every one in the locker room held hands and, Captain began to pray. She blessed God for not only victory on the court but also for being victorious in life. She also thanked him for a new beginning for all. When her prayer was over, the agents and coach left the girls alone.

Going back to her office, the agents decided to stick around for a while to observe how the girls handled themselves off court. They sat in her office and made small talk about the game and how the girls played with such veracity. "Look, you been my girl for ages, I have never seen you allow your team, any of your teams, to attack like the way them girls did tonight. And if my mind wasn't playing tricks on me, I swear I saw you give the slaughter sign." "Well, you all know me well. We didn't have any cause for settling for second best and besides that, it felt good to be able to really coach the way that best suits me. Even if it was for one night." They laughed as she poured each of them a drink.

As the victors prepared to leave the locker room, they hugged because they knew that this was an end of an era. The captains opened the doors and for the final time lead their team out to the court. The closer they got to the arena, the louder the noise became. They stopped by Coachette's and tapped on the door. Usually, it was the other way around. She opened her door and they shoved the trophy in her ample bosom. She took the trophy and lead her team into the arena.

They were happy to see the sea of people still in the arena, partying like it was 1999! They were mobbed and the music blared loud and hard. And to their surprise, their victims were still there. Their Rival Captain asked them, "Who turns down a good party? Not these girls. We them girls, ha." They hugged and laughed with one another before dispersing among the crowd.

Baby Girl, Girlfriend, Pastor, First Lady and Sr Deacon were still in the stands as the sisters made their way to them. They were showered with flowers and candy from their love ones. "We are so proud of both of you. You both did so well." "Them my girls." Baby Girl proudly proclaimed. The two girls were equally proud of their mom as well. With the help from her supporters, she had reached a new level of sobriety and he even rejoined the praise ministry!

They surrounded the two and the girls began to cry. The show of support was overwhelming. They embraced each other and the others joined in on the group hug. After a few minutes, they rejoined the celebration on the arena floor.

The festivities finally ended after a couple of hours even though the crowd was still rather large. The losing team had left already, but they did stay for a while because most of the girls on both teams knew one another. It was also refreshing that no hard feelings were left behind.

As the sisters left the arena for the last time as teammates, they met their family at the edge of the parking lot. First Lady, handed them bags and hugged them. "You two are the best and we love you so much. But the best is still yet to come." Their guys appeared and everyone left. They spent the rest of the night running a muck and just enjoying life. When the night ended they went home, thoroughly exhausted. They had decided to wait until the morning to share with their mom their good news in regard to their future.

They were awakened by the smell of bacon, eggs and pancakes. Their absolute favorites. Baby Girl was in the kitchen throwing down swaying to the music as she cooked. They walked up to her and kissed her on the cheeks. "Where the other brats?" "They over Ma Dears, we didn't know how long that we were going to be out, so we dropped them over there on the way to the arena last night."

They continued to talk as the girls set the table. They were so excited that it was hard to contain their emotions. When she sat the food before them, she knew that something was up. "Okay, out with it you two." "Mama, we have some very exciting news for you." "I ain't ready to be called Nana or granny just yet." "No it isn't anything like that." They grabbed her hands and Superstar said, "We are going pro. At least we have the prospect. We are meeting with agents next week to see just where we are slotted. And not only that, if we don't make a big league roster, there is a good chance for a team on the developmental league to pick us up. And we want you to go with us on the days that we are to meet with the agents."

Taking this information in, she didn't know how to react. Staying true to herself she sat back in her chair and whispered, "I was happy when both of you choose to stay local to help me and the kids. But when I started getting myself together I promised myself that I would never again hold any of my kids back. I even tried to reach out to y'all daddy without any success. I also wanted you all to go to college and become something other than a athlete.

My biggest fear, was when I encouraged the both of you to stay on campus. I wasn't worried about you, I was worried about me surviving and adjusting to a sober life. With y'all gone I would have to do better. Now there is a chance that both of you can become pro's. What on God's green earth did I do to deserve this?" She squeezed her daughters hands and began to pray. As they ate, they talked about some of life's curve balls, good and bad. After breakfast, they prepared for the afternoon event at the church.

"This morning when I awoke, I lay in my bed and could not go back to sleep. That's when it hit me that all things *do* work for the good of them that believe. I began to see things a lot clearer. For all of my set backs and set ups, I am still here with you all. Now that right there is a big blessing. Just imagine, my girls going pro. Where they do that at?"

Today was the day of the great celebration for one of the retiring members of the church. Baby Girl had been helping all week with the event after she got off of work. It had been built up and it was going to be a happening. No one was going to miss this. One thing the church did well was take good care of those that served the ministry well. They were known for having appreciation services for individuals as well as auxiliaries. It was the little things that helped the ministry grow as fast as it did. And when people joined, they rarely left unless they moved or passed on.

As she got dressed, Baby Girl looked at a picture of her kids. It was one of many, that she wasn't in or taking. This was one that represented her absentee in their lives. Doing her, was what she was doing and doing it well, as far as she thought. Why not let others pitch in and help her kids? She had done it for others. But now, she realized the major errors of her life. And as time passed since she had given her life back to Christ, it seemed as if He was really giving her another chance to get it right. The tears welled in her eyes and she clutched the picture and cried. She cried not in sorrow, but she cried in victory.

When they arrived at the church, people were already there and they were in a festive mood. They greeted many of them with hugs and kisses. This was going to be a fun event and they knew it. Some of his friends had special tributes and they had gotten together for one big surprise. One thing they tried to do was always to revere the grounds of the church. They tried to treat it as holy ground.

Once the event started, it was off with a bang. The lights dimmed and the guest of honor was lead in to take his seat at the table that was ornamented exquisitely. He and his wife looked at the full house and were overwhelmed with the outpouring of love for them. When they took their seats everyone applauded them. He leaned over to his wife of many decades and said, "No man is worth all of this." "Well, we have seen many others come and go, but you worked when others wouldn't. Now be quite and enjoy yourself." He took her advice and straightened up. He never liked being in the spotlight, he liked working from the shadows. Besides, this wasn't the first time they offered to do something nice for him, but he insisted that his staff was to be the recipient of any kind of appreciation.

After the dinner was served, it was time for the man of the hour to have some words. Taking his place behind the podium he cleared his throat and wiped his brow with his monogrammed handkerchief. "To all of you who have taken the time out of your busy schedule to help me and my family celebrate, I thank you from the bottom of my heart. I have seen faces that I hadn't seen in many years. One face in particular is my old friend Elder. I was here that night when his daughter talked about her dear daddy. Me and this cat go way back. But when he went down, I took it hard. To see a mighty man reduced to a shell of himself scared me. At one time, he even tried to convince me to get into politics. I told him, 'I fix things. That's all I do. Fix other peoples problems.' He never pressed me again. My brother, I have heard about your recovery and the work that you are doing for the Lord. If any one should be applauded, it should be people like him." He walked over to his old friend and hugged him. Before walking back to the podium, he held his arm high in the air. He finished with more thank yous and expressions of love for family and friends.

"Before we close. I want to personally thank you for all of your help through the years. You will be greatly missed on a daily level, but I'm sure that I will see you on some Sundays. Now lets get on with the gifts. Those that have something, please assemble to my left." Pastor directed.

About five people lined up and began to present him with gifts and words of encouragement. He received a suit, a round trip for two and some other wonderful gifts. First Lady was the last to come up. "Fixx, on behalf of all of us, we love you and before I start bawling all over the place, let me have your keys to the church and other buildings." With a look of surprise he stood up and removed the keys from the hook on his pants. "We don't want you to be tempted to unretire, so we are going to trade you those keys for these keys." She took his hand and the lights dimmed and the projector came down. In the parking lot, his pickup had an addition to it. It was a black and silver nine person pontoon with a custom hitch. The camera went over the entire boat and finally reached the back where it read, UMBEL BEGINNINGS.

He stood there in shock. Already one of few words, all he could do was hug her. As he let her go, she said, "This is the man that taught me how to hug. He never once saw me and didn't give me what belonged to me. I even call it, my hug." Overwhelmed, he let his wife approach the podium to speak on their behalf. "I know many of you are shocked to hear my husband talk this much. When I first met him, he didn't talk much and when I introduced him to family and friends, often they thought that he had a speech impediment." This caused a real heartfelt laugh throughout the assembly. She finished by thanking him for being hers for all of these years. After a little more talking, it was time to eat.

After the event was over, he went outside to check out his new boat. Checking it out up close, he knew that this was one of the high-end pontoons. It had all of the bells and whistles. He couldn't wait to get it out on the water, today! On the way back in, he saw Jr and Thickness. The men acknowledged one another with a hug. "Have the deed been done?" "Not yet, but everything is everything. Nice boat, Doc."

Within a couple of hours, the event was finally over and they were heading home with his brand new boat in tow. When they got home, he changed into something comfortable. As he sat on the bed waiting for Jr to arrive, a spider descended from the ceiling. He looked at the entire ceiling and saw no spiderwebs. Before he squished the infernal insect, he had an epiphany. Then he smashed the life out of the insect with a program for the retirement service.

"Wife, are you going to the waters with me?" "Nah, you and the guys go. I am kinda tired from the last week of running around. I'm going to have a little something before I lay it down. You know I ain't as spry as I once was. But didn't First Lady look good? Maybe, we should get with them soon. Just drop by unannounced one day." Not waiting for an answer, she walked away. As she walked past him, he patted her on her behind. Even after all of these years, the old girl still had her sexy on.

When Clean, Cook and the rest of the gang picked him up, he was ready. He just wanted to get out on the waters and test ride his beautiful vessel. As they approached the boat launch, he went into the harbor-master's office. He was sitting in a chair in his tiny office. Fixx, tapped on the bell. A lady came from behind the harbor-master's office door. "Mister, could you not ring my bell when you can clearly see there is someone here to help you." He smiled defiantly at her and rang the bell again. "Harbor-master, there is some old crazy man here that has a fetish for ringing bells that he know he shouldn't be ringing."

Harbor-master came to the counter and shook the retired maintenance man's hand. "Congrats, my friend. I guess we will be seeing you a lot more now, eh?" The two men walked into his office and sat down. Secretary closed his door and turned up the radio. Within minutes, the two men were walking outside and looking at the boat.

"My God man, this how the church sending people off now? Hell, if I would have known that they had it like that, I would have stuck it out with the young 'un. I just believe in old school and traditional values and he and his wife claimed to be such visionaries. To me all they are is cult leaders who want to control every thing. Why am I even talking about them. Besides, you knew that I would never set foot in that place again. So you do understand, right?" Fixx shook his head in agreement. They got into a golf cart and perused the docking area. When he saw a choice docking area he pointed towards it. After a few misses, he finally had a winner. On the way back to the office, they engaged in more pressing issues.

He went inside, payed the fees and thanked his buddy for looking out for him all of these years by letting him use *his* personal boat whenever he needed it. "So you got yourself a boat, huh?" Secretary asked. "It was a retirement gift from the church. Come on and check it out." "You mean with all of them out there? Are you crazy? How many years/decades we been hiding this thing of ours? Come back and get me when the boys are gone." She kissed him on the cheek and switched out the door. "Boss, I'm going to lunch. Be back in a hour or so." Standing there, he thought about how well he had taught her. After a few minutes, he walked outside.

"Let's get this bad girl out on the waters. What 'cha say?" he said to no one in particular. They slowly let the boat down into the water. When it leveled off, he fired her up after checking all of the gauges. They got on the boat with their gear and coolers. They had to wait for Brother to park the truck before they could launch. When he finally got on board they were ready for an adventure.

Before they launched, Fixx stood up. He was handed a huge champagne bottle for the christening. "She is much to beautiful to be smashed with a bottle. I know that traditionally that's the way that it's done. But whoever confused us with being traditional? No, I won't harm her as I haven't harmed any other woman. Let's pop the cork and have a dedication toast." The men agreed and he popped the top and poured the bubbly all around. They lifted their glasses to toast. "Long live the queen of the waters, UMBEL BEGINNINGS. They toasted, drank and pulled off. He loved this bunch of guys and he knew that even more good times were ahead for them.

They cruised on the waters for a few hours before getting ready to call it a night. Personally, he was ready, because he had some other business to take care of. When they tied the boat down to the dock cleats, they headed toward the parking lot. They were full of chatter and laughter. Often reminiscing about sporting events and sporting girls. Brother was quite verbal tonight. Something he hadn't been since breaking up with Nurse.

After every one else was gone, he needed to talk to his old buddy. "You got a minute? I really need to talk." "Yeah, but I got some other things to take care of before I go in the house. It's early yet. What's good, bro." "You know, I did everything to make her happy. But nothing seemed to be good enough for her. I mean all of the bull that she let the others get away with. But with me, if I didn't agree with her, it was like it was the end of the world. I never put my hands on her, called her out of her name, nothing like that. As a matter-of-fact, I had never raised my voice to her," Brother lit up a cigarette and offered the old man one. "She claims that I stopped talking to her for a little while and she didn't know where I stood in the relationship. I admit, when she told me about how she ran into her abuser and had the gumption to hold a conversation with him, I was livid. Here it is, I am being the best to her, but she has no problem catching up with some one who put her in harms way." As he listened to his story, he felt bad for the guy. He could tell that his heart was really broken. "What should I do? I miss her so much. The last time we were together, I wanted her to know just how much she hurt me. I was so pissed that I wanted to throw her into the water."

"Look, go home and we'll get up tomorrow. We'll sort this thing out, together." He walked Brother to his car and he jumped into his truck and sped off. On the way to get her, he thought about what he was going to do. As he pulled into the parking lot, he didn't see her car. Sitting for a moment, he thought to leave, but he decided against it. She was always a woman of her word and she was patient with him. Besides, she had been his other woman far longer than he could remember.

Lost in thought, he didn't even see her approach from the passenger side. When she tapped on the window it startled him. This retirement thing really had him on edge. She slid in and kissed him. "Let's go. I'm ready to experience you on the water." She jumped out in excitement. They held hands as they walked to the new water vessel. Ordinarily, they would get a golf cart, but he wanted to cherish this moment. He watched as the light of the moon hit her always well quaffed silver hair.

When they reached the vessel, he helped her aboard. "Before we pull off, I have something for you." she said reaching in her bag. She handed him the keys to her place and cars. "You been real good to me. And I know that all I ever was to you was your squeeze. Not your main squeeze, but your T and A. I have been a fool for you for a very long time. Even though I ain't a spring chicken, I could probably do a little better. You know what I mean? When you call, I come running no matter what time of day. I have given you the best days of my life and now I want some of these days for me."

He started the boat up and began to ease it out of the harbor. She slid a CD in and they listened to K'Jon's, On the Ocean. She stood behind him as he piloted the vessel at a moderate speed. When they got a good distance, he shut off the motor and they sat in silence.

Under normal circumstances, they would have been all over each other. Not this night. "I had a dream that you either killed me or had me killed. That was about a week before we attended the charity event at the aquarium. I have never been afraid of you and I still ain't. I have done for you as I am expected to do. Just tell me it was all a dream. Something in my head. Maybe, I wanted you too much. I don't know..." Before she could finish, he stood up and raised his hand to her. "As much as I love you, I love my right hand. And I would gladly give my right hand for you." She sat there in amazement. He had never raised a hand to her and he never would.

He started the boat again and they went out to the lighthouse. Out there all alone, they made love under the stars. He knew that he was making the right decision.

CHAPTER 34
A House Divided

Times around the church was a bit unusual. With the town hall meeting coming up and other activities as well. Something was amiss. The spirit surrounding the ministry was off, again. It was as if there was a lull in the atmosphere. The last couple of Sundays he had to minister very hard. A press it was indeed.

This Sunday was no exception. He called Asst. Pastor to come to his office. When he came in he stood at the door. Pastor beckoned him to sit. After all of this time, there was still a sense of uneasiness between the two men. "You're up today." He nodded his head and walked out of the office. Going down the hall to his 'tiny' office, he began to smile. As he passed some people, they noticed the strange look on his face. He hadn't been smiling much, at least in public. When he got to his office, he closed and locked his door. He began to make several phone calls. When his that was done, he began to go over his 'sermon' that he had been crafting for a time such as this.

There was still a little time before service, so Pastor, First Lady and Top Notch attended Sunday school. Occasionally, they tried to rotate between the Adults, Junior Adults and Future Adults. They believed in supporting those that stepped up and wanted to teach and help, and it seemed to work over the years. Of course, there was a glitch every once in a while. As they sat in on the Future Adults class, they watched how the teachers taught and handled the young children. The children were restless but attentive. At the end of class, the kids got a treat and prepared for the morning children service.

Children church followed. Asst. Pastor suggested this years ago and it was a success. The parents could attend their classes and morning service while the children were taught on their level. "That guy really had some good ideas. I just don't know what has come over him as of late." "Well, do you really think it was wise to give him the mic today?" "Maybe this will help us. I don't know. Let's just pray and hope for the best." "If he gets out of line, I swear I personally will pull the mic out of his hand." she laughed. Top Notch uneasily laughed with her leaders as they approached the teachers. After talking with the teachers and getting their feedback, they headed to the sanctuary. On the way, they were joined by #1 and #3.

Heading inside of the sanctuary, they prepared themselves for worship. To their surprise, Asst. Pastor was already in the pulpit. Pastor had long suspended the practice of all of the leaders walking in together. It happened more times than not, but it still was better to approach the pulpit individually. They knew people had to work or things came up. For them, it was better this way.

When it was time for praise and worship, they smiled when Baby Girl took her rightful place aside Praise Leader. Although she had walked away from the position, when she came back, she came correct. She humbled herself before God, submitted herself to her call and dedicated her life to serve Him in any way possible. When she first came back, she sought out the new praise leader and they talked. In fact, they became allies, because both had similar testimonies. One time they teased that between the two of them, they had probably serviced the entire region. "You know its good to have someone around that understands your plight in life." They would often share their experiences with one another.

Today, they were going to unveil a brand new worship experience. As they went forth, Asst. Pastor grew restless. He began to mumble under his voice. Finally, it was preaching time, on que, he made his way to the podium. He cleared his throat and began, "I promise not to be before you long. We have been taught that when the anointing is gone, start taking your seat. Our pastor also shared with us about teaching and preaching. So we know that we can't preach and teach the whole bible and the people shouldn't be held hostage. So with that being said, let us go forth, amen."

He used a familiar passage of scripture about Sodom and Gomorrah and Lucifer. Midway into his sermon, he took a drastic turn there was no turning back. "Brothers and sisters, if this God that we serve is so just and loving, why did he not forgive these wretched souls for failing to live up to his expectations? Isn't He suppose to be the god of a second chance? Look at what he did to Lucifer and his followers. If he was so close to god, why couldn't his transgressions be forgiven? What exactly is love? Is his love the same when god turns his back on someone that messed up? Is god the same one that allows good people to die young and be murdered? Who is this god that we claim to know? The one and the same that people love to say that he allows the rain to fall on the just as well as the unjust. So if that's the case, why serve him at all. Does god really need your money, time, tithes and the assembling amongst yourselves? Why of course he does. Because we fall into that erroneous trap and teaching."

It was right there that the Leader's knew that something was amiss and they were caught off guard. And Asst. Pastor knew their character and played on it. He went a little further and before anyone knew it, #1 and #3 were all over him. Pastor got up and tried to separate the men. "Let him go. Evidently, you have an agenda. And since we are all here, we are going to have Town Hall right now. Everybody that is here, please remain. Committee, staff and lay members before I relieve him of his position in *this* ministry, I will allow him to voice his thoughts." Pastor looked at his wife and some of the other elders and cut them a look that was all business.

Once the murmuring subsided, he handed the mic back to the former asst pastor. "What I am and have been trying to relay to the people is that this god that we serve is a god of opportunity. When he is done with us he casts us aside and we hope to get into some heavenly place where he and his gang reside. Take Sodom and Gomorrah for instance. He wiped them out for sexual impurities. Lot's wife was turned to salt because she looked back at a god forsaken and damned land. Why is that? What does god have against same sex love and marriage. Y'all remember a little while back at one of the town halls when a group wanted to have a auxiliary to help with same sex individuals and couples? And they shot it down without so much as a second thought. That got me to thinking about, what this god is all about. He creates something then destroys it. See, at least pagan gods had a plan. You pray to them and sacrifice to them and if all was done right, then you'd reap the harvest. If you didn't, you knew what time it was. All these people wanted was pleasure. Something that *he* designed, but turned around and destroyed. Just like you have done. I thought church was a place for everybody..." "Before you go any further, this ministry has always knew where we stood as far as the same sex community is concerned. Matter-of-fact, this is what I will do. All of those that are in favor of us having a alternative lifestyle auxiliary stand up."

He watched as several congregants stood to their feet. "Since we have a nice little group here, if you can get me two men or two women that can produce a baby together within a year, then we will be open for further consideration. Now, the key is that there is no adoption or fertility help. The two men and the two women have to do it all on their own. Deal?" "That's so absurd. Do you hear what you are saying?" "That's my position as well." Pastor took the mic from him and some women jumped to their feet. He had a cordless sent out to them. "Pastor, some time back a visiting minister came in and he spoke about rat droppings in the pulpit. We knew then what he was talking about. So we decided to come clean. All of us standing plus others that don't attend this church have been sleeping with him. He had promised us a lifestyle of a first lady when he opened his church. We fell for it. All of us did. Please forgive us for not sharing what we knew."

He stood there in horror, as his well designed plan unraveled before his eyes. Top Notch stood up with the other women. When she did, he knew that he was done for sure. She reached for the mic, "Not only did he make those kind of promises, he has also been physically abusive. It was him, not your son that brutally raped and beat me that time when you came to the hotel to help me. He give Son a pill and when he passed out he did all of those horrible things to me. I was to set Son up, that way, when he revealed his plan, he would have this as leverage against you and your wife. He was going to be pastor, me first lady and Son was to be his assistant. He wanted to destroy this ministry and divide the house." As she spoke #1 and #3 attacked him, right there in the pulpit.

Pastor called on security, but one of the ladies that stood up was one of their girlfriends. The whole security squad walked out of the sanctuary. #1 and #3 roughed him up pretty good before removing him from the pulpit. They hustled him to his office and to their surprise the security squad was there, waiting. "We got it from here, you cats go back with the leaders." Two of them grabbed both of his arms as he was forced to open his office.

They allowed him to open the door and they pushed him inside. "We ain't pastor, now open that file cabinet and let's see whats what." Before he could get the key in the lock, he was violently punched in the side. "Lock the door, we ain't got but a couple of minutes." When he unlocked the file cabinet, they began to beat him unmercifully. Once they got their fill, they decided to take him out to his car. They got in his car and drove out of the lot followed by one of the them. The others stayed behind to assist with the leaders.

When service was finally over, the leaders were rushed to their office. "He has been removed from the premises. But, he left everything in his office so if you need anything its in there." They went in his office and opened up the file cabinet. There wasn't much, but there was a couple of unmarked folders. They contained everything that he had been working on to destroy the ministry. Everything was in black and white. Names, events, you name it, it was there. They marveled at how thorough he was and how patient he was. Pastor picked up a two way and radioed out. "Yeah Pastor, we got him. We had to get him out of there before things got ugly. We'll be back in a few."

"Look dude, you get a pass this time. The only reason that I won't kill you now, is the fact that my old lady was involved and people saw us remove you from the church. Other than that, you'd be dead. Let's ride." "Speaking of rides, let's get with his. I mean some real diabolical gangster shiggitty." "His whip ain't the issue. There won't be no keying, window breaking or vandalism. Get his phone and smash it then punch a few holes in the gas tank. Take his shoes and clothes and use some of that gas to burn 'em, since he like being naked and all. Run him up the broken trail a few miles and leave him there. By the time he make it back to his car it should be cold and dark. To bad we don't have any syrup or molasses to put on his nuts and stuff."

Then, as if a light went off, Security remembered that he had groceries in his car. He went over and looked in the bags. Unfortunately, he didn't have anything sugary in the bags. But in the cup holder there were a couple of packets of honey. He took them and handed to his guy. "I'll wait here for you two to come back. When you get him up there, give him one to the temple then pour the honey all over his nuts and stuff."

"I thought you said that you weren't going to kill me. I thought I had a pass." He motioned for him to undress and watched as the troubled man undressed trembling uncontrollably. When he was naked, they got in Security's car and went up the trail. When they returned, they punched holes in the gas tank, and drained the oil out of the motor. Then they headed back to the church.

At the church, most of the congregants were gone. The three men went to Pastor's office. "He okay?" "He ain't dead." And with that, the three men left the office. Pastor sat rubbing his head thinking hard. He knew something was up, but not to this degree. He called for Top Notch. When she appeared, he told her to send out a memo to the committee and leaders for an impromptu meeting in the morning. "Sir, you have a meeting with your niece tomorrow morning." "No this is more important." "Why don't you schedule the meeting for the afternoon. She is meeting some powerful people, so you need to be there with her." "Make it for noon. And by the way, thanks."

She closed the door and let him be for a while. She knew that everything that happened could in fact split the congregation in half. As he sat in his office digesting the current events, he wondered why did he not see this coming. They had picked up on his lack of commitment long ago, but shrugged it off as a person who was going through something. They prayed and fasted for him and tried to stand in the gap as well.

Unaware that he was knocking on his wife's office door, he came out of his haze when he stepped inside. "The hell with him. Let the devil have him. He seemed to have made a deal with him, so let him keep it. This time, there ain't no coming back for him. Did you see what that ungrateful bastard did out there. He had really thought this one through. Not only that, we were warned! Babe, this could be real bad..." "Stop, stop that my covering. That is no way for the leader of this ministry to react. Two things about you. One, you're a praying man. Two, you are very cerebral. And as a bonus, you got what no other man has, me! Don't worry about anything because it will take more than this little outbreak to cripple us. Watch and see. At least we know who the Judas is. A house united we stand, a house divided we will fall. We are still standing and don't forget that!"

Soon they were on their way home. When they got there, Greg met them at the door. He had chewed up a brand new pair of her pink flip flops. "What is wrong with you, crazy cat?" she yelled as she chased him. Pastor laughed at her until he got to their bedroom. One of his slippers had been massacred. He stopped laughing and joined his wife in the hunt. "Oh, it ain't funny when he mauls something of yours is it?" After a few minutes, they called off the mission. "For that bad behavior, we are going to hit him where it hurts. Cut his rations to once a day. Let's see how the old boy likes that." They agreed and looked for something to eat. Later that evening they were sitting in the living room and they began to smell something burning.

They went to the kitchen and didn't see anything except the one eye that was burning on the stove. They looked around but found nothing so they went back to the living room. A few minutes later Greg walked in and sat down. At first they couldn't put a finger on it, but there was something strange going on with the cat. When he turned around, she finally realized what it was. She tapped her leg and Greg jumped into her lap. She looked at his face and laughed. "Husband, I now know what that smell was, look." And when he looked, he too began to laugh at the cat. Greg had jumped up on the stove and burnt his whiskers! "Now that's what you get. I bet that will teach you to jump up on stuff, won't it?" The poor thing looked even funnier with long whiskers on one side and short gnarled whiskers on the other.

After they finished watching the baseball game they went for a walk. As they walked, he watched as she pushed her hair back when the wind blew it out place. Grabbing her hand he stopped her. "I am blessed to have you as my wife. If your hair hadn't grown back, I would have loved you even more. Now I gotta get used to you having long hair again. Just promise me that you'll keep that sexy widow's peak." "You are so thoughtful. I remember when you promised me that you wouldn't let your hair grow longer than mine and I thought that that was so honorable. You helped me throughout this entire ordeal and I am thankful. I guess when you stood up in front of all those people many years ago and professed your love for me, you were serious and I still believe that to this day." They kissed and continued their walk.

The next morning he woke up and got ready for the day's many activities. He called his niece to make sure that she was ready for the big day. She was so excited that she hardly could contain herself. He was really happy for his favorite niece and how her families fortune was going to change within months.

They arrived at the agents office and got on the elevator to the sixty ninth floor. At the receptionist desk the two young ladies gave their names and sat down with their boyfriends. Then they began to look at the pictures on the wall of very well known celebrities and athletes. "Soon, you guys pictures will be among those other superstars. Come on, lets pray before they call for you two." They formed a small circle and he began to pray and in the midst of the short prayer, the receptionist joined in their circle. When he finished, Receptionist said, "Around here, one can never have enough prayer. They will be calling your names soon."

Captain was called in first. Her interview went well and she was informed of her potential draft position and she was speechless. As she left Agent's office she thanked her and walked out in a daze. "Girl, what happened in there? Why you looking like that?" Before she could answer, Agent called for Superstar. She and Pastor followed Receptionist to the office. When they went in, they sat down and Agent introduced herself and they did likewise.

"My dear girl, you have really put yourself in a favorable position. As I shared with your teammate, there is a great possibility that you will go in the top seven. Possible, top three. If you take me on as your agent we will work very hard to get you the best deals, all around. But, I suggest that if you feel a need to look around, by all means do so. Your coach and I have had a wonderful working relationship and she speaks highly of all of her girls. Either way, I wish you the very best and a hall of fame career. Is there any question that you have for me?"

"No ma'am, my uncle, is like my daddy and he was a great one in his day. My mamma couldn't make it because she was nervous. But she will be with me in all of my other meetings. I tried to convince her that this was just a preliminary meeting, but she wasn't having it. I would like to proceed with you as my agent. I trust coach, she been real good to all of us." "Well, if that's what you wish, we will start working on the paperwork for you. There will be a ton of meetings, so make sure that you are dressed to kill. One of our team members will give you a tour over lunch today. Okay?" As they shook hands, she opened the door for them.

Bursting into Captain's arms, the two girls hugged and jumped up and down, not worrying about who was looking. After they calmed down, Pastor informed her that he had to get to a very important meeting. She thanked him and kissed him on the cheek as he left. Receptionist, approached them to tell them what was going on from this point. "I will be having lunch with you four and by then I will know when to have you two back. I will be ready in a few."

When her replacement came, they headed to a conference room. There was a ton of food spread out. She showed them to the washrooms and then they went in to have lunch. They fixed their plates and sat down to eat. "I will be giving you a brief history of our agency and some of the names that we have worked for over the years. And to be honest, signing here will be life changing, trust me. But for right now, lets eat." As they ate, they made small talk and just basked in the joy of just being in this place. After everyone had eaten, they watched a promo about the agency.

When they were done, the young ladies asked if they could talk with Agent again. Receptionist called Agent's office and got the okay. She escorted the girls to the office, "Can our guys come in also?" "Sure." The four proceeded into the office and the girls sat in the seats while their guys stood on their sides. Receptionist, closed the door and left. "Ma'am, we want to share something with you that we feel is very necessary." "Okay, what's up?"

The girls reached out and held each others hand and the guys sat down on the couch. "We're an item. And we sorta want to be free in who we are." Agent, sat erect in her chair and placed her hands under her chin. "I have shared with you your possible draft slot. That is the reason why you are in *this* office, today. If you go public, it will be career suicide. Personally, I don't care what a person does with their lives but professionally, when it involves *this* agency, I do. Listen to me. You are not, and I stress, not the first to come in this office and tell me that. When draft day comes and you sign that multiyear contract, you are going to see a lot of green. Not pink or rainbows, baby. Green, that's what makes the world go around. You see what happened to the one that came out that was a sure top three. Where is that person now. Crooked is not the new straight, at least where this business is concerned. Let me ask you this question. Say you come out and fall further back than anyone thought and lose all of those millions. What they gonna give you? Are they going to replace all of those zeros that you are going to lose? So far I haven't heard about any athletes making that kind of scratch being elected to be the grand marshal. And as for endorsements, kiss all of that goodbye. We are just getting into the age where by-racial couples are featured in commercials in prime time. As your agent, get a big contract first then get a big dumb mansion and all four of you move in and keep the illusion going. Then after you sign your second contract, by all means do whatever you want to do. But I advise that you pay attention to history and history shows its better to come out after your career is over. That's just food for thought. If there isn't anything else, I have to get back to making a living." She buzzed and Receptionist knocked on the door then opened it. The four left the office and followed her to the front desk.

She handed them business cards with their next appointment times written on them. They thanked her and left. On the way out, they looked around at what could possibly be their new world. They were excited for the chance and didn't want to blow it.

Sitting in the car before they pulled off, they watched as one very famous face got out of a black Bentley Phantom. They saw the writing on the wall and decided that their families and futures were more important than anything else. "Let's go. If we kept it a secret this long, let's go a little while longer."

CHAPTER 35
Church Folks-There They Go!

Grimm sat on the deck of his boat as the boat drifted aimlessly on the open water. He had a lot on his mind and he knew that some major decisions had to be made. He was finally going to see his twins and he was a nervous wreck. No one had heard from their mother. When he went in she severed all ties with his family, dropping an occasional letter but never a picture. One day she just disappeared. The years of not knowing weighed heavy on him. But he rejoiced in believing that they were alive and well and kept him going. Since the time of his release, he had done everything in his power to find them. The last time that he held them, they were very small. It had been that long.

Soon it was time for him to head back. As he approached the dock, he saw a familiar face waiting on him. Thickness waved at him as he docked. As he tied the vessel down, she rubbed his back. "I came because I know that this is important to you. So what's important to you is important to me." Kissing her, "Thanks for being here for me. As a king once said, 'What is it that you want, up to half my kingdom, mt queen?' That Esther must have been some kind of fine, huh? Half a kingdom. If that monkey is that good, I don't want it." They laughed and as they walked to their cars she said, "As good as *this* is, I want at least half." She got into her car and followed him to the designated meeting place.

When they parked, he came over to her car and leaned in for a kiss. "Look, I'm going to go in and get a table. I'll be watching you, I know you want me by your side, but babe, you haven't seen your kids for fifteen almost sixteen years. I can meet them later, right now its all about you getting back in their lives." She got out and went inside of the restaurant. He went back to his car and sat on the hood. They were due to arrive shortly. He began to sweat and he hated when he did that. He remembered when his daddy found out when he was younger that he was trying to avoid sweating and his daddy told him, "Son, if you don't sweat your body will shut down." That scared the hell out of him, but he still refused to sweat if he could control it.

In the midst of his flashback a car pulled slowly past him. By the time his vision cleared, the car had passed by him. After the car parked, the occupants got out and they started walking towards the restaurant's door. He made his way toward them before they reached the entrance. For the first time in nearly a decade in a half, he and his estranged wife stood face to face. All four stood in silence as if the entire world around them had stopped. Without saying a word his children embraced him. He kissed both of them on their foreheads and wiped away some of their tears as they were overcome with emotions. Even Estranged was caught up in the moment, although she dared not to interfere in such a display of raw emotions. All he could say was, "Hollywood couldn't have scripted this any better." He opened the door for them and they went inside to be seated.

The first face that he saw was that of Thickness. She shot him a wink and he shot one back as she watched them being seated. She knew what he really did for a living but she didn't care. He was her knight in shining armor. But when she really got a look at Estranged, she felt a little inferior. Trying to shake herself free, she mumbled, "Hell, if I get half, she gotta get at least three quarters." She continued to nibble at her salad as she watched him interact with his family. That's when she decided that it was best for her to finish her meal and go. As she paid for her meal, she text him to let him know that she was leaving. She knew that he was in good hands. Leaving out of the door, she just had to take one more look at the beautiful woman with the well quaffed hair.

As the family ate, for a brief moment in time, this felt real. For about two point two seconds this was his world. Then he realized that his real life had walked out of the door. He started to get up but thought better of it. He needed to let his twins know that he was serious about starting a true relationship with them. They continued to eat and get reacquainted over the next hour. At first, the parents had agreed to only one hour for this initial meeting. Estranged was concerned for the welfare of her children. She had always told them that he was imprisoned, because one day he would be a free man. "I couldn't tell them that you were dead because if you came back into their lives, I would have to explain to them why their daddy is either a ghost or has risen from the dead. So I told them the truth. We are going to the fair. If you want to tag along its fine with me. The kids seem to like you." He called for the waiter to bring the bill so that they could leave. "Let me make a call and I'll meet you in the parking lot."

He called Thickness and told her about the opportunity to spend even more time with his kids and she could tell from his voice that he was excited. "Enjoy. I'll see you when you get home. Kisses." As she hung up she lay her head back on the sofa and imagined him and her with their own family and how nice that would be.

He walked up to Estranged and said, "I'll follow you." "No. I want to talk to you away from them so our son is going to drive him and his sister. He knows where it is. It's been one of our family traditions since they were very small." He looked deep into her eyes and all the contempt that he had for her subsided. "Now I realize what you did by staying away. It wasn't to hurt me but to protect them. I didn't see it like that before, my hatred for you was as deep as it could get. First, my freedom was taken..." "No, that's where you're wrong. Your freedom wasn't taken away from you. You gave it away. So stop and for once blaming me and everyone else for your shortcomings. It took me years to come to this place of security."

They got into his car and headed toward the fair. The fair was a state event that was always huge for the three weeks that it was set up. Every day there were surprise shows by major stars as well as local up and comers. No names were ever given because the founders learned that the element of surprise was rewarding. The only thing announced was the time and date. There was no ticket sales so this made it even easier to promote.

"I wonder who is going to be the surprise today. We have seen actors, recording stars, athletes and the whole nine. The kids have even taken some pictures with a few of them. Well, enough of this. Let's talk. Let us clear all of the air between us. I will go first." Clearing her throat she began. "I hated you for years because of your poor decisions in life that affected us. When I found out that you were sleeping around I found it in my heart to forgive you. But when you turned your back on the church I felt that you were trying to send us both to hell. I remember telling the devil, 'You can have him but you can't have me or my mind. And then when the twins were born, and when you did get them, you walked around like everything was all good. How could you be so callous? I loved you and everyone knew it. When you asked for my hand in marriage, my daddy gave you his blessing. I thought that you were finally coming around. But man was I wrong. You stood in front of close to two hundred people and told the biggest lie of your life when you said 'I do' on our wedding day. How long did it take for you to prove me wrong? Less than a year, that's how long it took. Then to rub it in my face at the reunion you showed up with her and our kids as if it was nothing. Look what you left me for. You wouldn't divorce me but you didn't want to be at home either. After a while I got it, the light bulb finally came on and I came to the realization that we were unreparable, not irreparable We were too fractured. I worked, cleaned, went to school and gave it to you as many times that you wanted it. But you were never satisfied. The church hoe is who you left me for. With all

213

of her baby daddies and kids, you mean to tell me that you couldn't have done better? Then as if that wasn't bad enough, you get busted and she turned on you to save her own skin. I remember your trial as if it was yesterday. The look on your face when she took the stand against you."

He started to interrupt but she held up her finger to stop him. "I'm not finished. If I stop now I will never get this off of my chest. Looking back now, it was hard watching you self destruct. When you was given that time, I knew that we were done. So after five years I filed for divorce as an abandonment. You proved that you did not want me so what else was I suppose to do? One of the hardest things that I had to do was to cut off your family but I needed to make a clean break. Maybe I was wrong but I did what was best for me and mine. Gratefully, the kids were too small to fully grasp what was happening when we packed up and left. Not one holiday or birthday passed that I didn't think or miss your family. But that was my mindset at the time. I couldn't understand how you could actually write *me* asking *me* to come and see you while you were down. What kind of fool would I have been to have stood by your side when you abandoned not only me, but your own kids. Thanks for allowing me to vent. I had to get this off of my chest. I needed this burden to be lifted off of me. I refused to let you and that tramp send me to hell because I was so full of hate."

As he took this all in, they approached the fairgrounds. Once he parked, he got out of the car and opened her door. Still silent, they walked to meet up with the kids. At the ticket booth, he purchased all day passes for them. "You want one?" "You know that I ain't getting on nothing here?" "Still afraid of heights, huh?" They laughed and followed the kids as they made their way to a ride. It was getting close to dusk and the lights on the rides started to take effect. The announcement boomed about the giant fireworks display coming up soon. But first, the special guest would get kick things off shortly.

By the time the special guest was announced, the kids had ridden a few rides so they made their way to the sound stage area. It was already packed and soon people were pushing their way to get closer to the stage. Finally, the lights dimmed and the special guest was revealed. When the curtain rolled back, a back drop of a church sanctuary was revealed. Then out of the crowd about twenty men and women took to the stage. The music began and the director stepped from among them and lead the choir. This choir had just reached critical acclaim and had won almost every major music award for gospel music, production & arrangement.

The crowd went wild as soon as the first notes were sang. The choir went forth with a three song opening set before the choir director calmed them to a hush. "Before we go any further, we would like to thank all of, our fans, old and new for helping us to achieve goals that we set and goals that we never imagined. I want to ask a question. What does a glutton, crackhead, dope find, fornicator, liar, alcoholic, gambler, prostitute, and weed-head have in common? Well, I'll tell you. The first thing they all have in common is that Jesus died for all of our sins! The second is, the voices that make up this awesome, award winning choir represent some of those sinners that I roll called. Period! Stop letting other people devalue your success. God knew you before you knew yourself. So, at this time I want to lead us in the Lord's Prayer. And after that, if you believe in your heart and speak from your mouth that Jesus died for you, you too will be saved." After Choir Director lead them, he turned back to the choir. "You know how we get up on Sunday mornings and go to church and sit all poised, knowing that we are as raggedy as anyone else. There isn't a sadder case than a member of the church of the poisened minds. Redeemed, let go and let God!"

Redeemed went at it as if this was going to be their very last concert. They sang under the anointing and people began to give their lives to Christ. Some spoke in tongues, others danced with the Holy Spirit not caring who was watching. Estranged, grabbed her children close and began to praise God. At the height of the experience, the firework show began. Once again, God's spirit moved upon the people.

When it was all of the singing was done the huge crowd lingered in the aftermath of this awesome move of God. Countless lives were changed and Redeemed had a helping hand in it. Just as they had taken the stage they went back into the crowd to worship with the others. Grimm looked at this mighty spectacle and almost gave in, but he felt that what he was all about wasn't worth saving. He knew God, but he also knew himself.

On the way to the car, he hugged his twins and reached for Estranged. "I have noticed that you have seen the ring on my finger. Of course, the one that you gave me is long gone." "So I guess this is the part when you tell me about him." "Yes it is. I met him years ago, way before I had met you. After we were no more, I sought him out and asked him to take me back. And he did with open arms. I attended a service and I became a Bride of Christ. It was good seeing you again, but my man wants me and I want Him. So you take care of yourself. The kids will be in touch and you have my number." She embraced him, then left. As her car faded into the distance all he could say was, "Almost."

The End or is it?

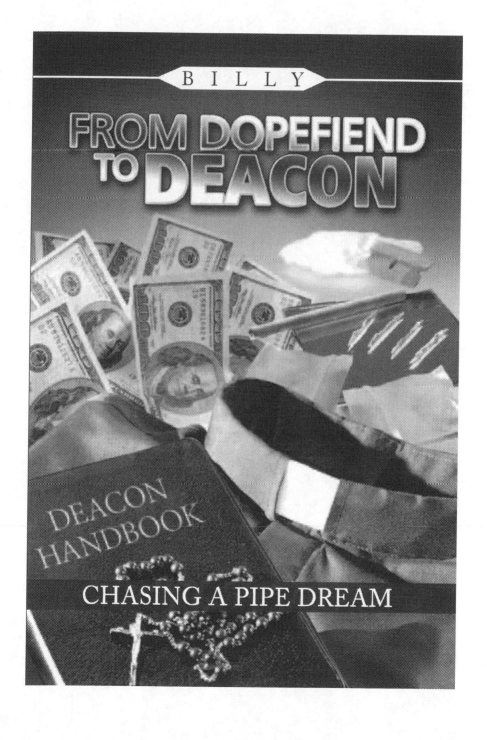

BILLY

FROM DOPEFIEND TO DEACON

DEACON HANDBOOK

CHASING A PIPE DREAM